SADDAM HUSSEIN
and the
CRISIS in the GULF

SADDAM HUSSEIN
and the
CRISIS in the GULF

JUDITH MILLER
and
LAURIE MYLROIE

TIMES ⓣ BOOKS
RANDOM HOUSE

*Grateful acknowledgment is made to the
following for permission to reprint previously
published material:*

Amnesty International: Excerpts from *Iraq:
Children: Innocent Victims of Political
Repression* (Index #MDE 14/04/89). Reprinted
by permission of Amnesty International.

The New York Times: Map from the August 26,
1990, issue of *The New York Times* and map
from the September 2, 1990, issue of *The New
York Times.* Copyright © 1990 by The New
York Times Company. Reprinted by
permission.

Yale University Press: Excerpts from *Human
Rights in Iraq* by Middle East Watch/Human
Rights Watch. Reprinted by permission of Yale
University Press.

ISBN 0-8129-1921-1
Manufactured in the United States of America
9 8 7 6 5
First Edition
Cover Photo Courtesy of AP/Wide World Photos, Inc.

Contents

Introduction

Why this book?
   Because of Corporal Sean M. Pulliam, a twenty-two-year-old American marine from Damon, Texas, who wasn't at his wife's bedside when their first child was born. Since mid-August, Corporal Pulliam, a tank gunner, has battled 120-degree temperatures and a variety of poisonous snakes which inhabit the Saudi desert. To avoid a confrontation, he has taken to sleeping on top of his tank.

   Because of Karin Oliver, age thirty, who has worked for nearly ten years in the public library in Bloomington, Indiana. A former Navy Seabee, Oliver was informed in mid-August that her reserve unit might well be called up on twenty-four hours notice for service in the Persian Gulf. She was told to be reachable by phone, day or night, and to ensure that her legal affairs were in order—including her will.

   Another reason is Barbara Bodine, an intrepid State Department foreign service officer who serves as the number two at the U.S. embassy in Kuwait. The embassy's skeleton staff refused to leave Kuwait City when the Iraqis ordered all diplomats out in late August and then cut off electricity and water to encourage their departure. With hundreds of Americans in hiding in the capital or held hostage in Iraq, Bodine and her colleagues were intent on staying. They survived from then on by drinking boiled water from the embassy pool and eating chicken and turkey they had smoked themselves to retard spoilage in the intense summer heat. In late August, Iraq permitted the first large group of hostages (or "official guests," as Iraqis call them) to leave from Kuwait. After Bodine saw off the first convoy of tired and terrified Americans, she allowed herself a small flouting of protocol. From that point on, she declared to her colleagues, no more high-heeled shoes.

Ashraf Bak, an Indian national, led what he called the good life in Kuwait City until August 2, the day Iraq invaded. Employed by a Kuwaiti investment bank, he earned about $15,000 a year and managed to send money to relatives in India. Two days after the invasion, his wife had a child. Unable to collect his paycheck and fearful of the hungry and marauding invaders, he and his wife decided to flee as soon as she was able to travel. In a minivan crammed with four other equally desperate families, they braved the desert heat, the car-killing sand pits, and the Iraqi patrols. Three days later, they crossed the border into Jordan, but soon after arriving at the refugee camp, Bak's infant daughter became severely ill. Homeless, penniless, and waiting endlessly on lines for a daily ration of bread and water, this once proud man was transformed into a beggar, a mere statistic in a pool of human misery—one of some 400,000 Asian and Near Eastern refugees who fled Kuwait and Iraq and who do not know whether, when, or how they are to return home.

Mohammed al-Sager had it all until Iraqi tanks rolled into his country and took over, among other things, his newspaper. A member of one of the sheikdom's wealthiest and most influential families, Sager was a happily married man with a large family, a thriving investment business, an elegant home in Kuwait City, vacation houses in Europe, and friends in the Gulf, Europe, and

America. Educated at the University of Southern California and fascinated by the Western press, he helped turn his family's newspaper, *al-Qabas,* into one of the Arab world's most respected journals. Like so many Kuwaitis, he and his family were vacationing in Europe when the Iraqis invaded. But even he feels the pangs of luxurious exile, which he fears may be permanent. With Saudi help, the Kuwaiti government began republishing *al-Qabas* in late August as an opposition newspaper from London. In its pages, the outrage of the dispossessed has found a voice.

Samir al-Khalil is not his real name. A slight man with fine features, wavy hair, and sensitive eyes, he has been living in Europe under this pseudonym for many years, ever since he decided to oppose Saddam Hussein's regime; life in Baathist Iraq, he explained, was unbearable for an intellectual with integrity. Khalil received more than sixty rejection slips before a university press agreed in 1989 to print a token number of copies of his aptly titled book on Iraq, *Republic of Fear.* Academic in tone, relentless in its hatred of pan-Arabism, loaded with insights about Saddam's use of terror and intimidation to secure legitimacy, Khalil's book has been rescued from obscurity by the invasion. But personally he has not been as fortunate. Fearful of the regime's revenge, he has continued to live in virtual seclusion, with only a few friends knowing his real name, address, or telephone number.

For all of these people—Americans, Asians, Kuwaitis, Iraqis, and other Arabs—life has changed dramatically (for some, permanently) because of Saddam's invasion of Kuwait on August 2, 1990. Many Americans have already been or soon will be affected by this event more than 10,000 miles from our shores. Some have friends or relatives involved in what has been the single largest deployment of American forces overseas since Vietnam; for others, the effect has been limited to paying more for gasoline at local pumps. But the crisis that unfolded throughout August and September has potential implications for many people in the United States, Europe, and the Middle East that go far beyond what was experienced in the immediate aftermath of Iraq's action.

The Bush administration, which has won praise for its management of the crisis, has nonetheless offered curiously shifting and often grandiosely vague descriptions about what is at stake in the Gulf for the United States and the West. President Bush, who initially stated that no American intervention was contemplated, corrected himself only hours later. When on August 8 he announced his decision to send American forces to the area, he stressed they were for "purely defensive purposes." Gradually, however, the list of goals—some implied, others explicit—expanded, as did their ambitiousness. Bush subsequently described the stakes in Saddam's invasion of Kuwait as a threat to no less than "our way of life." He did not hesitate to compare Saddam's territorial conquests with those of Adolf Hitler. A half century ago, Bush said, "our nation and the world paid dearly for appeasing an aggressor who should, and could, have been stopped. We are not going to make the same mistake again."

Secretary of State James A. Baker 3d, testifying before a congressional committee in early September, elaborated on these statements. The Iraqi invasion, he said, was a "political test of how the post–Cold War world will work." This, he said, was a "critical juncture in history . . . one of the defining moments of a new era." The end of the Cold War did not mean an end to violence or conflict, he argued. America and its allies had a simple choice: "Do we want to live in a world where aggression is made less likely because it is met with a powerful response from the international community, a world where civilized rules of conduct apply? Or are we willing to live in a world where aggression can go unchecked, where aggression succeeds because we somehow cannot muster the collective will to challenge it?"

But others saw different motives. What was really at stake, wrote Thomas L. Friedman, diplomatic correspondent of *The New York Times,* was free access to and effective control over the price of oil—indispensable to the West's economic engine. In an assessment that shocked official Washington barely ten days after the Iraqi invasion, Friedman bluntly stated that American boys were being asked to be willing to die for oil, "five cents more a gallon."

Throughout the crisis, the administration has vigorously rejected arguments that what was really at stake was President Bush's standing in the polls, his reelection prospects, or most significant, low energy prices that would allow Americans to continue their voracious gas guzzling. "This is not about increases in the price of a gallon of gas at the local service station," Baker retorted, his voice laced with anger. "It is rather about a dictator who, acting alone and unchallenged, could strangle the global economic order, determining by fiat whether we all enter a recession or even the darkness of a depression." The burden of higher energy prices, he warned, would threaten not only the United States, but the 1989 anti-Communist revolutions in Eastern Europe, as well as the poorer nations of Central America, South Asia and Africa.

Which interpretation is accurate? Has this crisis really been about whether aggression will be tolerated in a critical and highly volatile part of the world? Or is it really, as Republican analyst Kevin Phillips has asserted, "the first war this country has fought over economics—

that is, over oil"? What is really at stake for the United States in the Persian Gulf?

And who is Saddam Hussein? A modern-day Hitler, the demented irrational "Butcher of Baghdad" portrayed in early breathless articles that followed the invasion? Or, as Arab and Western diplomats have described him, a ruthless, cunning, rational thug intent on dominating the Middle East and the West through a stranglehold on the supply of oil?

What kind of country is Saddam Hussein's Iraq? What do Iraqis really feel about their leader? Why, after eight long years of war with Iran, would his people support his attack on the Arab neighbor that had helped pay for the weapons which enabled Iraq to claim victory over the Iranians? Why did so many ordinary Arabs not oppose Saddam's blitzkrieg invasion, the first such incursion by one Arab state against another in modern times? Why were America's allies so slow to respond and, in some cases, so niggling in their contributions to the campaign to force Iraq to withdraw?

Why was almost every government stunned by Iraq's action? Why did America, Europe and the Soviet Union believe that the support they had given Saddam would moderate his policies toward Kuwait? Has Western assistance helped turn Saddam into a monster by building his powerful military? How many chemical weapons does he have? What kind of biological weapons does he have? Does he possess a nuclear bomb?

Finally, will the Arab world ever be the same? Or will America? How will the crisis affect American interests—its presence in the Persian Gulf and its relations with Arab states and with Israel? Indeed, how does Israel fit into this state of affairs?

At the beginning of the summer, few Americans had thought much about Iraq, let alone about such questions. Today, after the abrupt dispatch of more than

100,000 U.S. troops to the Middle East, many Americans hunger for answers and a deeper understanding of the conflict. Unfortunately, there are almost no books available for a general audience about Saddam Hussein, Iraq, and Persian Gulf politics. And the few that exist are written by scholars for scholars. This book, written quickly, before the resolution of the crisis and therefore without the benefit of hindsight, raises some of these key questions. It also attempts to offer some preliminary answers. And it seeks to provide some basic insight into Saddam Hussein—the kind of man he is, the kind of society he has built, and the way in which his Arab neighbors, the United States, and the Western European nations have reacted to him. In sum, it seeks to be a primer, a guide to appreciating the immediate and deeper roots of this conflict.

After the United Nations voted in late August to support the limited use of force against Iraq, to give teeth to the economic sanctions it had previously approved, Thomas R. Pickering, the American ambassador to the United Nations, called the action a "historic" moment for the United States and the international organization. "We have drawn a firm line in the sand," Mr. Pickering told one reporter.

"Fine," a sympathetic Arab diplomat replied, upon hearing his colleague's statement. "Now let us pray we can control the winds."

SADDAM HUSSEIN
and the
CRISIS in the GULF

I

Hijack

In the eighth century, Abu Jafer al-Mansur, the second caliph of Iraq, decided to build a capital befitting his powerful kingdom, the ancient site of Sumer and Babylon. So he summoned his finest architect and instructed him to design a city like nothing that had ever been built before.

The architect produced a unique plan: a city in the shape of a circle. The design would ensure that the caliph's subjects would be equidistant from one another, and that those at the farthest reaches of the capital would be equal distances from the city's center—the caliph's palace.

But Mansur could not imagine such a city. So the architect ordered his assistants to dig a vast trench around the perimeters of the future city and fill it with wood and straw. Then he escorted the caliph to a promontory not far from the area. At his command, the workmen set the trench ablaze so that the caliph could envisage his future capital, Baghdad. The flames raced through the trench and formed a perfect ring—a circle of fire.

In mid-September 1990, Saddam Hussein sat in his innermost sanctum—the presidential compound in central Baghdad—encircled yet again by a political firestorm of his own making.

3

His invasion and seizure of tiny Kuwait, or "The Revolution of August 2," as it was trumpeted in the Iraqi state-controlled press, had enraged the world in a way he had not anticipated. The United Nations, at the behest of the Americans, had quickly approved five resolutions condemning his invasion, demanding his unconditional withdrawal from Kuwait and the immediate release of the three thousand Americans and thousands of other Westerners taken hostage, some of whom he had sent to military and chemical production facilities to serve as human shields in case of attack. And the U.N. Security Council, traditionally paralyzed by ideological and often petty disputes, had unanimously endorsed a financial and trade boycott of Iraq and its oil, 95 percent of his country's foreign exchange. The world was closing in on him.

To his north was hostile Turkey. The Turks, members of NATO, deeply in debt to the Americans and eager to join the ranks of the European Community, were among the first to side with the United States. President Turgut Ozal had personally assured President Bush in a telephone conversation the night of the invasion that he would block oil in the pipeline that ran from Iraq through Turkey, cutting off one-third of Iraq's export capacity from reaching its markets. Ozal had also taken to the phone the next morning, urging others, including King Fahd of Saudi Arabia, not to yield to Iraqi intimidation.

To the west was Syria, a fellow Baathist state headed by Saddam's most bitter adversary, Hafez al-Assad. Syria and Iraq had long been divided by ideological and personality conflicts between their leaders and by recent memories of Syria's ardent support for Iran, a non-Arab state, in the Iraq-Iran war. Syria was a hard-line foe of Israel and of what it called American imperialism in the region, as well as a haven for terrorists, including those who had masterminded the 1988 bombing of Pan Am flight 103 over Lockerbie, Scotland—the most deadly action ever staged against American civilians. But Damascus, too, had eagerly joined the American-led boycott. President Assad agreed to aid his newfound enemy-of-his-enemy by sending an initial installment of 3,200 Syrian troops to help defend Saudi Arabia from Iraqi aggression, one of initially only three Arab states outside the Gulf to do so. And in early September, Syria promised the Saudis it would send an armored division of about 20,000 troops and an additional 270 Soviet-made tanks and artillery.

Jordan also lay to the west, just south of Syria. After the invasion, King Hussein astounded the Bush administration by criticizing Washington for sending troops to defend Saudi Arabia. The king, Saddam knew, could ill afford to offend the country that protected Jordan from Israeli intimidation and which provided Amman with 95 percent of its oil and roughly 25 percent of its gross national product. Moreover, the king had grown close to Saddam during Iraq's long war and stood in awe of Saddam, whom he viewed as the first Arab to stand up to the West since Gamal Abdel Nasser. But even the "plucky little king" (as Hussein had long been known in diplomatic cables) had agreed to honor the embargo. And he had rushed off to Kennebunkport in late August to explain to an unmoved President Bush why he could not be more forthcoming. No, King Hussein, Saddam's namesake but no blood relation, could not be trusted to help Iraq.

To Saddam's east was Iran, the Shiite fundamentalist rival for hegemony in the region whom he had attacked in 1980 and had fought to a standstill after eight long years. Tehran had also initially endorsed the embargo. To neutralize Iran, Saddam was forced in August to relinquish the precious Shatt al-Arab waterway he had won in the war—his only access to the Gulf before his seizure of Kuwait and the only trophy from a conflict that had reportedly cost more than a million casualties. The Iraq-Iran war had been the region's bloodiest since the Mongol invasion in the thirteenth century.

Tehran seemed to appreciate Saddam's gesture. On September 12, Ayatollah Ali Khamenei, Iran's supreme religious leader, called in a broadcast for a "holy war" against the United States to force American troops to leave the Gulf. He also said that Iran would provide food and medicine and other "humanitarian assistance" to Iraq. But Saddam knew that the Iranian government was deeply divided, and that it was still unclear whether Tehran, desperate for Western credit, aid and technology to rebuild its war-ravaged country, would risk alienating the West by openly flouting the embargo. Maybe a little cheating, yes. But real support was unlikely. Moreover, Iranian officials were already pressing Gulf states to see what price could be extracted for Iran to adhere diligently to the embargo. Besides, the enmity between Iraq and Iran was so great, the mistrust so deep, that Saddam knew to be wary of Iranian pledges.

His most pressing concern though, was Saudi Arabia to the south. Before the invasion, Riyadh had not permitted a single American soldier to be stationed on Saudi soil. Even keeping enough technicians on the ground to maintain the billions of dollars worth of exotic military equipment the Saudis had purchased from America had been a source of tension. The invasion had stunned Riyadh, which had attempted to mediate a solution to the crisis. The night of the invasion King Fahd was said by a source who knows him well to have been "quaking with fear." But by mid-September, the ever-cautious Saudis were privately calling upon fellow Arabs and George Bush to get rid of Saddam—permanently. They were also playing gracious host to more than 200,000 soldiers from more than twenty countries, more than 140,000 of them American.

The Kuwait government in exile, for its part, courted American help by dangling an offer of a permanent base in the sheikdom if the ruling Sabah monarchy were restored to power. And Bahrain had decided to permit the United States and Britain to station some military personnel there permanently to operate base facilities. Oman, which after the fall of the shah of Iran had become a major intelligence-collecting base for the Americans, was being very helpful as well. And Egypt, Iraq's historic rival, whose army was second only to Saddam's own in the region, agreed in early September to bolster its paltry initial deployment of 2,000 airborne forces in Arabia with two more army divisions—about 30,000 troops—along with eight commercial ships carrying tanks and artillery.

In addition to the American and Arab armies, Saddam faced an awesome American arsenal on or within striking range of the Saudi border: hundreds of M-1 tanks and armored personnel carriers; AWACS radar planes to help Saudi and American fighter pilots spot Iraqi aircraft; EF-111 and EC-130 electronic jamming planes to confuse Baghdad's electronic systems; more than 1,000 helicopters; fighters, fighter-bombers, ground-attack planes and bombers including F-15s, F-16s, A-10s, and Harriers; F-111s and F-117s stationed in Turkey; F-14s, F/A-18s and A-6s aboard the aircraft carriers *Eisenhower, Independence,* and *Saratoga;* and even B-52 bombers operating out of the tiny island base of Diego Garcia in the Indian Ocean.

By mid-September, Saddam, the self-proclaimed supreme commander and leader of the Arab forces, found himself surrounded in a military and economic vise that threatened his very survival.

How had it come to this?

7

Western and Arab analysts disagree about when and why Saddam decided to move against his neighbor. In Washington, many government officials and Middle East experts argued that Saddam's move was "spontaneous," that although he had moved 30,000, then 70,000, then 100,000 troops up to the Kuwaiti border less than a month before the invasion, he had really been "saber-rattling," trying to bully Kuwait into complying with his demands. But knowledgeable Arab sources and some American officials dispute this interpretation. There was nothing impromptu or spontaneous about Saddam's moves, they insisted, conceding that they, too, had failed to gauge his true ambitions. In retrospect it was fairly straightforward, they argued: Saddam Hussein had invaded Kuwait for money and territory; the action was well planned; and his strategy began to be implemented in February 1990, six months before the invasion.

Western and Arab analysts agree on this much—Iraqi resentment toward Kuwait and his other Gulf neighbors had been building since the cease-fire in the Iraq-Iran war in August 1988. Throughout that conflict, said Richard W. Murphy, former assistant secretary of state for Near Eastern and South Asian affairs under the Reagan administration, Saddam and his clique resented what they saw as inadequate support for Iraq's fight against the nation whose virulent Islamic fundamentalist credo had threatened the entire region.

"I was struck by the constant theme we heard from the Iraqis in 1988," Murphy recalled. "They were clearly nettled and aggravated that the Arabs and, indeed, the world were not sufficiently grateful for Iraq's sacrifice in the war, that none of us appreciated what Iraq had done for all of us," complaints that the United States itself would soon be uttering with respect to its own allies in the confrontation with Iraq.

8

To Saddam, the Iraqis had bled and died in Iran in a war, albeit one he had started, that had protected the sheikdoms from subversion and conquest by the non-Arab Persians. For Gulf Arabs, life had continued relatively uneventfully. True, the Gulf states had supplied money and arms for his war. But not nearly enough, Saddam told colleagues and diplomats after the cease-fire.

Only eight days before he invaded Kuwait, Saddam had vented his rage in a meeting with April Glaspie, America's ambassador to Baghdad. "Who else was there to protect the Gulf states against Iran?" he had lectured her, according to sources familiar with her cable back to Washington. "Who else would have fought a ground war to stop Iran? Would you have been able to lose 10,000 men in a single battle one week, and then turn around and lose another 10,000 the next without concern that public opinion might force you to change your policy?"

Yes, Iraq had emerged victorious, more or less. Iran had failed to achieve the Ayatollah Ruhollah Khomeini's vow of driving Saddam from power. Tehran had sued for peace. But the victory was futile: Iraq was a wreck, its population decimated by almost a decade of war. According to the most reliable estimates, some 120,000 Iraqis died in the conflict, about 300,000 were wounded, many of whom were left permanently disabled.

Even more troublesome was Iraq's financial outlook. The country was broke. At the start of the war, Saddam had some $30 billion in cash on hand; by the war's end, according to Marshall Wiley, who heads the U.S.-Iraq Business Forum, Baghdad owed the world more than $70 billion, about half of that to the Gulf states. Saddam and all the Arabs knew that this debt would never be repaid. Saudi Arabia no longer even bothered to keep the loans on its books, one diplomat said. But Kuwait had repeatedly raised the debt issue as a bargaining chip whenever Iraq reiterated demands for territory or more money after the war's end. The Kuwaitis were accustomed to pressure from Iraq; after all, the dispute over the Iraq-Kuwait border had continued, on and off, for more than fifty years. What about your debt to us, the Kuwaitis would politely, but firmly, reply. And what about recognizing Kuwait's borders in exchange for forgiving the debt, Kuwaitis would press. What was perceived as insulting Kuwaiti intransigence infuriated Saddam. With hindsight, some diplomats said, Kuwait might have prevented, or at least deferred, Iraqi aggression if it had heeded its powerful neighbor. "When the lion is hungry," a U.S. official said, "you don't tell it that there isn't going to be any dinner."

The situation had deteriorated sharply by February, though few diplomats and analysts realized it at the time. The Israelis detected worrisome Iraqi movements at least a year before the invasion. Military sources were alarmed, for example, when Iraq deployed three new clusters of missile launchers to each of its borders. But American analysts say that February was the month that Saddam embarked on what in retrospect seems a calculated policy of heightening tensions between Iraq and the West in part to build popular Arab support and to disguise his true agenda—gaining a larger slice of his neighbor's vast wealth and Gulf-front property. Saddam's actions seem to have been aimed at pressuring the weak Gulf states to yield to his demands. If Saddam were willing to challenge Israel and the United States, what might he do to the weak, defenseless Gulf states if they did not submit to his will? The stronger he appeared, Arab sources agreed, the more intimidated the Gulf states were likely to be. In addition, his defiant harangues against Zionism and imperialism appealed to what Arab intellectuals call the "the Arab masses," projecting Saddam as a spokesman for causes dear to the Arab heart, which as the proverb goes, beats with a single beat. The attacks also made it difficult for the Gulf states to call upon America, Israel's defender, for support. Finally, the tirades against Israel and the United States served as an effective smoke screen for his more pressing agenda of money and territory.

The strategy worked well, as events since February suggest. On February 12, John Kelly, the American assistant secretary of state for Near Eastern and South Asian affairs, made a tour of the Persian Gulf region that ended in Baghdad. According to both Arab and American accounts, the meeting was a success. Kelly seemed to have received little indication that Saddam was so deeply troubled by his financial straits, or that his anger had intensified toward the Gulf states. In Washington, U.S. officials confirmed, the trip was seen as a positive step in American efforts to "moderate" Saddam by building a good relationship between Washington and Baghdad. Two days later, however, the Voice of America broadcast an editorial calling for the overthrow of dictators around the world, including Saddam Hussein. Ambassador Glaspie assured the Iraqis that the editorial did not reflect official American policy. But it had been approved by Washington. On the heels of the Kelly visit, it infuriated the Iraqis, who made their displeasure known.

On February 19, prime ministers of the Arab Cooperation Council (ACC) assembled in Baghdad to mark the group's first anniversary. A regional organization consisting of Iraq, Yemen, Jordan and Egypt, the ACC had been established after the Iraq-Iran war to promote economic and security cooperation among Iraq's close allies. The Saudis had always been wary of it, but Kuwait approved, arguing that it would divert Iraq's attention from the Gulf to the Arab world's "fertile crescent." In fact, the undersecretary of Kuwait's Foreign Ministry said in an interview in February 1989 that Iraq had been "looking for a role to play in the region" and that, happily, the "ACC showed the way."

At the meeting, Saddam surprised the group by demanding that the United States remove its ships from the Persian Gulf. American officials in Washington were perplexed by Saddam's remarks, but largely dismissed them as an overreaction to the VOA editorial. Five days later, at the ACC summit meeting in the Jordanian capital of Amman, Saddam expanded with vehemence on what had seemed his passing remark in Baghdad. He warned fellow Arabs that the increasing weakness of the Soviet Union would leave the United States as the only remaining superpower in the Middle East; America's main interest, he said, would be to advance Israel's interests. Repeating his call for the United States to leave the Gulf, Saddam warned that Israel might attack the Arabs in the next five years. "We can see the bright lights of holy Jerusalem," he told the Arab leaders. "Thus the signs on the path of liberating Jerusalem are clear."

That was Saddam's public stance. Privately, however, Saddam's preoccupation was money. At a closed session of the summit, one prominent diplomat recounted, Saddam said that not only did it not matter whether the Gulf states were willing to forgive his debts (since he had taken such forgiveness for granted and had no intention of repaying them), but that he also needed more money. "I need $30 billion in fresh money," Saddam told fellow Arab leaders, according to this reliable account. "Go and tell them in Saudi Arabia and the Gulf that if they don't give it to me, I will know how to take it."

Egyptian President Hosni Mubarak, not a man

known for outbursts, was said to have replied angrily, "I won't be a party to extortion."

Saddam left abruptly; the meeting broke up in disarray.

On March 9, Saddam made another unexpected and seemingly unrelated move. Farzad Bazoft, an Iranian-born, British-based journalist for *The Observer,* was suddenly brought to trial after five months of languishing in an Iraqi prison on charges of spying for Israel. Bazoft was arrested after he foolishly visited an Iraqi missile plant south of Baghdad to try to report on the cause of a mysterious explosion there in September. Most diplomats thought that Iraq would not risk angering Britain, which had also provided aid in the Iraq-Iran war, by putting a British journalist on trial. Thus, Bazoft's sudden appearance in an Iraqi courtroom shocked Western journalists and analysts. The show trial was particularly provocative since it took place just as prominent Iraqis were meeting in London with British scholars and diplomats at a conference aimed at improving relations between the two countries. Within the week, Bazoft, who like most people accused of crimes in Iraq had confessed to spying months earlier, was sentenced to death and executed.

A few chance incidents also served Saddam's goal of raising tension within the region and focusing attention on strains between Iraq and the West. On March 22, Gerald Bull was assassinated in Brussels, apparently by professionals. He was found in front of his building, face down, with five bullets in his neck and $20,000 in cash in his pockets. Bull, a naturalized American citizen, was the key developer of Iraq's program to build a supergun that would fire artillery shells thousands of miles. It was widely reported that agents for the Israeli intelligence service, Mossad, had killed Bull. Then, on March 28, the United States and Britain arrested several Iraqis in a well-publicized sting operation aimed at breaking up an Iraqi ring that was attempting to smuggle capacitors—highly sophisticated components that among other things could be used to separate the stages of missiles—to Baghdad.

On April 2, Saddam, in a long rambling speech, deplored the murder of Gerald Bull, asserted that Iraq possessed binary chemical weapons, and made the following threat: "By God," he said, "we will make fire eat up half of Israel if it tries anything against Iraq." Suddenly the world's attention, including Washington's, was focused on Iraq and on its chemical weapons program, just as it had been in 1988, when Saddam used chemical weapons against his Kurdish civilians to help quell a rebellion in northern Iraq.

In mid-April, Saddam sent a private letter to Iranian President Hashemi Rafsanjani, offering to give Tehran unspecified territory and to return some of its prisoners of war in order to settle the conflict between their nations permanently. Western intelligence sources learned of the offer months after the fact, and U.S. officials eventually saw the letter as a bid by Iraq to settle with its former enemy before engaging a new one. Also that month, Iraq placed orders for American wheat and other commodities, in quantities far greater than normal consumption would seem to warrant.

In late May, at the Arab League summit in Baghdad, Saddam issued another threat. To portray himself as a hero of the Arab nation, he publicly repeated his call for the Arabs to liberate Jerusalem. He also blamed the enslavement of the Palestinian people on U.S. military and economic support for the "Zionist entity," a hardline term for Israel long abandoned by many Arab leaders. But his speech made no mention of his more immediate priority: the liberation of some territory and a substantial amount of cash from Kuwait. Reflecting once more the gap between his public and private agendas, Saddam chose to issue his demand for money in a closed session of the summit. "We cannot tolerate this type of economic warfare which is being waged against Iraq," Saddam said, according to a report in September in *The New York Times.* He wanted some $27 billion from Kuwait alone. The Kuwaitis are reliably reported to have replied, again privately, that they did not have such huge sums available.

Kuwait, however, was rattled by Saddam's belligerence. Soon after the summit, Sheik Jaber al-Ahmad al-Sabah, the Emir of Kuwait, shifted his long-time oil minister and relative, Sheik Ali Khalifa al-Sabah, to become minister of finance. Khalifa, an American-educated official, had been closely associated with the policy of high levels of oil production to keep the world price low and stable.

At the end of June, one month before an important meeting of the Organization of Petroleum Exporting Countries, Saddoun Hammadi, a senior Iraqi official, toured Kuwait and the other sheikdoms, ostensibly to press other Arab oil producers for lower OPEC production quotas and strict adherence to them so that the price of oil would rise. But according to a senior Arab official, in each state that he visited Hammadi also pressed Saddam's demand for a contribution of $10 billion in aid. To underline his seriousness, he produced a list of Kuwaiti assets to demonstrate that Kuwait had sufficient funds to permit such a gift. Kuwait stonewalled, and offered instead a paltry sum (in Iraqi eyes) of $500 million over three years.

On July 10, Gulf oil ministers met in Jidda to discuss Iraq's demands. The two largest violators of OPEC quotas—Kuwait and the United Arab Emirates—agreed, under pressure from Iran, Iraq, and Saudi Arabia, to abide strictly by their quotas. But that did not deter Iraq from pursuing its demands for more cash. Six days later, on July 16, Iraqi Foreign Minister Tariq Aziz sent a letter to the Chadli Klibi, the Arab League secretary-general, again accusing Kuwait of violating its quotas and of stealing Iraqi oil from the Rumaila field, which both countries share. That same day, Aziz told an Arab summit meeting in Tunisia that "we are sure some Arab states are involved in a conspiracy against us. We want you to know our country will not kneel, our women will not become prostitutes, our children will not be deprived of food."

On July 17, in a speech to the nation, Saddam repeated his threat to Kuwait and the U.A.E. for overproducing, despite their assurances of good faith. For the first time, Saddam threatened military action if they failed to comply: "If words fail to afford us protection, then we will have no choice but to resort to effective action to put things right and ensure the restitution of our rights."

On July 18, Kuwait's cabinet met. Notes taken at the meeting, first published by *The Financial Times* of London, reflect the sheikdom's intense state of disarray, its confusion over Saddam's objectives. Having rejected Iraq's demand for $10 billion in aid, the cabinet was formulating a response to yet another Iraqi demand—this time an Iraqi memorandum demanding compensation for the $2.4 billion of oil allegedly "stolen" from the Rumaila oil field shared by both states. The field is situated mostly in Iraq, but the tiny section in Kuwait had enabled the emirate to lift what Iraqis claimed was far more than its fair proportion of oil from the field.

"The Iraqi memorandum is just the beginning. God knows how far they will go," said Dhari al-Othman, the minister of justice. He argued that the oil price issue was a pretext for something else. Badr al-Yacoub, the minister of state for the National Assembly and Abdul-Rahman al-Awadi, the minister of state for cabinet affairs, both argued that Iraq was simply intent on extorting money. A military strike was possible, some of the ministers asserted. The cabinet decided to cancel all military leaves and call an alert. The foreign minister, Sheik Sabah al-Ahmad al-Sabah, then called for an emergency session of the Gulf Cooperation Council, a defense group formed during the Iraq-Iran war that includes Kuwait, the U.A.E., Oman, Qatar, Bahrain, and Saudi Arabia. He also urged that the Arab League be asked to intervene. Even those who argued that military intervention was likely thought that Saddam would seize only a small amount of disputed territory, not the whole country.

In Washington, the CIA reported on July 21 that Iraq had moved some 30,000 troops to the Iraqi border near Kuwait. But the agency initially concluded that Saddam was merely saber-rattling to raise the price of oil and to achieve his other demands, according to William H. Webster, the director of central intelligence, who discussed the crisis at a private conference this summer in Aspen, Colorado.

On July 22, Iraqi Foreign Minister Aziz repeated his criticism of Kuwait and the U.A.E. after Saddam had met in Baghdad with Egyptian President Mubarak, who had gone to mediate the dispute. Mubarak told President Bush that his trip had been successful, that he had "assurances" from Saddam that Iraq would not move against Kuwait. Iraqi officials later claimed that Saddam had said only that nothing would happen to Kuwait as long as negotiations continued.

On July 24, the United States, in response to continued movement of Iraqi troops and supplies to the Kuwaiti border, deployed six combat vessels in joint maneuvers with the U.A.E. The Bush administration warned that "there is no place for coercion and intimidation in a civilized world." State Department spokesperson Margaret Tutwiler said that the United States was committed to supporting the individual and collective self-defense of American friends in the Gulf. But, she added, "we do not have any defense treaties with Kuwait, and there are no special defense or security commitments to Kuwait."

The next day, U.S. Ambassador Glaspie was summoned to a meeting with Saddam—her first meeting alone with him since her arrival at the end of 1988. He lectured her for an hour, stressing his view that he was misunderstood in Washington and that his country desperately needed cash. From this point on, accounts of what happened at the meeting conflict. According to an Iraqi transcript of the session, released after the invasion and first disclosed by ABC News, Saddam made clear that an invasion could not be ruled out unless Kuwait yielded to some of his demands. Glaspie reportedly said, "We have no opinion on the Arab-Arab conflicts, like your border disagreement with Kuwait." But in her cable back to Washington, she said that Saddam had told her that there would be a meeting the following week in Jidda at which Saudi Arabia would try to mediate the dispute. She had received assurances, she wrote, that Saddam would not move unless Kuwait proved stingy. She left the meeting convinced that Saddam would not invade, or, according to a source familiar with her cable, that at the very worst he would seize a small amount of disputed territory or one of the islands off Kuwait's coast. As she later remarked to *The New York Times*, "I didn't think—and nobody else did—that the Iraqis were going to take all of Kuwait." President Mubarak of Egypt also said that day that Saddam had assured him that he had no intention of invading.

On July 26, OPEC met in Geneva. The news was reassuring: Kuwait had agreed to lower production quotas and higher prices. But Saddam had begun moving another 30,000 troops to the border.

On Saturday, July 28, an American oil expert and former government official discussed the crisis in the Gulf with a senior Iraqi official whom he knew well. What did Iraq have up its sleeve? he asked his Iraqi contact. "You'll see by next week," came the reply. The expert pressed further. Was Iraq contemplating military action? "By next week," the Iraqi said, "we will be protecting the people of Kuwait." But what about the Americans? The Iraqi paused. "The Americans are a paper tiger," he said. "They won't do anything."

The expert called the State Department to report on his conversation. He was told not to be concerned; the government was aware of Iraq's actions, but was persuaded that Saddam was only blustering. He would not invade.

On July 30, the CIA reported that Iraq's forces on the Kuwait border stood at approximately 100,000, with some 300 tanks. Both Iraqi force estimates were reported prominently in *The Washington Post*, accompanied by government assertions that the Iraqis were bluffing. Ambassador Glaspie and her Soviet counterpart left Baghdad for vacations that day.

On July 31, Assistant Secretary Kelly told a congressional hearing that while the U.S. position was to do "all we can to support our friends when they are threatened and to preserve stability," he agreed with Representative Lee Hamilton of Indiana that the United States had no defense treaty with any Gulf country. On August 1, a crisis meeting at the White House heard the CIA's conclusion that invasion was "probable": "They're ready; they'll go."

Meanwhile, Kuwait and Iraq met under Saudi auspices in Jidda on July 31 to mediate their differences. Kuwait's crown prince and prime minister, Sheik Saad al-Abdullah al-Sabah, said he was "looking forward with an open heart" to the meeting that, he hoped, would resolve their differences.

What happened at this crucial meeting remains in dispute. Mohammed al-Mashat, the Iraqi ambassador to the United States, said in effect that the Kuwaitis had come to the meeting in bad faith, that they had been unwilling to listen or to negotiate seriously. "They were arrogant," said Mashat. "The Kuwaitis were conducting themselves like small-time grocery-store owners. The gap was irreconcilable, so the meeting collapsed."

The Kuwaiti version of events, not surprisingly, differs. According to Kuwaiti officials, the head of Iraq's delegation opened the meeting with a list of demands. He wanted Kuwait to cede some disputed territory and oil-pumping rights, and to give Baghdad $10 billion. The Kuwaitis replied that these were not negotiations, but orders. Iraq told Kuwait to consider the demands overnight. Having slept on it, Crown Prince Saad met one-on-one with his Iraqi counterpart. But during the meeting, the Iraqi developed a severe headache and retired in a huff to his room. Saad pleaded with him not to leave, to no avail. Then Saudi Crown Prince Abdullah tried to sway the Iraqi, who refused. "Nothing of substance was ever discussed in Jidda," a Kuwaiti official said.

Kuwait, he continued, had been prepared to make concessions, if necessary. Specifically, the Kuwaitis were prepared to write off Iraq's debt and to lease one of the Kuwaiti islands in the Gulf to Iraq, but the delegation needed further instructions. Both sides agreed to talk further in Baghdad in a few days.

At 2:00 A.M. the next morning, Iraqi forces swept across the border and in the space of six hours had seized and annexed Kuwait.

Saddam's tactics had worked. The sudden attacks on

Israel and the United States in early spring had stunned and perplexed American diplomats, who had long courted Iraq. Had the United States during the war not tilted decisively toward Iraq? Had it not helped finance hundreds of millions of dollars in wheat and grain sales to feed the Iraqi people, 75 percent of whose food was imported? Had it not provided critical intelligence information to Saddam about Iranian troop deployments and movements when the war turned against Baghdad? Had it not put American lives at risk by sending carriers and destroyers to the Persian Gulf in 1987 to keep the Gulf open after Iran threatened to close the vital waterway to Iraqi oil exports? Had it not looked the other way when an Iraqi missile accidentally blew up the U.S.S. *Stark,* killing thirty-seven sailors? And had that assistance not continued even after the cease-fire? Despite chemical weapons attacks on the Kurds, had the United States not maintained a good relationship with Baghdad? Given all this, the State Department was confounded by Saddam's about-face. American policymakers had failed to pay sufficient heed to Iraq's bullying of its Gulf state neighbors.

The smoke screen had worked. The West was focused on Israel. The Arabs were focused on oil production quotas and pricing. And Iraq was focused on Kuwait.

The invasion came as a shock to Kuwait, America, and the world. Only the CIA had warned that Iraq would invade. But one White House official said that the warning was hedged and that it came only the day before the invasion. Finally, leading government analysts had agreed that if Iraq did invade, it would only be to grab a limited amount of disputed territory. The Arabs could probably have lived with that, so Washington could have done so as well.

Those who argue that Saddam had not intended to

invade, that he simply "blew his stack," as former State Department official Richard Murphy put it recently, cannot account for his steady buildup of troops and tension in the region. And this charitable interpretation conflicts with that of Israeli and American military analysts, who said that Saddam needed at least two weeks to prepare for his invasion. It also belies the weeks and months of secret Iraqi demands for money—in effect, extortion money—that Saddam made before he pounced.

Saddam was correct in assuming that his move would confound the world. What he failed to anticipate was the extent of American fury and concern about his aggression in the West's primary source of oil. This was not the first time that Saddam had made such a major miscalculation. In 1980, he thought he could invade Iran, a nation weakened by Khomeini's purges of the military and ruling classes and by the flight of thousands of its most talented citizens, and score a victory within two weeks. He had failed to anticipate the depth of the Iranians' determination to defend their country, or the lengths to which the regime would go to stave off defeat. Saddam was saved only by the Arab and Western world's fear of an Iranian and Shiite extremist victory in the Middle East, and by their perception that he was the lesser of two evils.

Both of Saddam's misjudgments, a decade apart, concerned the reaction of non-Arab players. He had correctly anticipated the initial reaction of most Arab states, which was to wait and see what the United States would do. He knew the Arabs would be stunned, but suspected that they would ultimately come around to his side—but he had failed to understand men like the Ayatollah Khomeini and George Bush. And in both cases he had also overestimated his strength.

The misjudgments, moreover, reflect Saddam's ap-

palling lack of knowledge of the world beyond Iraq.
Given his origin and backround, his rise to power is
itself impressive. A peasant boy from a backwater village whose stamp he has borne throughout his life, Saddam Hussein has caused two major world crises in a
decade in a relentless quest to wield power and win
respect.

II

The Don from Takrit

Saddam Hussein loves *The Godfather*. It is his favorite movie, one he has seen many times. He is especially fascinated by Don Corleone, a poor boy made good, whose respect for family is exceeded only by his passion for power. The iron-willed character of the Don may perhaps be the most telling model for the enigmatic figure that rules Iraq. Both come from dirt-poor peasant villages; both sustain their authority by violence; and for both, family is key, the key to power. Family is everything, or "almost" everything, because Saddam, like the Godfather, ultimately trusts no one, not even his next of kin. For both, calculation and discipline, loyalty and ruthlessness are the measure of a man's character.

There is, however, a difference. Where the Don was a private man, obsessed with secrecy, seeking always to conceal his crimes behind a veil of anonymity, Saddam is a public figure who usurped political power and seizes every opportunity to advertise his might in order to impress upon his countrymen that there is no alternative to his rule. To visit Iraq is to enter the land of Big Brother. Enormous portraits of Saddam Hussein, black-haired and mustachioed, full of power and a strange serenity, stare down all over Baghdad. His photograph is everywhere—even on the dials of gold wristwatches. In the land where the Sumerians invented writing, discourse has been degraded to a single ubiquitous image.

But perhaps this difference matters not at all. For both the Don and Saddam relish power and seek respect, the more so because each knows what it means to have none. Neither ever forgot any insult, however trivial or imagined, both secure in the knowledge that, as Mario Puzo observed of his fictional character, "in this world there comes a time when the most humble of men, if he keeps his eyes open, can take his revenge on the most powerful." And in this likeness there perhaps lies the key to understanding Saddam Hussein's ambition.

Saddam Hussein was born fifty-three years ago on April 28, 1937, to a miserably poor, landless peasant family in the village of al-Auja, near the town of Takrit, on the Tigris River, a hundred miles north of Baghdad. (Although Muslims do not generally share the Western custom of celebrating birthdays, Saddam has made his a national holiday in Iraq.) The Arab town of Takrit lies in the heart of the Sunni Muslim part of Iraq. But in Iraq, the Sunnis are a minority. More than half the country is Shiite, the Sunnis' historical and theological rivals. Takrit had prospered in the nineteenth century, renowned for the manufacture of kalaks, round rafts made of inflated animal skins. But as the raft industry declined, so did the fortunes of the town. By the time Saddam was born, it had little to offer its inhabitants.

Communication with the outside world was difficult. While the Baghdad–Mosul railway ran through Takrit, the town had but one paved road. Saddam's nearby village was even worse off. It had only dirt roads. Its people, including Saddam and his family, lived in huts made of mud and reeds and burned cow dung for fuel. No one—either in Takrit or in al-Auja—had electricity or running water. The central government in Baghdad seemed far away, its authority limited to the presence of some local policemen.

Iraq was then a seething political cauldron, governed by a people who knew little of government. The Ottoman Turks had ruled Iraq for 500 years, before a brief decade of British rule. Britain's mandate over Iraq ended in 1932, only five years before Saddam was born. Within four years of Iraq's independence, hundreds of Assyrians, an ancient Christian people, would perish at the hands of the Iraqi army. Five years later, similar atrocities would be committed in Baghdad's ancient Jewish quarter. Between independence and Saddam's first breath of life, the Iraqi army had doubled in size. It saw itself as the embodiment of the new Iraqi state, "the profession of death" that would forge a nation out of the competing religious, tribal, and ethnic factions tearing at one another's throat. It was into this volatile world that Saddam Hussein was born.

Accounts of Saddam's early years are murky. Official hagiographies shed little light. The unsavory aspects of Saddam's harsh and brutal childhood are not something he wants known. It is usually said that Saddam's father, Hussein al-Majid, died either before Saddam's birth or when he was a few months old. But a private secretary of Saddam's, who later broke with him, has suggested that Saddam's father abandoned his wife and young children. Whatever the truth, after her husband was gone, Saddam's mother, Subha, was on her own until she met Ibrahim Hassan, a married man. Eventually she convinced him to get rid of his wife, and to marry her instead. By Muslim law, Ibrahim was permitted four wives, but Subha insisted on being the only one.

Saddam's stepfather was a crude and illiterate peasant who disliked his stepson and treated him abusively. Years later, Saddam would bitterly recall how his stepfather would drag him out of bed at dawn, barking, "Get

up, you son of a whore, and look after the sheep."
Ibrahim often fought with Subha over Saddam, complaining, "He is a son of a dog. I don't want him." Still,
Ibrahim found some use for the boy, often sending Saddam to steal chickens and sheep, which he then resold.
When Saddam's cousin, Adnan Khayrallah, who would
become Iraq's defense minister, started to go to school,
Saddam wanted to do the same. But Ibrahim saw no
need to educate the boy. He wanted Saddam to stay
home and take care of the sheep. Saddam finally won
out. In 1947 at the age of ten, he began school.

He went to live with Adnan's father, Khayrallah Tulfah, his mother's brother, a schoolteacher in Baghdad.
Several years before, Khayrallah had been cashiered
from the Iraqi army for supporting a pro-Nazi coup in
1941, which the British suppressed, instilling in Khayrallah a deep and lasting hatred for Britain and for "imperialism." Whether Saddam's stepfather kicked him out
of the house or whether he left at his own initiative for
his uncle's home in Baghdad is unclear. What is certain
is that Khayrallah Tulfah—who would later become
mayor of Baghdad—would come to wield considerable
influence over Saddam.

Having started elementary school when he went to
live with Khayrallah, Saddam was sixteen when he finished intermediary school, roughly the equivalent of an
American junior high school. Like his uncle, he wanted
to become an army officer, but his poor grades kept him
out of the prestigious Baghdad Military Academy. Of
the generation of Arab leaders who took power in the
military coups of the 1950s and 1960s, only Saddam Hussein had no army experience, though his official biogra-
phy notes his love of guns starting at the age of ten. In
1976, he would correct the deficiency by getting himself
appointed lieutenant general, a rank equal to chief of
staff. When Saddam became president in 1979 he would

promote himself to field marshal and would insist on personally directing the war against Iran.

Baghdad was utterly different from the world he had left behind in al-Auja. Yet Saddam still lived with Takritis. Khayrallah's home was on the western bank of the Tigris, in the predominantly lower-class Takriti district of al-Karkh. As in most Middle Eastern cities, peasants from the same region tended to cluster in certain neighborhoods when they moved to the city, giving each other support and maintaining their rural clan connections.

Times were unusually turbulent when Saddam was a student in Baghdad. In 1952, Lieutenant Colonel Gamal Abdel Nasser led a coup that toppled Egypt's monarchy. Though there had been considerable sympathy in the United States for the Egyptian officers, Nasser and the West were soon at odds. Nasser's purchase in 1955 of huge amounts of Soviet arms and his nationalization of the Suez Canal in 1956 led France, Britain and Israel to attack Egypt that year. Most Egyptians—indeed, most Arabs—believed that Arab nationalism, through Nasser, won a tremendous victory when the invasion was halted, Israel forced to withdraw from the Sinai, and the canal returned to Egyptian control. That the United States was almost single-handedly responsible for that outcome did not reduce the tremendous popular enthusiasm for Nasser among the Arabs.

Saddam soon found himself swept up in a world of political intrigue whose seductions were far more compelling than the tedium of schoolwork. In 1956 Saddam participated in an abortive coup against the Baghdad monarchy. The next year, at the age of twenty, he joined the Baath party, one of several radical nationalist organizations that had spread throughout the Arab world. But the Baath in Iraq were a tiny and relatively powerless band of about 300 members in those days.

In 1958 a non-Baathist group of nationalist army officers, led by General Abdul Karim Qassim, succeeded in overthrowing King Faisal II. The fall of the monarchy intensified plotting among Iraq's rival dissident factions. A year after Qassim's coup, the Baath tried to seize power by machine-gunning Qassim's car in broad daylight. Saddam (whose name translates as "the one who confronts") was a member of the hit team. He had already proven his mettle, or in the jargon of the American underworld had "made his bones," by murdering a Communist supporter of Qassim in Takrit. The Communists were the Baath's fierce rivals—in fact, the man Saddam killed was his brother-in-law. There had been a dispute in the family over politics, and his uncle Khayrallah had incited Saddam to murder him. Although Saddam and Khayrallah were arrested, they were soon released. In the anarchic confusion of Baghdad after the monarchy's fall, political crimes were common and often unpunished.

Iraqi propaganda embellishes Saddam's role in the attempt on Qassim's life, portraying him as a bold and heroic figure. He is said to have been seriously wounded in the attack. Bleeding profusely, he orders a comrade to dig a bullet out of his leg with a razor blade, an operation so painful it causes him to faint. He then disguises himself as a Bedouin tribesman, swims across the Tigris River, steals a donkey and flees to safety across the desert to Syria.

The truth is less glamorous. Iraqi sources present at the time insist that Saddam's role in the failed assassination attempt was minor, that he was only lightly wounded, and that the wound was inadvertently inflicted by his own comrades. A sympathetic doctor treated Saddam and several others much more seriously hurt at a party safe house. Saddam would later have the opportunity to reward him for his help. When the Baath party finally succeeded in taking power in 1968, the doctor was made dean of the Medical College of Baghdad University, a post he held until he broke with Saddam in 1979.

From Syria, Saddam went to Cairo, where he would spend the next four years. The stay in Egypt was to be his only extended experience in another country. Supported by an Egyptian government stipend, he resumed his political activities, finally finishing high school at the age of twenty-four. In Cairo he was arrested twice, and both times quickly released. The first arrest occurred after he threatened to kill a fellow Iraqi over political differences. He was arrested again when he chased a fellow Baathist student through the streets of Cairo with a knife. The student was later to serve as Jordan's information minister.

Saddam entered Cairo University's Faculty of Law in 1961. He eventually received his law degree not in Cairo, but in Baghdad in 1970, after he became the number two man in the regime. It was an honorary degree.

While in Cairo, Saddam married his uncle Khayrallah's daughter, Sajida, in 1963. His studies in Egypt ended abruptly in February when Baathist army officers and a group of Arab nationalist officers together succeeded in ousting and killing General Qassim, a figure of considerable popularity, particularly among the poor of Iraq. Of Qassim, Hanna Batatu, the author of an authoritative history of Iraq, has written: "The people had more genuine affection for him than for any other ruler in the modern history of Iraq."

Many people refused to believe that Qassim was dead. It was rumored that he had gone into hiding and would soon surface. The Baathists found a macabre way to demonstrate Qassim's mortality. They displayed his bullet-riddled body on television, night after night. As

Samir al-Khalil, in his excellent book *Republic of Fear,* tells it: "The body was propped upon a chair in the studio. A soldier sauntered around, handling its parts. The camera would cut to scenes of devastation at the Ministry of Defense where Qassim had made his last stand. There, on location, it lingered on the mutilated corpses of Qassim's entourage (al-Mahdawi, Wasfi Taher, and others). Back to the studio and close-ups now of the entry and exit points of each bullet hole. The whole macabre sequence closes with a scene that must forever remain etched on the memory of all those who saw it: the soldier grabbed the lolling head by the hair, came right up close, and spat full face into it."

Saddam was elated. He hurried back to Baghdad to assume his part in the revolution. He was twenty-six years old.

Saddam quickly found his place in the new regime. He became an interrogator and torturer in the Qasr-al-Nihayyah, or "Palace of the End," so called because it was where King Faisal and his family were gunned down in 1958. Under the Baath the palace was used as a torture chamber.

Few in the West are aware of Saddam's activities there. But an Iraqi arrested and accused of plotting against the Baath has told of his own torture at the palace by Saddam himself: "My arms and legs were bound by rope. I was hung on the rope to a hook on the ceiling and I was repeatedly beaten with rubber hoses filled with stones." He managed to survive his ordeal; others were not so lucky. When the Baath, riven by internal splits, was ousted nine months later in November 1963 by the army, a grisly discovery was made. "In the cellars of al-Nihayyah Palace," according to Hanna Batatu, whose account is based on official government sources, "were found all sorts of loathsome instruments of torture, including electric wires with pincers, pointed iron stakes on which prisoners were made to sit, and a machine which still bore traces of chopped-off fingers. Small heaps of blooded clothing were scattered about, and there were pools on the floor and stains over the walls."

During the party split in 1963, Saddam had supported Michel Aflaq, a French-educated Syrian, the party's leading ideologue and co-founder of the party. Saddam was rewarded the next year when Aflaq sponsored him for a position in the Baath regional command, the party's highest decision-making body in Iraq. With this appointment, Saddam began his rapid ascent within the party.

His growing prominence was also due to the support of his older cousin, General Ahmad Hassan al-Bakr, the party's most respected military figure and a member of the party from its earliest days. It is said that Saddam's wife helped to cement Saddam's relations with Bakr by persuading Bakr's son to marry her sister, and by promoting the marriage of two of Bakr's daughters to two of her brothers. The party's affairs were rapidly becoming a family business. In 1965, Bakr became secretary-general of the party. The next year, Saddam was made deputy secretary-general.

During the period of his initial rise in the party, Saddam spent a brief interlude in prison, from October 1964 to his escape from jail sometime in 1966. There, as Saddam later recounted, in the idleness of prison life he reflected on the mistakes that had led to the party's split and its fall from power. He became convinced that the "Revolution of 1963" was stolen by a "rightist military aristocracy" in alliance with renegade elements of the Baath party. Divisions within the party, which had less than 1,000 full members at that time, had to end. Unity was essential for power, even if it had to be purchased by purge and blood. He determined to build a security force within the party, to create cells of loyalty which answered to no one but himself, to ensure that victory once won would be kept.

Upon his escape from prison, Saddam quickly set about building the party's internal security apparatus, the Jihaz Haneen, or "instrument of yearning." Those deemed "enemies of the party" were to be killed; unfriendly factions intimidated. Saddam's reputation as an architect of terror grew.

Two years later, on July 30, 1968, Saddam and his Baathist comrades succeeded in seizing and holding state power. Bakr became president and commander in chief in addition to his duties as secretary-general of the Baath party and the chairman of its Revolutionary Command Council. Saddam was made deputy chairman of the council, in charge of internal security. He quickly moved to strengthen control and expand his base within the party. The security services graduated hundreds of Saddam's men from their secret training schools, among them his half brothers, Barzan, Sabawi, and Wathban; another graduate, his cousin Ali Hassan al-Majid, would earn notoriety years later for his genocidal suppression of the Kurds during the Iraq-Iran war and his leading role in the invasion of Kuwait; another graduate was Arshad Yassin, his cousin and brother-in-law, whom the world would come to know as the bodyguard who repeatedly stroked the head of Stuart Lockwood, the young British "guest," as Saddam tried to get him to talk about milk and cornflakes.

Saddam was thirty-one. His penchant for asserting his authority by title—today he holds six—was evident even then. He insisted on being called "Mr. Deputy." No one else in Iraq was Mr. Deputy. It was Saddam's title, his alone. Although he would remain Mr. Deputy for a decade, he was increasingly regarded as the regime's real strongman.

The hallmarks of the new regime soon became apparent. Barely three months after the coup, the regime announced on October 9, 1968, that it had smashed a major Zionist spy ring. Fifth columnists were denounced before crowds of tens of thousands. On January 5, 1969, seventeen "spies" went on trial. Fourteen were hung, eleven of whom were Jewish, their bodies left to dangle before crowds of hundreds of thousands in Baghdad's Liberation Square. Even the Egyptian newspaper *al-Ahram* condemned the spectacle: "The hanging of fourteen people in the public square is certainly not a heartwarming sight, nor is it the occasion for organizing a festival." Baghdad radio scoffed at the international condemnation, of which there was shockingly little, by declaring, "We hanged spies, but the Jews crucified Christ." Over the next year and a half, a tapestry of alleged treason was unraveled, providing a steady spectacle of denunciation and execution. The victims were no longer primarily Jews. Very soon they were mostly Muslims. The Jews had been but a stepping-stone to the regime's real target, its political rivals. The Baath began their rule with an inauguration of blood.

Saad al-Din Ibrahim, a respected Egyptian scholar, was later to call such regimes "new monarchies in republican garb." Disillusioned with what he regarded as the failure of the new breed of "revolutionary leaders" to deliver on the radical promises they had made for transforming Arab society when they seized power, Ibrahim concluded: "Despite the presence of a political party, popular committees, and the president's claim that he is one of the people . . . the ruler in his heart of hearts does not trust to any of this nor to his fellow strugglers of all those years. The only people he can trust are first, the members of his family; second, the

34

tribe; third, the sect, and so we have arrived at the neo-monarchies in the Arab nation.

"The matter is not restricted to the appointment of relatives in key positions, but to how those relatives commit all sorts of transgressions, legal, financial, and moral without accounting, as if the country were a private estate to do what they like."

From the beginning Saddam's base was the security services. Through them he controlled the party. Saddam established the financial autonomy of his power base early on, in an innovative way. Although Islam forbids gambling, horse racing had been a popular sport under the monarchy. Qassim had banned horse races; Saddam reintroduced them. He used the funds that betting generated to provide an unfettered, independent source of revenue. After 1973, when the price of oil quadrupled, Saddam's resources rose accordingly. He began to stash away considerable sums for the party and security services, often in accounts outside the country, which are today frozen because of international sanctions imposed in response to the invasion of Kuwait.

If Bakr continued to live modestly after 1968, Saddam and his associates were bent on reversing a lifetime of personal indignities, real and imagined. He used his new political power to acquire the social and economic standing he had long coveted. Years of struggle and deprivation filled him with a measure of greed far greater than those whom he had usurped. It made him far more ruthless in his determination to hold on to power and to break all who stood in his way or who might one day challenge his rule.

Saddam and his associates became social climbers. In 1969, Saddam's oldest half brother, Barzan, was made the new director of the prestigous Aliwwiya club, the traditional haunt of the servants of imperial Britain, frequented earlier in the century by such historical figures as Sir Percy Cox, Britain's first high commissioner, and the intrepid Gertrude Bell, the embassy's Oriental secretary. According to Iraqi sources, Baath party members and their wives would enjoy coming to the club in expensive, ostentatious clothes. They were fond of matching jewelry—his and hers cufflinks and earrings cut from the same stone. Saddam hired an Armenian tailor who sewed the lining of his jackets from the same silk as his ties. As Saddam's tastes grew more sophisticated, the tailor was sent to Europe to have the clothes made there.

Far from the public image of asceticism in the service of nationalism which it was the party's official duty to project, Saddam and his closest colleagues became better known for their vulgarity. Mafia-like stories of their extreme clannishness and brutality are legion inside Iraq. But rarely have they been told beyond its borders. Here are a few:

A passion for social respectability, its intensity betraying an awareness of its absence, was apparently one reason Saddam took a second wife from an old distinguished Baghdad merchant family. The tall and blond Samira Shahbandar was already married to Nurredin al-Safi, an Iraqi Airways official, when she was first introduced to Saddam. Safi prudently stepped aside so that Saddam could marry her. He was later promoted to director of the airline company.

After the marriage, a member of the Shahbandar clan named Farouk told his wife in what he thought was the intimacy of their bedroom that Samira was not a real Shahbandar. Her father, he explained, had simply taken the family name. Farouk was unaware that the bedroom was bugged. He and his wife were arrested and sentenced to life imprisonment. They are still in jail.

Saddam is not a man to tolerate aspersions on his

character or slights to members of his family. On one occasion, another Takriti, General Omar al-Hazzah, boasted to a woman friend, while visiting her home, that he had once slept with Saddam's mother. The woman's home was wired. When Saddam acquired the tape recording, he called a conclave of the Takriti clan and played it for them. According to one eyewitness, Saddam openly wept, crying: "What do you expect me to do with a man like that?" The response was predictable. Hazzah and his son, an officer in the presidential guard, were executed. Their homes were bulldozed and reduced to rubble. The woman was executed and hanged.

Saddam is cut from the same cloth as his mother, Subha. When one of Subha's married daughters had a problematic pregnancy and came down with a high fever, the daughter was taken to a private hospital for women in Baghdad, headed by a prominent gynecologist. After the doctor had examined the woman, Subha stopped him in front of several members of the hospital staff standing in the corridor and screamed, "You son of a bitch, if my daughter dies, I will erect your gallows outside your hospital and hang you!" The man fainted.

Saddam's uncle Khayrallah Tulfah ranks among the greediest of the clan. He made his fortune as mayor of Baghdad, a position to which he was appointed soon after the Baath took power. His corruption became so notorious that Saddam was eventually forced to remove him from office. But he is still a man of immense wealth, with a near monopoly of the country's citrus production. Accustomed to expropriating property by making landowners offers they refuse at their peril, Khayrallah was taken aback when one Iraqi whose land had been taken in 1981 threatened to sue. According to the hapless landowner, Khayrallah replied with a shrug: "Why waste your time? If we are in power, you will get nothing and you will only hurt yourself. If we are overthrown, you won't get one centimeter of my flesh, because there are so many people waiting to cut me up."

Khayrallah is a crude and ignorant man who is unembarrassed by his prejudices. In 1981, for example, the government publishing house distributed Khayrallah's pamphlet entitled *Three Whom God Should Not Have Created: Persians, Jews, and Flies.* Persians, Khayrallah writes, are "animals God created in the shape of humans," Jews are a "mixture of the dirt and leftovers of diverse peoples," and flies are a puzzling nuisance "whom we do not understand God's purpose in creating."

Iraq is run as a private preserve of Saddam and his inner clique. He distributes wealth, assigning sectors to his family and other close associates to control and to milk. His cousin and son-in-law Hussein Kamel al-Majid is responsible for military purchases. Arab sources report that on a 1987 purchase of 120 Chinese Scud missiles, Hussein Kamel pocketed a "personal commission" of $60 million. Khayrallah, as noted, makes his money on land. Saddam's first wife, Sajida, makes hers on trade. His eldest son, Uday, now twenty-six years old, has free rein over local business ventures and has built up an extensive commercial empire. He is the owner of Super Chicken, a food-processing chain, which in addition to monopolizing the fowl market, produces cheese, eggs and beef, according to an article in *The Observer.* He also owns an ice cream company called The Wave. In 1988, the newspaper reported, as part of the regime's effort to take its bloated and inefficient public sector private, the National Meat Company was put up for sale. Uday went to the acting governor of the Central Bank, Subhi Frangoul, and told him to transfer 10 million dinars out of the country at the official rate of three dollars to the dinar. Given the country's hard currency shortage, the request was highly unusual. Frangoul stepped out of the room to call Saddam, who told him, "Sure, let him do it. It's his money." Uday then proceeded to sell $8.5 million of the $30 million he received on the black market, where the dollar fetched nine times its official rate. Not only did he manage to raise the cash to buy the meat company, he still had $20 million left over.

Uday's talents as a businessman are perhaps matched only by his capacity for violence. His murder of his father's valet is a case in point. He was well known for his hot temper, having already "made his bones" by killing two men who had objected to his treatment of women. Now it was the valet's turn to feel his wrath. Over the years, Kamal Hana Gegeo had performed many favors for Saddam, including acting as go-between for Saddam and the woman who was to be his second wife. Uday feared that their union might mean that he would not inherit his father's position. In October 1988, Uday decided to take his revenge at a party in honor of Suzy Mubarak, the wife of Egypt's president. Although the party's host, Iraqi Vice President Taha Mohyiden Maruf, had learned of Uday's intentions, he was powerless to stop Saddam's reckless son, who arrived at the party with his bodyguards. Pushing Maruf aside, he bludgeoned Gegeo with a heavy club. When Saddam learned what had happened, it is said that he became so enraged, his first wife Sajida had to call upon her brother Adnan Khayrallah, the defense minister, to stop Saddam from killing Uday himself.

The incident jolted the family, and tensions grew. When a high-ranking Kuwaiti delegation went to Baghdad in February 1989, four months after the feud, Adnan confided to the Kuwaitis that he was in personal danger. He was no longer involved in military purchases, he said, or in military intelligence, and he had lost his authority over the Republican Guards, the elite military units. The next month *The Sunday Times* of London reported rumors that Adnan would be dismissed. Two months later he died in a helicopter crash.

It is instructive to recall that Adnan was Saddam's cousin, the son of his uncle and foster father Khayrallah Tulfah, a companion since boyhood, and, of course, his brother-in-law. Saddam trusts no one. Those who have had long experience with him know that. Egyptian President Hosni Mubarak has called him a "psychopath." The Saudis have called him "psychotic."

When Saddam travels abroad, which is infrequently and almost always to other Arab countries, he makes sure to take his own food and food taster. He is said to take his own chair to prevent an enemy from embedding a poisonous tack or needle in the cushion. Before he sits down, a trusted guard brings in the chair, and as soon as the session is over and he rises, his aide removes it.

At the Arab Cooperation Council summit in February 1990, the lights went out briefly. According to Arab sources, Saddam, fearing an assassination attempt, dove under the table for cover. Of the four heads of state present, he was the only one to hit the floor.

Saddam is equally suspicious when he receives visitors. An Arab professional delegation visited Baghdad in 1986. Suddenly they were summoned to a rare interview with Saddam. According to a member of that delegation, they were all obliged to strip naked and were searched. The security check was so humiliating that it caused one woman to start crying in protest that she did not even want to meet Saddam.

Saddam Hussein has come a long way. He fought hard to get to the top. Survival has not been easy. It has required cunning and patience, fortitude and a willingness to risk everything. A weaker character, with less

ambition and intelligence, might have ended up no
more than a scoundrel and a petty thief. But Saddam
never lost confidence in his own destiny. He carries
about him the air of a man who commands absolutely
the world in which he lives. As his power has expanded,
his dreams and pretensions have grown. Saddam's reluctance to confess his rough-hewn peasant origins has
prompted him to claim the noblest lineage. He has presented a family tree to the Iraqi public. It traces his
roots to the prophet Mohammed. Saddam Hussein has
said: "The glory of the Arabs stems from the glory of
Iraq. Throughout history, whenever Iraq became
mighty and flourished, so did the Arab nation. This is
why we are striving to make Iraq mighty, formidable,
able and developed."

The means to be used are graphically spelled out in
the words of al-Hadjadj, the governor of what is now
Iraq in seventh century A.D., whose reign is described
by Marshall Hodgson in *The Venture of Islam* as one of
"frank terror." These lines are known to every Iraqi
schoolchild: "I see heads before me that are ripe and
ready for the plucking, and I am the one to pluck them,
and I see blood glistening between the turbans and the
beards."

III

Prime-Time Terror

No episode better reveals the essence of Saddam's regime than the baptism of blood that accompanied his ascension to absolute power in July 1979. For eleven years Saddam had waited, working in apparent harmony with his older cousin, head of the Baath party, and president of the republic, Ahmad Hassan al-Bakr. For years Saddam had worked to build a loyal and ruthless secret police apparatus. On the surface, all was well. Behind the scenes, trouble was brewing for Saddam.

The triumph of the Ayatollah Ruhollah Khomeini over the shah of Iran in January 1979 had aroused Iraq's Shiites, politically powerless, although they comprised 55 percent of the population. Deadly riots had erupted in a huge Shiite slum in east Baghdad, after the government had arrested the Shiites' foremost religious leader. The Baath party organization had collapsed in that sector of the city. The disturbances were so serious that Bakr concluded that it would be unwise to defy Shiite opinion within the party. But Saddam opposed any concessions. The party's Shiites, he felt, had failed to control their co-religionists. He suspected them of leniency toward the rioters, and he felt they must be purged and punished. Shiites within the party, who had been associated with Saddam, began to gather around Bakr. They were joined by some non-Shiites and army officers. They began to cast about for a way to check Saddam.

Ironically, Saddam himself had provided them a way. In the fall of 1978, Iraq and Syria, ruled by murderously rival Baath parties, suddenly announced that they would unite. Saddam was the architect of that policy. He wanted the Arab states to break their ties with Egypt, ostensibly to punish Cairo for the peace treaty it was about to sign with Israel. If he could force the Arabs to ostracize Egypt, the most important and populous Arab state, he could open the way for Iraq's dominance of the Arab world. Saddam succeeded, at least in his first step. At the November 1978 Arab summit in Baghdad, Saddam threatened to attack Kuwait, while Syrian president Hafez al-Assad warned the Saudis, "I will transfer the battle to your bedrooms." The Arab states agreed to break all ties with Egypt.

Unity with Syria, however, threatened to undermine Saddam within Iraq. It soon became apparent that Bakr could become president of a Syrian-Iraqi federation, Assad could be vice president, and Saddam would be number three. His rivals urged unity with Syria as a way of blunting his ambitions, while Saddam became increasingly apprehensive that they might succeed.

While Saddam saw the danger to himself in the proposed union, the Takritis saw their monopoly of power threatened, along with their immense privileges. Saddam decided to press the sixty-four-year-old Bakr to resign so that he could become president and leaned heavily on the family to support him. According to Iraqi sources, Khayrallah Tulfah, backed by his son Adnan, urged Bakr to step down for the good of the clan. Reluctantly, Bakr came to agree, although not before sending Assad a secret request to hasten union negotiations because "there is a current here which is anxious to kill the union in the bud before it bears fruit," according to British journalist Patrick Seale.

On July 16, 1979, President Bakr's resignation was announced, officially for reasons of health. Saddam Hussein was named president, as well as secretary-general of the Iraqi Baath party, commander in chief, head of the government, and chairman of the Revolutionary Command Council.

Saddam had succeeded in carrying out his putsch. On July 22 he staged an astonishing spectacle to inaugurate his presidency when he convened a top-level party meeting of some 1,000 party cadres. This meeting was recorded and the videotape distributed to the party. A few minutes of that tape have appeared on American television and it has been briefly described elsewhere, but no full account of that extraordinary meeting has been published before. The following account is based on an audiotape made available to the authors and the testimony of an individual who has seen the video.

The meeting begins with Muhyi Abdul Hussein al-Mashhadi, secretary of the Revolutionary Command Council and a Shiite party member for over twenty years, reading a fabricated confession detailing his participation in a supposed Syrian-backed conspiracy. Muhyi reads hurriedly, with the eager tone of a man who believes that his cooperation will win him a reprieve. (It did not.) Then Saddam, after a long, rambling statement about traitors and party loyalty, announces: "The people whose names I am going to read out should repeat the slogan of the party and leave the hall." He begins to read, stopping occasionally to light and relight his cigar. At one point he pronounces a first name, "Ghanim," but then changes his mind and goes on to the next name.

After Saddam finishes reading the list of the condemned, the remaining members of the audience begin to shout, "Long live Saddam," and "Let me die! Long live the father of Uday [Saddam's eldest son]." The cries are prolonged and hysterical. When the shouting dies down, Saddam begins to speak, but stops suddenly to retrieve a handkerchief. Tears stream down his face. As he dabs his eyes with the handkerchief, the assembly breaks into loud sobbing.

Recovering himself, Saddam speaks: "I'm sure many of our comrades have things to say, so let us discuss them." Party members call for a wider purge. One man rises, and says, "Saddam Hussein is too lenient. There has been a problem in the party for a long time. . . . There is a line between doubt and terror, and unbalanced democracy. The problem of too much leniency needs to be addressed by the party." Then Saddam's cousin, Ali Hassan al-Majid, declares: "Everything that you did in the past was good and everything that you will do in the future is good. I say this from my faith in the party and your leadership." After more appeals from the party faithful to search out traitors, Saddam brings the discussion to a close. More than twenty men, some of the most prominent in Iraq, have been taken from the hall. Saddam concludes, "We don't need Stalinist methods to deal with traitors here. We need Baathist methods." The audience erupts into tumultuous applause.

In the days following, Saddam obliges senior party members and government ministers to join him in personally executing the most senior of their former comrades. The murdered include Mohammed Mahjoub, a member of the ruling Revolutionary Command Council; Mohammed Ayesh, head of the labor unions, and Biden Fadhel, his deputy; Ghanim Abdul Jalil, a Shiite member of the council and once a close associate of Saddam's; and Talib al-Suweleh, a Jordanian. Saddam's two most powerful opponents were dispatched before the July 22 meeting took place: General Walid Mahmoud Sirat, a senior army officer and the core of the opposition to Saddam, was tortured and his body mutilated; Adnan Hamdani, deputy prime minister, who had been in Syria on government business, was taken from the airport on his return and promptly murdered. Some sources believe that as many as 500 people may have been executed secretly in Saddam's night of the long knives. The true figure may never be known.

The savagery of Saddam's victory was meant to make him seem invincible. His rivals had been smashed; his primacy as absolute leader secured. He had replaced the state with the party, and now the party with himself, the giver of life and death. The terror that was his to dispense would make people fearful, but it would also inspire awe, and in a few, the appearance of mercy would even evoke gratitude. Saddam had made good his promise of 1971 when he had declared that "with our party methods, there is no chance for anyone who disagrees with us to jump on a couple of tanks and overthrow the government." From 1920 until 1979, Iraq had experienced thirteen coups d'état. Saddam was determined that his would be the last.

The key to understanding Saddam's rule, in the opinion of Samir al-Khalil, author of *Republic of Fear,* lies in the sophisticated way the regime has implicated ordinary people in the violence of the party by absorbing them into the repressive organs of the state. As Khalil writes: "Success is achieved by the degree to which society is prepared to police itself. Who is an informer? In Baathist Iraq the answer is anybody." A European diplomat stationed in Baghdad once told a reporter from *The New York Times* that "there is a feeling that at least three million Iraqis are watching the eleven million others."

His assessment may not be exaggerated. The Ministry of Interior is the largest of twenty-three government ministries. Khalil estimates that "the combined numbers of police and militia . . . greatly exceed the size of the standing army, and [is] in absolute terms twice as large as anything experienced in Iran under the shah." And this in a nation whose population is just under one-third the size of Iran's.

In 1984, about 25,000 people were full members of the Baath party; another 1.5 million Iraqis were sympathizers or supporters. The former are generally prepared to embrace the party line; the latter are often in the party for some peripheral reason. Party membership may be a requirement for their jobs. However lukewarm their attachment to the party, and it is for many of these, they are still part of the system, obliged to attend the weekly party meetings. If one multiplies each member by four or five dependents, the Baath can be said to have implicated slightly under half the entire population. About 30 percent of the eligible population is employed by the government. If one includes the army and militia, the figure jumps to 50 percent of the urban work force—this in a society in which 65 percent of its citizens now live in urban areas. For all practical purposes, state and party are synonymous.

"Oppressed people always deserve their fate; tyranny is achieved by a whole nation, it is not the accomplishment of a single individual," remarked the Marquis de Custine, after visiting Czarist Russia in the first part of the nineteenth century. His judgment is perhaps too severe. And yet it is not wholly false. As Simon Leys has observed of Mao's China, but which is equally true of Saddam's Iraq: "If totalitarianism were merely the persecution of an innocent nation by a small group of tyrants, overthrowing it would still be a relatively easy matter. Actually, the extraordinary resilience of the system resides precisely in its ability to associate the victims themselves with the all-pervasive organization and management of terror, to make them participate in the crimes of their executioners, to turn them into active collaborators and accomplices. In this way the victims acquire a personal stake in the defense and preservation of the very regime that is torturing and crushing them."

Police work of one kind or another is a major profession in Iraq. In 1978 more than 150,000 people worked in the Ministry of Interior and its various agencies. They comprised 23 percent of all public-sector employees. (The East Germans long advised and trained the Iraqi security forces. Iraq's security police is probably similar to that which East Germany had, and the populations of the two countries are roughly the same size. In East Germany over 1,000 people worked as telephone tappers, 2,000 in mail surveillance, and 5,000 following other people. The figures in Iraq are at least as high, and perhaps higher, as Baghdad is an even more controlled society than East Germany was.)

The Iraqi security organizations have many branches, with overlapping, competing functions, each replete with its own prisons. They are designed to spy on each other as much as on the citizenry. The following are among the most important:

•The General Intelligence Department (or Mukhabarat), which grew out of the Baath party's secret police, the Jihaz Haneen, founded by Saddam Hussein in the mid-1960s. It is now a state organization and is concerned with both external and internal affairs. It was headed by Barzan Ibrahim al-Takriti, Saddam's half brother, from 1974 to 1983. He was succeeded by Fadel Barrak, a close aide to Bakr, who was chief until the summer of 1989. Fadel Selfeeg, a maternal cousin of Saddam's, then became acting head until Saddam's middle half brother, Sabawi, took over at the end of 1989.

•State Internal Security (or Amn al-Amm) is mostly concerned with internal operations, although it has occasionally participated in foreign missions. Its chief is reliably reported to be Saddam's youngest half brother, Wathban.

•The Military Intelligence Department (or Istikhbarat) supervises security within the army, spies on foreign armies and runs the military attachés in Iraqi embassies abroad. Along with the General Intelligence Department, it operates terrorist actions against dissident Iraqis in exile and other targets abroad, carrying out Saddam's threat that "the hand of the revolution can reach out to its enemies wherever they are found." Disaffected Iraqis have been killed in at least the following countries—Lebanon, Sweden, England, Egypt, the Sudan, and the United States. At least one assassination was attempted in Paris. At least four assassinations of Iraqi exiles in Detroit between 1977 and 1983 are suspected to be the work of Saddam Hussein. A Military Intelligence agent was convicted by a British court for leading the hit team which attacked Shlomo Argov, the Israeli ambassador to London. That incident provided the pretext for Israel's invasion of Lebanon in 1982.

•The Presidential Affairs Department (or Amn al-Khass) is directly attached to the office of Saddam Hussein. It controls foreign bank accounts and runs dummy companies for investment and procurement of contraband items. Saddam's cousin and son-in-law, Hussein Kamal al-Majid, who is also minister of military industry and industrialization, has close ties with the organization.

•Party Security (or Amn al-Hizb) coordinates intelligence on party members and controls party cells and offices in various districts of the country.

•Finally, there are the Border Guards, the Mobile Police Strike Force, the General Department of Nationality, and the General Department of Police.

The cynical manipulation of the Iraqi people, the abuses to which they have been subjected, and the torments they have endured, have been convincingly detailed in the reports of Amnesty International and Middle East Watch, a division of Human Rights Watch. Both are non-profit independent human-rights monitoring groups. Extracts from their recent reports are included in the appendix to this book.

Middle East Watch, in its 1990 report, *Human Rights in Iraq*, observes that "Iraq under the Baath party has become a nation of informers. Party members are said to be required to inform on family, friends, and acquaintances, including other party members. . . . All teachers were required to join the party, and those who refused or were deemed ineligible were fired. . . . Teachers reportedly ask pupils about their parents' views, with the result that parents feel obliged to disguise their thoughts in front of their children." The penalty for refusing to inform is severe. According to the London-based *Index on Censorship:* "One reliable report concerns a member of the ruling Baath party related to a former senior official, arrested in Baghdad in August [1987] after government informers reported that he had been present at a gathering where jokes were made about President Saddam Hussein. [The party member] was arrested for not informing the authorities, as were the male members of his family: three sons and a son-in-law. During interrogation they were subjected to torture. . . . All five were subsequently executed and the family's home was bulldozed."

Public insult of the president or of the top institutions of the state or party is punishable by life imprisonment or death. The Iraqi government lists twenty-four offenses that carry the death penalty. According to the Middle East Watch report, "collective punishment is routinely practiced in Iraq. In Kurdish areas, people have been rounded up randomly and shot in reprisal for attacks on Iraqi troops or officials. When persons wanted for political or security crimes could not be found, family members have frequently been arrested and in some instances tortured and murdered." People in Iraq "disappear." As Khalil describes the scene in *Republic of Fear:* "What one assumes to be the corpse is brought back weeks or maybe months later and delivered to the head of the family in a sealed box. A death certificate is produced for signature to the effect that the person has died of fire, drowning, or other such accident. Someone is allowed to accompany the police and the box for a ceremony, but at no time is he or she permitted to see the corpse. The cost of the proceedings is demanded in advance, and the whole thing is over within hours of the first knock on the door."

Accounts of torture are persistent and well-documented. In 1981, Amnesty International reported that in November 1978 the authorities arrested a young journalist: "During the first two days he was taken to different rooms and beaten with fists, rods and a whip. . . . In one room he was caressed and sexually fondled, before being taken out and beaten and kicked. The torture then became more systematic, taking place every one or two hours. His head was whipped and beaten so hard that he lost consciousness. . . . After regaining consciousness on one occasion he was aware that his trousers had been removed and realized that he had been raped. He was then made to sit on a cold bottle-like object which was forced up his rectum."

The regime also tortures family members as a means to punish those it cannot catch, or as a way of increasing the pressure on those already in prisons. When the authorities cannot capture the suspects they seek, relatives are rounded up as hostages. Children are arrested and tortured to force confessions from their parents.

The Kurds have been the special object of the regime's repression. Largely Sunni Muslim by religion, but non-Arab, they comprise about 20 percent of Iraq's population. The victors in World War I promised the Kurds the possibility of a state of their own carved out of the fragments of the Ottoman Empire. But a Kurdish state did not materialize, and tensions have always existed between Baghdad and the Kurds. Yet no Iraqi regime has been as brutal as Saddam's.

The vicious fight against the Kurds has been conducted without regard to any notions of human rights. In one well-documented atrocity, for example, sixty-seven women and children who had sought shelter in a cave to escape artillery shelling were knowingly incinerated. In March 1974, two Kurdish towns of about 25,000 and 20,000 inhabitants were utterly razed. Napalm was routinely used. Hundreds of thousands of Kurds were forced to flee. Edward Mortimer, who covered the war for *The Times* of London, estimates that up to half of the overall population of 1.5 million became displaced persons, and that more than 100,000 were forced into Iran.

Kurdish rebels who surrendered to government troops were often massacred once they had laid down their arms. Mass deportations of entire families and villages were carried out; families were resettled in the southwestern desert region of Iraq. The number of people affected is unknown, although estimates range from a low of 50,000 by *The Economist* to as many as 350,000 by opposition sources.

A particularly gruesome feature of Saddam's willingness to wage war without scruple is his unhesitating use of chemical weapons to suppress the Kurds, making Iraq the only state in the world ever to have used them against its own citizens. Survivors were interviewed by Amnesty International officials in October 1988, who reported: "Some of those interviewed said members of their families, including children, had died instantly as a result of chemical attacks, while others were too seriously wounded to flee. Iraqi troops were said to have first used chemical weapons, then entered the affected villages, dynamiting the houses or razing them to the ground with bulldozers."

Saddam's use of terror as a routine instrument of state policy is intended to destroy the fabric of civil society, to throttle all centers (or potential centers) of opposition. He promotes a climate of suspicion in the country so that no one can trust another enough to combine together against him. Terror is the solvent of an autocratic and egalitarian culture. Individuals have no rights; they are entirely subordinate to the demands of the state. The state is subordinate to Saddam.

Since the invasion of Kuwait, many people have been shocked by Saddam's actions, in blatant violation of international law and convention. Saddam has sought to change the demographic character of Kuwait, in violation of the Geneva conventions. Records of Kuwaiti citizenship have been taken to Baghdad. Kuwaitis have been harassed into fleeing, while Iraqis have been encouraged to move into Kuwait. Saddam holds foreign nationals against their will, as shields for military targets. Iraqi troops have not scrupled to respect the sovereignty of foreign embassies, entering them by force and seizing their occupants. Previously, Saddam distinguished between the methods he used on his own population and those he employed with the outside world. Now he deals with the world in the same way he has long dealt with Iraqis—through naked force and the threat to escalate his use of force to the limits of his brutal capabilities.

Saddam understands that his ability to project power outside the country helps maintain his authority inside the country. Threatening and intimidating other states contributes to an aura of invincibility at home. Adventures beyond Iraq's borders provide a rationale for the terror of a police state. They keep a restless and disgruntled population busy. And they keep busy the very army he has built up, partly to impress his authority on the population. The ancient Greeks, familiar with the many tyrants of their day, cast light on this age-old phenomenon. Plato wrote: "A tyrant is always setting some war in motion so that the people will be in need of a leader." Aristotle said tyrants are "warmongers with the object of keeping their subjects constantly occupied and continually in need of a leader."

Saddam has had to take care that his huge army does not turn on him. He has used methods similar to those he used with the internal security forces to establish his control over the army. He sought first to hollow out the institutions of the military, to ensure that only party stalwarts would survive to form a new and trustworthy officer corps. Quick military courses raised hundreds of officers from Baath party ranks. A system of political commissars was established to supervise the army officers, and the commissars themselves were supervised by the Baath's military committee. Political loyalty became the primary criterion for officers' promotion. But Saddam can never be sure that he has the army's loyalty or respect. His hold over the army has always been a problem. He has no military experience and began with no base in the army. Thus, Saddam has been careful not to let any individual military leader become too powerful. Officers are frequently rotated and those that might become dangerous are executed.

It is said that in the wake of the early reversals suffered by Iraq during its war with Iran, Saddam personally rebuked an officer who lost his nerve when confronted by the human wave assaults mounted by fanatical Iranian youths. Saddam shot the man point-blank with his revolver. In 1982, Saddam had the following exchange with a reporter from the West German magazine *Stern*:

Stern: It is known that your excellency is not satisfied with the Iraqi military command. Is it true that in the recent period three hundred high-ranking military officers have been executed?

Hussein: No. However, two divisional commanders and the commander of a mechanized unit were executed. This is something very normal in all wars.

Stern: For what reason?

Hussein: They did not undertake their responsibilities in the battle for Khorramshahr.

These methods of ensuring obedience became difficult to maintain during the long war with Iran, as they seriously compromised the army's ability to wage war efficiently. Saddam found himself increasingly obliged to turn over more independent authority to the army. Generals inevitably became popular public figures, but when the war ended, Saddam redoubled his efforts to secure control. Between December 1988 and March 1989, he had hundreds of officers arrested and many executed. Iraq's most celebrated war hero, General Maher Abdul Rashid, whose daughter was once married to Saddam's son, Qusay, disappeared from public view.

The inquisition Saddam has loosed on his people is perhaps difficult to understand. After all, with Iraq's immense oil wealth, why squander the nation's youth, its resources, and its future in a self-inflicted bloodletting extreme even by the standards of the Middle East? There is something elemental in Saddam's behavior. Robert Conquest, the author of *The Great Terror*, the classic work on Stalin's Gulag, has perhaps described one part of the answer: "One does not establish a dictatorship in order to safeguard a revolution; one makes the revolution in order to establish the dictatorship. The object of persecution is persecution. The object of torture is torture. The object of power is power." Still, the unending purges, each more brutal in its fury than the preceding one, elude comprehension. Perhaps Alexandre Vialatte captures something at the heart of such a despotism when he tells of the fate of cannibals in a remote tropical land, and remarks, "There are no more cannibals in that country since the local authorities ate the last ones."

IV

The Legacy of
Nebuchadnezzar

Saddam's unhesitating use of terror to solidify and justify his rule is deeply rooted in history. Unlike such homogeneous and authentic Arab nations as Egypt, Iraq was cobbled together by foreign powers from a diverse set of fractious tribes and peoples. The paradox of Saddam's rule is that from this patched-together country he has sought to forge a single nation in the name of a pan-Arabism which denies the legitimacy of national borders imposed earlier in this century by European colonialism. Appeals to patriotism are couched in the name of a pre-colonial past, a past in which Iraq itself didn't exist.

Saddam's campaign to enroll the past in the service of future glory is obsessive. He has embarked on a giant project to reconstruct a version of ancient Babylon. Millions of bricks have been baked, many of them inscribed: "The Babylon of Nebuchadnezzar was reconstructed in the era of Saddam Hussein." Saddam is widely portrayed as a latter-day Nebuchadnezzar, the sixth century B.C. Babylonian ruler, whose memory the Old Testament has preserved as the conqueror of Jerusalem, the leader who carried the Hebrews into captivity. During one official nighttime celebration, diplomats and invited guests were asked to cast their eyes upwards into the black desert sky. There above them hung twin portraits of Saddam and Nebuchadnezzar etched against the night by laser beams. Saddam's features were rendered unusually sharp and hard in order more closely to resemble the ancient carved images of Nebuchadnezzar.

The destiny of Iraq is inextricably bound up with mystical notions of Mesopotamian antiquity. The Greeks gave Iraq the name Mesopotamia, meaning the land between the rivers. And indeed, the Tigris and Euphrates rivers form the core of present-day Iraq. Baghdad lies on the Tigris, which flows southward from Turkey to join the Euphrates, coming from Syria in the west. The rivers meet above Basra, Iraq's second largest city and the capital of the south, where they merge into one waterway, the Shatt al-Arab, "the river of the Arabs." South of Basra, the Shatt al-Arab forms the border between Iran and Iraq.

Somewhat larger than the state of California, Iraq, with a population of 17 million, is a country of diverse terrain and peoples. Sunni Arabs are 20 percent of Iraq's population, most of whom live in the area north of Baghdad between the two rivers. The fertile, densely inhabited river plain south of Baghdad is home to Shiite Arabs, 55 percent of the population, who form a small majority and an overwhelming plurality. Kurds, a non-Arab and largely Sunni Muslim people, reside in the mountains in the north and constitute another 20 percent of the population. Western Iraq, sparsely populated by Bedouin tribes, is part of the Great Syrian Desert, arching through eastern Jordan and Saudi Arabia up to central Syria.

While the two rivers define Iraq's core, they do not delimit its outer boundaries, which for the most part are without historical basis. The contemporary state of Iraq arose from the infamous Sykes-Picot agreement of 1916, under which the British and the French divided the spoils of their anticipated victory over the Ottoman

Empire in World War I. After the war, Britain merged three former Ottoman provinces, centered on Baghdad, Basra, and the northern city of Mosul, to form the new state of Iraq.

Only Iraq's border with Iran is not artificial. It existed for 250 years as the boundary between Persia and the Ottoman Empire. But most of Iraq's other borders—those with Kuwait and Saudi Arabia in the south, and those with Jordan and Syria in the west—are little more than straight lines in the sand, drawn by the British. Iraq's border with Turkey corresponds to an Ottoman administrative division, the boundary of the former Mosul province. But that line is also artificial, as it arbitrarily divides the Kurdish population living on the Iraqi-Turkish border.

Geography has been cruel to Iraq. As an independent state, Iraq suffers handicaps that did not exist when it was a province of the far-reaching Ottoman Empire. First, Iraq lacks natural defenses. Like Germany, to which Iraq has often been compared, it faces the problem of encirclement by hostile powers. Given the openness of the land surrounding the two rivers, it is not surprising that the Mesopotamian region has historically been vulnerable to invasion from all sides.

Moreover, Iraq's two largest cities are highly vulnerable. Baghdad is seventy miles from the Iranian border; Basra, merely thirteen. During the Iraq-Iran war Baghdad was subject to Iranian missile attacks long before Iraq's missile program gave it an equal capacity, while Basra was under near-constant siege. Finally, Iraq is practically landlocked. Its access to the sea is limited to a scant twenty-six miles of Persian Gulf coast, and the Shatt al-Arab is the only maritime route to Iraq's interior. The outbreak of the Gulf war in 1980 closed the Shatt, and Iran cut access to Iraq's Gulf ports. During the war Iraq became entirely dependent on its neighbors, particularly Jordan, for the transport of vital supplies.

It is one of the ironies of history that Saddam Hussein rules the land where civilization began. The Sumerians, living in the Mesopotamian plain south of present-day Baghdad in the third millennium B.C., developed the world's first system of writing and the world's first urban culture and administrative bureaucracy.

A thousand years later, two empires divided Mesopotamia. The Babylonians, renowned for their cultural and scientific achievements, ruled in the south. The great king Hammurabi (1792–1750 B.C.) was the first to codify and write down a legal framework for society. Outstanding astronomers, the Babylonians developed the system of measuring time that we continue to use today. The hour is divided into sixty minutes and the minute into sixty seconds because sixty was the basis of the Babylonian number system.

Babylon's rival, Assyria, controlled the northern half of Mesopotamia, with its capital at Nineveh, near present-day Mosul. Warlike and keen on conquest, the Assyrians developed the world's first militaristic culture. Assyria's greatest conqueror, Tiglath-Pileser III (744–727 B.C.), developed the key concept behind their rule—a permanent military force controlled by a permanent political bureaucracy. The Assyrians were also notorious for their cruelty, which had the undesired effect of inspiring near-constant revolt among their subject peoples, making their empire fragile.

Like other ancient rulers, the Assyrians had their images carved in huge stone reliefs. The images of the seventh-century king Asserbanipal (668–627 B.C.) testify to the harshness of Assyrian rule. Like Saddam's monumental bronze arms rising above the battered helmets of dead Iranian soldiers in Baghdad today, Asserbanipal is shown in one relief standing before the head of his enemy hanging from a tree, with bodies piled around him. Although today considered great works of ancient art, the Assyrian stonework served the same purposes as Saddam's videotapes and his cult of personality in general—to remind the subjects of the ruler's power and brutality in order to make his authority unchallengeable. Another parallel exists as well between the ancient Assyrians and the modern Iraqis. A distinguished archaeologist has argued that internal problems lay behind the Assyrians' unceasing conquests and that their expansion derived "solely from the weakness of the system."

Around 500 B.C. Mesopotamia's ancient civilizations came to an end. Babylon and Assyria fell to Cyrus the Great. Over the next eleven centuries, a variety of Greek and Persian rulers controlled Mesopotamia, until the seventh-century Arab-Islamic invasion brought something entirely new.

Saddam Hussein called his war with Iran "Qadissiyat Saddam," evoking memory of the battle of Qadissiyat in 637, when Arabian tribes, newly converted to Islam, defeated the Zoroastrian Persian rulers of Mesopotamia. The Muslims not only brought their religion but established Arab dominance in the country, giving it its modern name, Iraq. Yet Iraq's first century of Muslim rule was troubled. Early divisions within Islam reflected themselves in tensions in Iraq. The greatest such division was the Sunni-Shiite schism. The origins of that split lay in a dispute over the succession to the prophet Mohammed. One group, the Shia, or "party" of the prophet's cousin and son-in-law Ali, favored him as Mohammed's successor. The second group, the Sunnis, sought to accommodate the old aristocracy of Mecca, Islam's birthplace and its holiest site. The Sunnis prevailed, and three men of their choosing governed Islam in succession. But in 656 mutinous Arabian soldiers, bridling at what they considered the injustice and nepotism of Othman, the third caliph, murdered him and proclaimed Ali caliph.

Civil war followed. Ali retreated to the capital city of Iraq, Kufah, southwest of present-day Baghdad. Muwayah, the governor of Syria and a cousin of Othman, called for revenge, and Ali marched with his forces to meet him. After a few inconclusive skirmishes, Ali accepted mediation with Muwayah, but his more fanatical supporters viewed negotiation itself as a compromise with injustice and murdered him. Muwayah thereupon became caliph, founding the new Umayyad dynasty, and shifting the seat of Muslim rule to Damascus. Ali was buried in Najaf, which became an important shrine city for the Shiites. Ayatollah Khomeini would spend many years in exile there in the 1970s. A generation passed and Ali's son Hussein, grandson of the prophet, rebelled against Muwayah's son, who had become caliph on his father's death. In 680 Hussein was invited by the population of Kufah to lead a revolt. But before Hussein's arrival, the Kufans were cowed by the Umayyad authorities and at the crucial time failed to support him. Betrayed, Hussein and his small band of followers were massacred by an overwhelming army on the nearby plains of Karbala. Hussein's martyrdom became a focal point of Shiite doctrine and his bravery in facing certain death the subject of deeply rooted emotional passion plays. In turn, Karbala became a second shrine for the Shiites in Iraq.

Iraq did not achieve a measure of stability until 694, when the Umayyads appointed as governor the ruthless al-Hadjadj. Upon his arrival, al-Hadjadj summoned the population of Kufah and addressed them: "O people of Iraq, O people of discord and hypocrisy . . . You have been swift to sedition; you have lain in the lairs of error and have made a rule of transgression. By God, I shall strip you like bark, I shall truss you like a bundle of twigs, I shall beat you like stray camels. . . . By God, what I promise, I fulfill; what I purpose, I accomplish; what I measure, I cut off." Though notoriously brutal, al-Hadjadj is considered to have been an efficient governor who brought peace to Iraq and promoted trade and agriculture.

The new Muslim leaders built the city of Baghdad and made it their capital. Under the Abbasid Caliphate (750–1258), Islam reached its cultural apogee. Abbasid rule also marked the high point of Iraq's political and cultural development in the 2,500-year period between the end of the ancient Mesopotamian civilizations and the present day.

The Abbasids ruled a vast area from present-day Afghanistan to North Africa, and they encouraged the synthesis of Persian, Greek, and Arab learning. There followed a terrific burst of creativity in many disciplines—mathematics, chemistry, astronomy, medicine, geography, and literature. The Abbasids established a renowned research library, Bayt al-Hikmah, the House of Wisdom. Abu Nawwas, the eighth-century libertine poet, dedicated his verse to love and wine. Idrisi drew the first map of the world. The mathematician al-Kawarizmi, from whose name we derive the terms algorithm and logarithm, synthesized the study of algebra, and his book, *al-Jabr,* gave that field of mathematics its name.

Yet for all their glory, the Abbasids also reflected a darker side of Iraq's rulers. The ancient Persians had shared with their Assyrian contemporaries a tradition of harsh, absolutist monarchy, and the Abbasids, while Arab, had absorbed this aspect of Persian rule. Upon the overthrow of the Umayyad dynasty, the first Abbasid caliph, al-Saffah (750–754), slaughtered indiscriminately and ruthlessly as many members of the former ruling family as he could. Even the Abbasids' allies did not fare well under their harsh rule. The Shiites, for example, had been key supporters of the Abbasid revolt and had thereby gained a measure of autonomy, but the caliph al-Mansur (al-Saffah's successor) murdered their leaders to eliminate any source of authority not entirely subservient to him. Al-Mansur assembled a vast bureaucracy to supervise every province in minute detail, and he built a network of spies to prevent any conspiracies like the one that brought his own family to power.

The Abbasids consciously adopted from the Persians a court routine which elevated the caliph to a magnificent figure whose casual word was to be obeyed like divine law. Only the most privileged could speak with the caliph, and he could be approached only after an elaborate ritual, which included kissing the ground before his feet. All this stood opposed to the Arab and early Islamic tradition, according to which the caliph was supposed to be one of the people. It roused the ire of the religious leaders and the pious, including the Shiites, who were in intermittent revolt throughout the centuries of Abbasid rule.

The Abbasid caliphs eventually brought in Turkish mercenary soldiers to enforce their absolutist rule. By the end of the ninth century, however, the Turks came to dominate the court. They became the real rulers of Baghdad, reducing the caliph to a figurehead, whom they changed frequently and at will. In turn, government grew weak and lawlessness became endemic.

Abbasid glory had thus long passed from the scene by the time the Mongol armies appeared at the frontiers of Iraq. Alone among the Arab states, Iraq faced the devastation of the terrifying Mongol conquests. The invasions sealed a decline from which the country has never fully recovered. In 1258 the Mongol leader Hulagu, grandson of Genghis Khan, sacked Baghdad and laid the country waste. Ordinary Iraqis were put indiscriminately to the sword for over a week, and the Tigris flowed with blood. Historians estimate that more than 100,000 were slaughtered. Baghdad was looted, and all vestiges of Abassid culture and learning were destroyed. The centuries that followed were a dark period as political chaos, economic depression, and social disintegration set in. Iraq was subject to the depredations of foreign armies and nomadic incursions. The historian Phebe Marr has observed that it has not been Abbasid glory, but rather "the centuries of stagnation" that has most powerfully shaped the environment and character of twentieth-century Iraq.

Not until the sixteenth century did enduring government return to Iraq, but that rule did little to alleviate the country's distress. The Ottomans, originally a Turkish tribe from Central Asia, had built a vast empire in the fourteenth and fifteenth centuries, culminating in their conquest of Constantinople in 1453, which they renamed Istanbul, and where they established their capital. The Ottoman Sultan eventually assumed the title of caliph and the Ottomans, a Sunni people, became the dominant power in Islam.

The Ottoman Turks first conquered Iraq in 1534, in the initial phase of a long conflict with the Shiite Savafid dynasty in Iran. Iraq became a battlefield as Baghdad changed hands numerous times during the next two centuries.

In the course of the conquests and reconquests, the flames of sectarian hatred in Iraq were fanned. Whenever the Persians conquered Baghdad, they took revenge on the Sunni population, who had looked to the Ottomans as their champions. And with every Ottoman reconquest of the city, the Sunni population's calls for revenge could not be ignored and it was the Shiites' turn to become the victims. This deadly minuet went on until the final conquest of Baghdad in 1638, when Ottoman rule was finally established without interruption.

But intermittent hostilities between the Turks and Persians would last until the early nineteenth century. The Ottomans continued to distrust the Shiites and came to rely on a class of civil and military bureaucrats from the local Sunni population, or more frequently from non-Arab functionaries in the service of the Sultan. The descendants of this latter group subsequently became an important part of the urban Sunni aristocracy of modern Iraq.

Throughout the Ottoman period, southern Iraq was populated by fierce and independent Shiite Arab tribes. The holy centers of Shiism, Karbala and Najaf, exercised a strong religious and cultural influence on the surrounding countryside. It was during the Ottoman period that the ancestors of the Arab tribes of southern Iraq moved north from Arabia in the last phase of the periodic migrations that have long charactrized the relationship between Arabia and Mesopotamia. These Arab tribes came under the influence of the religious centers of Najaf and Karbala and became Shiite.

The Ottomans' power base was consequently restricted to the major cities, and their rule did not extend beyond them. As long as the tribal chieftains that dominated the countryside allowed them certain rights of transport and access and maintained some fiction of allegiance to the sultan, the Ottomans left them to their own ways. When the modern state of Iraq was formed, most of the population had little familiarity, or loyalty, to any central authority. Tribal, sectarian, and regional loyalties were much stronger than the new, unfamiliar, and artificial sense of Iraqi nationhood.

The destructive impact of war and sectarianism were compounded by Iraq's remoteness from Istanbul. (Vienna is closer to Istanbul than Baghdad is.) And in those days of primitive transportation and slow communications, such distances seemed far greater than they do today. Iraq was a true backwater of the empire; Ottoman bureaucrats whose fortunes had waned in the court were sent into semi-exile there. Social, economic, and political developments in the Ottoman Empire arrived in Iraq many years later and much diluted. Iraq, of course, was even further from Europe than it was from Istanbul. While some Europeans settled in the Mediterranean parts of the Ottoman Empire, few came to Baghdad. In the nineteenth century, when European advances in technology were spreading to Cairo and Damascus, Baghdad lagged far behind.

Ottoman rule in Iraq came to an end in 1917. Istanbul had entered World War I on the side of the central powers (Germany and Austria-Hungary), and British forces invaded Iraq in the course of their desert warfare against the Turks. The pressures of the war and the prospect of future gain led the British to seize the whole country, although not without some heavy fighting. By war's end, Great Britain had supplanted Turkey as the ruler of Mesopotamia.

In 1920, the Allied powers met in San Remo, Italy, to divide the spoils of war. The announcement that Iraq would be placed under British mandate sparked a widespread revolt in the country. Tribal chieftains, Shiite religious leaders, and Sunni officers all roused their followers. It was testimony to the Shiites' lack of political aptitude, fostered by long years of oppression by Sunni rulers, that they did not take advantage of the Ottoman defeat to secure political rights for themselves. Instead, they rejected British rule solely on the grounds that Muslims should not be ruled by non-Muslims. Thus, even though the rebellion was fought largely by the Shiite tribes of southern Iraq, its outcome was yet another form of Sunni domination.

In response to the demand for Arab rule, the British

installed the Emir Faisal as king of Iraq. Faisal, a scion of the Hashemite family that ruled over the Islamic holy places in western Arabia, had fought alongside the British against the Ottomans during the Arab Revolt of World War I (later glamorized in David Lean's 1962 film *Lawrence of Arabia*). The British had led Faisal's father to believe that after the war the Hashemites would rule an independent Arab state, stretching from the Persian Gulf to the Mediterranean coast. It was in that context that during the war Faisal met with the head of the World Zionist Organization, Chaim Weizmann, and reached agreement in principle on the implementation of the Balfour Declaration, the British promise of a national home for the Jewish people in Palestine. But the British never kept their wartime promises to the Hashemites, and that unique accord, if it had ever had a chance of success, was stillborn.

Instead, after the war the former Arab provinces of the Ottoman Empire were placed under British or French mandates, according to the Sykes-Picot agreement. The Europeans set up governments like their own in the Arab states. In Iraq, the British established what was formally a constitutional monarchy, with a parliament, alongside King Faisal. But what worked in Europe did not necessarily function in other places. Through their status as mandatory power, the British maintained dominant influence. Britain's role in Iraq, and elsewhere in the Arab world, was never acceptable to the local population. There was a fundamental contradiction between the democratically expressed will of the people and British control. There was constant agitation against the British position, which became a source of instability for the fledgling state as demonstrations occurred regularly in the streets of Baghdad. Iraq's politicians constantly sought to undermine their rivals by cynically outbidding each other in opposing the British, even though they knew that they had no means to impose their program against Britain's determination to maintain its position in Iraq.

Even apart from the British question, parliamentary democracy never took root in Iraq. Elections were a sham. Political parties were small cliques with no mass following, and government quickly degenerated to a game of musical chairs among Baghdad's Sunni urban elite. The average life of a cabinet under the monarchy was less than eighteen months.

Although Faisal had been installed to meet Iraqi demands for an Arab ruler, his roots in the country were shallow. An Arabian prince, he relied to an unusual degree on those officers who had fought with him in the Arab Revolt against the Ottomans. These Iraqi officers were strong Arab nationalists, yet they were willing to work within the terms of the British mandate. Surprisingly, some of them were passionately pro-British, particularly Nuri Said, who was to serve frequently as prime minister.

The officers in Faisal's entourage were all Sunni Arabs. Aside from a genuine commitment to principles of self-determination and dignity for their country, their support for Arab nationalism linked Iraq to the broader Sunni-dominated Arab world and served as a rationale for perpetuating their rule over a country whose majority was not Sunni Arab. These officers were careful to maintain their control of the army through limiting recruitment to the military college and ensuring that Iraq's army officers remained overwhelmingly Sunni Arabs.

Even as Sunni Arabs kept political control in their own hands, the new Iraqi kingdom was fragmented along ethnic, religious, sectarian and social lines. The early years were plagued with many armed insurrections, in Kurdistan in the north and among the Shiite tribes in the south. Reflecting on this situation, King Faisal wrote in the early 1930s that "this government rules over a Kurdish group most of which is ignorant and which includes persons with personal ambitions who call upon this group to abandon the government because it is not of their race. It also rules a Shiite plurality which belongs to the same ethnic group as the government. But as a result of the discriminations which the Shiites incurred under Ottoman rule, which did not allow them to participate in the affairs of government, a wide breach developed between these two sects. . . . There are also other huge blocks of tribes . . . who want to reject everything related to the government because of their interests and the ambitions of their sheiks. . . . I say with my heart full of sadness that there is not yet in Iraq an Iraqi people."

Yet at the same time as Faisal penned his lament, Iraq was becoming an independent state. In response to unceasing agitation over the past decade, Britain agreed to terminate its mandate, and in 1932, Iraq became the first Arab state to rid itself of mandatory status and the first to enter the League of Nations. However, Britain still considered its position in Iraq to be of great strategic importance, and Iraq's independence was coupled with a treaty of alliance that maintained much of British privilege, particularly its military bases in the country. The British position was to remain a source of discord and instability for years to come.

One year after Iraq's independence, King Faisal died unexpectedly at the age of fifty-six. Iraq lost a man of vision and principle, the one person with sufficient prestige to hold the country together around an idea of national interest and to balance conflicting national and British pressures. Faisal's son and successor, Ghazi, was too young, weak, and impetuous to be an effective ruler. Ghazi died in a car crash six years later. His young son

Faisal II was crowned king, with his uncle Abdul Illah appointed regent.

With Faisal's death, the army, which had been an important pillar even during his reign, quickly established its ascendancy in Iraq's political life. The army's first major act was the brutal and bloody suppression of an Assyrian insurrection in the north.

The Assyrians were an ancient Christian community who had lived in Turkish Kurdistan before rebelling against the Ottomans during World War I. They were then forced to flee their homes and were settled by the British in northern Iraq. They came to provide the main recruits for the British military levies. Over the next decade, many causes for friction arose between the Assyrians and the Iraqis. Finally, a border incident occurred in August 1933 that led to a clash in which thirty Iraqi soldiers died. Anti-British and anti-Assyrian sentiment flared. The Kurds and other northern tribes were incited to attack the Assyrians, who were rounded up and shot on sight. Finally, the Iraqi army moved in to suppress the revolt, and, under the command of General Bakr Sidqi, massacred over 300 unarmed Assyrians, looting and destroying many of their villages.

Sidqi, until then a little-known general, became an Iraqi hero. On his way back to Baghdad, he was given an enthusiastic reception in Mosul, where memories of the Assyrians' role in suppressing local unrest had especially contributed to inter-ethnic tensions. Triumphal arches greeted Sidqi, some decorated with melons stained with blood, with daggers stuck in them. Baghdad likewise gave Sidqi a tumultuous welcome. He was hailed as a champion of national unity, the army's action as token of its fulfillment of a great duty.

Sidqi's newly won popularity was quickly translated into political gain. In 1936, in cooperation with Hikmat Suleiman, a prominent reform-minded Iraqi politician,

Sidqi took up arms to force the king to install a new government. Suleiman became prime minister; Sidqi, chief of staff. It was the first modern Arab coup. From then on Iraqi politicians succumbed to the temptation of gaining office through military interventions, allying themselves with various officer factions. Iraqi officers manipulated cabinets behind the scenes, and the army, having tasted power, was unwilling to relinquish it.

As Samir al-Khalil notes with great incisiveness, the Assyrian affair represented the crystallization of traditional religious antagonisms into a new sentiment, which was given the respectable title of "anti-imperialism." The brief decade of rapid modernization under British rule had only compounded tensions and unease. The anti-imperialist slogan set comforting limits on modernization. As Khalil observes, "This was a world that had been catapulted across the centuries, with dizzying results."

By the 1930s, throughout much of the Arab world, including Iraq, the old ways had been undermined. Yet what would replace them was unclear. While liberal nationalism has at its core the idea of popular self-government, in many places, beginning with the French in 1789 and including Germany, Italy, and Eastern Europe, nationalism led to authoritarianism, chauvinism, and political extremism.

The same happened in Iraq. Communism's prestige in Moscow, and particularly fascism's rise in Europe, provided explosive and attractive models to a younger generation eager for change. Syrians and Palestinians at odds with the mandatory authorities in their countries took refuge in Iraq. The growing tensions between Arabs and Jews in Palestine strengthened nationalist, anti-British sentiments in Iraq, although clearly there was sufficient ground for such passions had the Palestinian question never existed. As the Syrian-born scholar Bassam Tibi explains, "While Arab nationalism in the pre-colonial period . . . sought the introduction of liberal freedoms and bourgeois democracy . . . it developed into an apologetic, reactionary, populist and frequently aggressive ideology under colonial rule."

Germany in particular held a powerful attraction. Sunni Arab nationalists, including the military officers, came to see Iraq as the Prussia of the Arab world. The dream was that Iraq, by virtue of its early independence and through its army, would unite the Arabs. The Nazis actively cultivated the Iraqis, and Hitler's success in defying Britain and France further enhanced the pro-German sentiments of the young urban elite and the army officers.

But there was more to fascism's appeal than simply revenge against the British. Militarism emerged in Germany and Japan as a consequence of a rigid, conservative social order undergoing the stress of rapid modernization. The same factors were at work in Iraq. It was a sign of the times in 1938 when an ardent Arab nationalist, Sami Shawkat, was appointed director-general of education. Shawkat was a fascist who admired Mussolini. "If we do not want death under the hooves of the horses and the boots of the foreign armies, it is our duty to perfect the manufacture of death, the profession of the army, the sacred military profession," he had once proclaimed.

Indeed, fascism had broad appeal throughout the Arab world at that time. Initially, Gamal Abdel Nasser was a member of Egypt's "Green Shirts," and when George Habash founded what is now the Popular Front for the Liberation of Palestine, its slogan was "Blood, Fire, Iron." After fascism's defeat in World War II, those like Nasser and Habash who had embraced it began to express their discontent through more respectable leftist ideologies. These ideologies all appealed to the same sentiments—a resentment of European dominance, a sense that something was wrong at home, and for some, a desire for a more equitable social order. But their substantive programs, to the extent that they existed, could not easily be realized. The most significant distinction underpinning Iraq's ideological politics was that it was community-based. The Communists, who became prominent after World War II, tended to be Shiites, Kurds and other minorities. None of these groups had an interest in union with other Arabs, and were content to consider Iraq their country. Arab nationalists were upper- and middle-class Sunnis, for pan-Arabism rationalized their monopoly of political power. The Baath appealed to lower-class Sunnis and to some Shiite elements, because of its special claim to nonsectarianism and its supposedly socialist program.

The outbreak of World War II led to open confrontation between the nationalists and the British. Events in Baghdad came to a head in April 1941, when Iraqi army officers forced the regent and Prime Minister Nuri Said to leave Baghdad. The officers sought help from Germany, and Hitler sent a few planes through Vichy-occupied Syria. British forces then proceeded to occupy Iraq a second time, supported by the British-officered Arab Legion, which came across the desert from Transjordan, and the regent and his government were restored.

Upon their defeat, rebel officers took their revenge by instigating the mob into attacking the city's prosperous and ancient Jewish community. For several days, army elements ran amok. One hundred and eighty of Baghdad's Jews were killed and several hundred were wounded amid wide-scale looting. However, the times were still more civilized than they were to become. The newly restored Iraqi government instituted a judicial investigation of the affair. The inquiring magistrates squarely blamed elements in the army for the atrocities and recommended penalties, including stiff jail terms. Baghdad would remain quiet for the rest of the war. In 1943, in a largely symbolic move, Iraq declared war on the Axis powers, and contributed to the Allied effort by facilitating the passage of American military assistance to Russia.

The end of the war brought with it the more or less permanent ascendancy of Nuri Said. His policy was strongly pro-Western, despite anti-British sentiment among significant elements of the population and anti-Western feelings engendered by the establishment of a Jewish state in Palestine. In 1948, Iraq sent troops to fight in the Arab-Israeli war. The Israeli victory was a source of dissatisfaction everywhere in the Arab world. In Egypt, it precipitated the 1952 officers' coup. In Iraq, the myth grew that Israel had won because of the treachery of the government leaders, who refused to give the necessary orders for the Iraqi army to wipe out the Zionist forces, a myth that was to play a major role in undermining the loyalty of the armed forces to the monarchy.

The ever-painful question of relations with Britain was made more troublesome by the rise of Egypt's new President Gamal Abdel Nasser as an Arab nationalist figure. The government of Iraq was aligned firmly with Britain and the United States in international politics, and Iraq was prepared to accommodate the Western powers' desire for a regional security pact in the Middle East. Nasser, however, firmly opposed this idea, and an intense rivalry between Nasser and Nuri soon developed.

In the period between 1955 and 1958, Nasser reached the peak of his popularity among the Arabs. In September 1955 he became the first Arab leader to acquire Soviet arms; the Arab populace applauded his defiance of the West and expected that he would use those arms to liberate Palestine. Tensions between Egypt and the West continued to rise, and in May 1956, the United States cut funding for a major Egyptian project, the Aswan High Dam. In July Nasser retaliated by nationalizing the Suez Canal, thereby acquiring the necessary revenues to fund the dam.

Britain and France, who were still the dominant Western powers in the Middle East, decided that the region would be better without Nasser. So did Nuri Said, who had been in London at the time of the canal's nationalization and urged British Prime Minister Anthony Eden to "hit him fast and hit him hard." In October, Britain and France combined with Israel to attack Nasser, keeping their plans secret from the United States.

For reasons that are still not entirely clear (the U.S. government continues to withhold the diplomatic papers from that period), President Dwight D. Eisenhower felt obliged to force the allies out of Egypt almost unconditionally. Eisenhower's actions made Nasser a great hero. The Arab people forgot that Nasser had been unable to defend the Sinai peninsula, which had quickly fallen to Israeli forces. Nor did the fact that the United States was responsible for the return of Egyptian territory reduce their sense that Arab nationalism had won a tremendous victory. Less than two years later, Egypt and Syria joined to form the United Arab Republic. The union of the Arabs, the overcoming of colonially imposed frontiers, seemed at hand.

In that heady atmosphere, a group of Arab nationalist army officers, led by General Abdul Karim Qassim, succeeded in overthrowing the Iraqi monarchy on July 14, 1958. Although the armed force that attacked the palace was small (less than 100 people) and lightly armed, the regent, Abdul Illah, failed to order the 2,500-man contingent of well-armed Royal Guards, stationed a mile away, to fight back. Abdul Illah's resignation and defeatism has never been satisfactorily explained. The commander of the guard sought Abdul Illah's permission to attack the rebels, but it was denied. After a two-hour siege, the regent, the young King Faisal II, Abdul Illah's mother and his sister, along with some household servants, were mowed down by machine-gun fire.

While the coup was in progress, an announcement was read over the radio by Qassim's co-conspirator, Colonel Abdul-Salam Arif, proclaiming the death of monarchy in Iraq. Within an hour, a huge mob, the poor and dispossessed of Baghdad, was in the streets, shouting, cheering, and calling for vengeance. They raged through the city, attacking the British embassy and other targets, killing several Jordanian ministers and a Western businessman caught in a local hotel. The mob seized the body of Abdul Illah and proceeded to mutilate it and drag it through the streets. When Nuri Said, who had tried to escape dressed as a woman, was discovered the next day, he was immediately shot. The mob subsequently disinterred his body and treated it as it had Abdul Illah's.

The new regime proclaimed that it had overthrown a "corrupt clique" subservient to the imperialists, and that the new government would be a "people's republic." Yet the "republic" soon degenerated into an authoritarian regime with Qassim as "Sole Leader." Rifts appeared immediately within the original coalition. The most troublesome faction was the Arab nationalist wing, encouraged by Nasser, who repeatedly challenged Qassim.

Although the Egyptian president had applauded the demise of his rival Nuri Said and had welcomed Iraq's new government, Qassim had no intention of following Nasser's lead. He particularly had no plans to join the

United Arab Republic, the Egyptian-Syrian union formed in February 1958. Although Qassim's father was a Sunni Arab, his mother was a Shiite Kurd, and Qassim reflected that element within Iraq that was oriented toward the country and not toward pan-Arabism. Qassim's coolness on this issue soon set Nasser and the Nasserites in Iraq against him. The first troubles began with Qassim's partner, Arif. An Arab nationalist, and more in tune with the views of the Sunni Arab officers, Arif sought better ties with Nasser. He traveled to Damascus two days after the coup to seek support against any counterrevolutionary attack. But he also appeared in public holding Nasser's hand, proclaiming that Iraq would join the United Arab Republic.

Arif soon gave every evidence of seeking Qassim's position for himself. Qassim wanted him out of the country, offering him the post of ambassador to West Germany, but Arif refused. Matters came to a head in October at a meeting in Qassim's office. After five hours of fruitless discussion, Arif suddenly reached for his revolver. Only with the help of another man did Qassim succeed in wresting the gun away from him. But Qassim did not eliminate this determined foe. Evincing a compassion that most of his successors would not share, Qassim repeated his demand that Arif leave the country. When Arif continued to refuse, he was arrested.

Meanwhile, Qassim's struggle with the pan-Arabists continued. Rashid Ali, who had served as prime minister of the pro-Nazi government suppressed by the British in 1941, returned to Baghdad in September from his exile in Cairo, and was hailed by Qassim himself as a national hero. With money from Nasser, and with the support of tribal sheiks and pan-Arab officers, Rashid Ali, by now an old man, began to conspire against Qassim. However, Qassim discovered the plot in December and had him arrested. Although Rashid Ali was sentenced to death, the sentence was never carried out. Yet it remained a great irony that the hero of so many Iraqis, including Saddam's uncle Khayrallah, was jailed by Iraq's first self-styled revolutionary government.

The pan-Arab opposition caused Qassim to seek support elsewhere. He invited the Kurdish leader Mustafa Barzani back from exile in Moscow, seeking partly to balance the nationalists. Barzani was royally treated, housed in the former palace of Nuri Said's son, and provided a car and an allowance. Yet Barzani began to suspect that Qassim would not meet his demands for Kurdish autonomy, and indeed Qassim had begun to fear that such demands would lead to Kurdish independence. Relations between Baghdad and the Kurds deteriorated, and by September 1961 civil war between the Kurds and the Iraqi army had broken out. The conflict became a serious drain on Qassim's regime.

But the most important pillar of Qassim's rule, at least initially, was the Iraqi Communist party. Communists throughout the Middle East were at bitter odds with Nasser, because he had suppressed them in Egypt and again in Syria after the 1958 union. The Iraqi Communists thus quickly backed Qassim's coup. Moreover, the party, with its membership consisting largely of Shiites, Kurds, and other minorities, shared Qassim's Iraqi orientation.

The Communist party mushroomed after the coup, and the Communists were able to bring out huge crowds into the streets to counter the Nasserites. The Communists also formed a "Popular Resistance Force," a people's militia, ready to back Qassim as well. Although he occasionally tried to curb their excesses, Qassim nonetheless needed the Communists' support. The Resistance Force, acting with unlimited powers of arrest, began to terrorize a frightened public.

The rising strength of the Communists increased political tensions, and the rivalry with the Nasserites reached a bloody peak in March 1959. Sunni Arab officers and tribal sheiks based in the north, again backed by Nasser, were planning a revolt against Qassim. They chose to launch their rebellion while Communist sympathizers held a major rally in the northern city of Mosul. More than 200,000 people had poured into the city from all over Iraq. The rebels attacked them, but the government forces quickly succeeded in repelling the assault and suppressing the revolt. The Communists, however, took immediate revenge, massacring the nationalists and looting some of the wealthier homes in Mosul. About 2,000 people died in the carnage.

Qassim now realized that the Communists had become too strong, and he slowly began to curb their authority. Yet by doing so, he compromised his only institutional base, as he possessed no other structure that could effectively mobilize his popularity among the Iraqi masses.

The Communists' growing strength caused the small and previously insignificant Baath party to make its first bid for power. The Baathists began planning for an assassination attempt on Qassim in October 1959, in which the twenty-two-year-old Saddam Hussein participated. The Baath worked in concert with a group of nationalist officers and received Nasser's clandestine support. In the assassination attempt, Qassim's driver was killed and one of his aides seriously wounded. Qassim himself was hit as well, and his injury proved serious enough that he remained hospitalized for a month.

Still, Qassim survived, and the plotters scrambled for their own safety. Some, including Saddam, succeeded in fleeing Iraq, but seventy-eight others were arrested and put on trial. Many of these men were jailed, a few receiving death sentences. However, no executions were carried out.

As Qassim's rule progressed, it began increasingly to reflect the limits of good intentions. He was, by all accounts, a decent and nonviolent man. There were many he could have killed, but he refrained from doing so. Few doubt his sincerity in seeking to improve the lot of his country's poor. His most cherished project was the building of "little houses" for the people, perhaps the most important and enduring of his economic policies. Nearly 25 percent of each annual budget was allocated for public housing. When later confronted by his enemies and facing death, Qassim defended himself, stating, "I exerted myself on behalf of the poor. I built thousands of small houses for the poor."

But Qassim was a mercurial and erratic figure. In other fields, most notably agrarian reform, he had no clear idea of how to implement his program, leading to drastic declines in production. By 1961, Iraq no longer exported barley, as it once had, and imported nearly half the rice and wheat it consumed. Qassim's most fundamental problem, however, was a basic naiveté. One man who served as a cabinet minister under Qassim later reflected that he and his colleagues had no idea of the enormity of the task of governing Iraq. The simplistic notion that overthrowing an established order like the monarchy would necessarily bring a benevolent and forward-looking regime, he felt, was an unforgivable error.

Even Qassim's notorious Mahdawi court was less harsh than circumstances might have suggested. Presided over by Fadil Abbas al-Mahdawi, a cousin of Qassim's, the court was originally established to try leaders of the old regime. Yet in time the court became a circus—and one whose proceedings were televised to the entire nation. The audience was allowed to participate in the proceedings by giving speeches and threatening the accused. The court frequently suspended proceedings while Mahdawi listened to sycophantic poetry that praised himself and Qassim. The Soviet Union awarded Mahdawi the Lenin Prize of Justice, which he was pleased to display in the court. In fact, it was during only one brief period that the judgments of the court resulted in executions, and even then the bloodshed was limited, compared to what would transpire later. In August and September 1959, fourteen people were executed on order of the Mahdawi court, less than the number Saddam had killed at the 1979 party meeting.

Thus, as Qassim moved to curb the power of the Communists, he possessed little organized support for his regime. And through his erratic ways he soon managed to alienate every group within the political elite. Still, he was tolerated. He was not Stalin, the Iraqis would say. They somehow knew it could be worse, and they were right.

On February 8, 1963, during the Muslim holy month of Ramadan, Qassim was overthrown. As in 1959, Baathist officers joined with Arab nationalist officers against him. Arif, whom Qassim had recently released from jail, led the coup in the name of the nationalists. He became the new president; Colonel Ahmad Hassan al-Bakr, the leading Baathist officer, became prime minister.

The coup was dramatic and bloody. Air Force pilots sympathetic to the nationalist cause bombarded Qassim's office in the Ministry of Defense. An army brigade moved toward Baghdad and encircled the ministry. Baathist civilian assassination squads attacked assigned targets at dawn, while other squads arrested leading officials of Qassim's government.

Waking to the sound of gunfire, Qassim drove around the city to raise the population. He was well met and generally supported. Then, however, he went to the

Ministry of Defense and barricaded himself inside. This was a fatal mistake; by doing so he cut himself off from his base of popular support in the city, relying solely on the army to suppress the coup. The army, though, with its Sunni Arab orientation, had been heavily penetrated by the Baathists and the Nasserites, and it failed to support Qassim, who was quickly defeated and captured along with many of his supporters.

Qassim was taken to the television station in Baghdad and charged with high treason by a special court. A swift death sentence was passed. When informed of the verdict, he asked to see his old comrade, Arif, to implore him to spare his life, as he had done for Arif in 1958. But Arif replied that the matter was out of his hands. Qassim was placed before a firing squad in the Arabic music room of the television station and summarily executed. Killed along with Qassim were several of his officials, including Mahdawi, who was kicked to death on the orders of Ali Saleh al-Saadi, then secretary-general of the Baath party and deputy prime minister in the new regime.

Qassim's death was by no means sufficient to guarantee the new regime control over the nation. Battles raged in several quarters of Baghdad. People fought bitterly for two days against the coup. The army bombarded the city with artillery and liberally sprayed the streets with machine-gun fire. More than a thousand civilian casualties ensued. The conduct of the coup, moreover, was a harbinger of things to come. Thousands of people were rounded up from their homes. Communists were particularly targeted. As the prisons filled up, the overflow was diverted to sports stadiums. Terrible methods of interrogation were used and many Iraqis were killed under torture.

And in a macabre way, Qassim's ghost haunted the new regime. People would not believe that he was dead, and this belief inspired his supporters to continue fighting. The Baathists then resorted to a grotesque use of the media. As noted in an earlier chapter, they displayed Qassim's dead body in uniform, sitting in a chair. A soldier held his limp head by the hair, repeatedly dropping it to prove beyond doubt that the man was dead.

"The internal life of Egypt is characterized by moderation, that of Syria by tensions, and that of Iraq by extremism," observed Eliezer Berri, the Israeli historian. There is a temptation within the Arab world to consider the Iraqis to be of different mettle than other Arabs. In some respects they probably are. There is an Arabic verb *tabaghdad,* derived from the word Baghdad, and meaning "to swagger, throw one's weight around." An Iraqi sociologist, Ali al-Wardi, has offered a sober reflection on his society. "The personality of the Iraqi individual contains a duality," he observed. The Iraqi "is enamored more than others with high ideals which he calls for in his speeches and writing. But he is at the same time, one of those who most deviates from these ideals. He is among those least attached to religion, but deepest in sectarian strife. . . . There are two value systems in Iraq. One upholds strength, bravery, and arrogance, all qualities of the conquering hero, side by side with another value system which believes in work and patience. . . . The Iraqi people were known to be a people of discord and hypocrisy . . . but the Iraqi is not really different from other men. The difference lies in his idealistic thinking. He thinks of principles which he cannot execute and he calls for aims which he cannot reach."

V

"We Came to Stay": The Rise of the Baath

The February 1963 coup against Qassim marked the arrival of a new and ruthless player in Iraqi politics—the Baath party of Ahmad Hassan al-Bakr and, later, Saddam Hussein. The Baath (Arabic for "renaissance") began as a political movement in Syria in the 1930s. It soon came to be dominated by two Damascus high school teachers, Michel Aflaq and Salah Bitar, who had studied together at the Sorbonne between 1928 and 1932. Aflaq was the party's leading ideologue, and he would remain closely associated with the Iraqi regime until his death in 1989. He is buried at the Baath's national party headquarters in Baghdad.

As a student in Paris, Aflaq was attracted to the fascist ideas then fashionable in Europe. He was "full of enthusiasm for Hitler" and other German fascists, according to the Syrian-born historian Bassam Tibi. Aflaq saw in Nazi Germany a model for his ideas of a synthesis between nationalism and socialism. At the time of the 1941 coup of the pro-German Rashid Ali, he and Bitar formed a "Society to Help Iraq," the nucleus of what later became that country's Baath party, according to the Princeton historian Bernard Lewis. Aflaq's view of Arab nationalism was quite romantic and far more radical than that of the liberal nationalists. Aflaq exalted the glory of the Arabs as a race, as expressed in the Baathist slogan, "One Arab nation with an eternal mission." The party's credo consisted of three words: "Unity, Freedom, Socialism." Yet neither in those formulations nor in Aflaq's highly abstract writings was there put forth a concrete political program.

Though the Baath were strongly anti-Communist, they were organized as a secret political party along Leninist lines. The basic unit of the party was the cell, composed of not more than four members and a leader. Cell leaders were organized in cells of their own in a hierarchical order extending all the way to the party's regional command in each Arab country. The regional commands were joined in a national command for the entire Arab "nation." In practice the regional commands dominated Baathist political activity in each country. Whenever the Baath came to power, the national command quickly became subservient to the ruling regional command.

Under the new Baath regime in 1963, Iraq was officially ruled by a body called the National Council for the Revolutionary Command. The membership of the council remained a secret, adding to the sinister character of the regime. Although the army had carried out the coup and Colonel Abdul-Salam Arif was nominally the regime's top official, the Baath dominated the Revolutionary Command. A Baathist member of the command was later to recount, "We passed the resolutions. Arif didn't like them. But we didn't listen to him." Baath party membership was thin, and their influence totally disproportionate to their numbers in Iraqi society. When they seized power, their total membership was less than 1,000. Furthermore, they were young; members of the party's regional command averaged only thirty years of age.

The Baath also moved to secure their hold on power through the expansion of the National Guard. On the morning of the coup, the new regime called for recruits to the guard, and several thousand young men were quickly enrolled. An Iraqi Communist leader described the Guard as "adolescents befuddled by jingoistic propaganda, declassed elements and all sorts of riffraff." But it was not long before the army came to see the guard as a serious threat.

Despite the bloodiness by which the Baath had seized power, they initially enjoyed the support of those elements in Iraqi society who had opposed the Communists, including the business community and the Sunni Arabs, whose champion was Colonel Arif.

The success of the Baath in Iraq encouraged the Baath party in Syria to make a similar bid for power, and in March 1963 they succeeded in overthrowing the parliamentary regime in Damascus, again in cooperation with Nasserite army officers. Both Baathist regimes were committed to an ideology of Arab unity, and they sought to strengthen their positions at home by securing Gamal Abdel Nasser's seal of approval.

After some initial Egyptian reluctance, the negotiations on Arab unity convened in Cairo in April. Nasser, embittered over the failure of the UAR, from which Syria had seceded in 1961, was not interested in giving his imprimatur to Baathist rule. The talks dragged on, and Nasser used them to discredit the Baath. Recorded excerpts from the sessions were broadcast on Cairo radio, portraying the Baath delegates as fumbling adolescents manipulated by a sinister éminence grise, Michel Aflaq.

The failure of the unity talks and Nasser's increasingly hostile attitude began to undermine the Baath in Iraq. At the same time, friction was growing between the army and the Baath, and public opinion in Iraq was growing restive. The Baath's popularity was further diminished when the National Guard inaugurated a campaign of harassment in the cities. Members of the guard broke into homes, intimidated the occupants and stole their property. They accorded themselves the power to arrest people without warrant and to take them for interrogation to the Palace of the End, where the young Saddam Hussein was a torturer.

The growing resentment worked in Colonel Arif's favor. Through the summer of 1963 he bided his time as tensions grew inside the Baath—partly a power struggle, partly a civilian versus military dispute, and partly a question of doctrine. At the sixth National (all-Arab) party conference in October, Ali Saleh al-Saadi and his faction won primacy in the party. Saadi was a young doctrinaire Baathist, radical in his interpretation of party doctrine. Iraqi army officers within the Baath reacted harshly to Saadi's victory, voiding it by force of arms and calling for the election of a new, less extreme command within Iraq. They then arrested Saadi and four of his associates, putting them on a plane to Madrid with passports invalid for return to Iraq.

The National Guard responded with a rampage lasting several days. A pro-Saadi member of the air force bombarded the presidential palace. The Iraqi Baath called in Michel Aflaq and other high-ranking party members from Syria. They arrived in Baghdad November 13. Capitalizing on the disarray and the sense that foreigners had been brought in to conduct Iraqi affairs (Aflaq was not only a Syrian but a Christian as well), Arif made his move on November 18. Army units loyal to him seized control of Baghdad and arrested the leaders of the Baath.

Arif remained president, but the Baathists were now gone. However, some Takriti army officers, initially allied with the Baath, chose to stay on in Arif's government. They were never forgiven by Bakr and Saddam. Thus ended the Baath's first attempt at government in Iraq. It had lasted nine months.

The nation heaved a sigh of relief with the departure of the Baath. Optimism and hope greeted the new regime, which allowed greater freedom of speech and of action, and which now set about dismantling the repressive apparatus of the Baath, including the National Guard.

But the perennial problems that had bedeviled Iraqi society quickly reasserted themselves. The internal war against the Kurds continued, despite Arif's attempts to arrange a cease-fire. Fear of the Shiites still caused the regime to treat them with suspicion. The predicament of relations with Nasser remained unresolved. Despite his professed pan-Arabism, Arif found that Iraq's interests precluded any meaningful union with Egypt. But Nasser continued to press for influence and control in Iraq, urging Arif to take some measures to bring Iraq closer to Egypt's policies of nationalization and socialism. Nasser's ambassador in Baghdad pressed for the adoption of such programs, and he found support among Nasserite officials high in the Iraqi bureaucracy.

Although in July 1964 Arif nationalized the Iraqi economy, he quickly came to regret his decision, as his support eroded among the traditional leaders and business groups. But still it was not enough to satisfy Nasser and his supporters in Iraq, who still pressed for more.

With Egyptian support, the Nasserites attempted a coup against Arif in the autumn of 1965. But Arif survived, and in the months that followed Nasserist influence in Iraq waned. Arif embarked on a liberal policy to be implemented by Abdul Rahman al-Bazzaz, the first civilian prime minister since the monarchy's overthrow in 1958.

The discrediting of the Nasserites following the failed coup attempt opened the way to renewed Baathist activity. The repression of the Baath under Arif was not very severe. Takriti elements sympathetic to the party continued to wield influence in the government, where they could aid and give protection to the Baathists. Then, in April 1966, Arif died in one of those mysterious helicopter crashes which take place with some regularity in Iraq and are attributed to "sudden sandstorms." He was succeeded as president by a weaker man, his elder brother Abdul Rahman Arif, while Bazzaz continued as prime minister. They secured a cease-fire with the Kurds, offering them the most generous agreement to date, which finally brought peace to the north. During the second Arif presidency, government control was further relaxed and human rights abuses largely curtailed.

A second Nasserite coup was attempted in June 1966, but again without success. The Baath supported Abdul Rahman Arif in crushing the rebels, making him and his government even less inclined to restrict their activity. Bakr, who had become secretary-general of the party after Saadi's exile in 1963, deputized Saddam to organize the civilian branch of the party and to set up the party's internal secret police. Under Bakr's patronage, Saddam began to emerge as a power within the newly invigorated Baath.

Two years later, on July 17, 1968, the Baath succeeded in seizing state power for the second time in five years. As before, they made their move in coalition with Arab nationalist officers, this time the Republican Guards. A gullible and ambitious young officer, Colonel Abd al-Razzaq al-Nayif, deputy director of military intelligence, had been looking for partners who might join him in a coup. Eventually he chose the Baath. Nayif brought along the Republican Guard by promising high positions to its commander and to other guard officers.

Even so, that support alone would not have been enough to propel the Baath to power. The commanders of critical tank units were at first unwilling to sign on.

However, a dispute arose between Tahir Yahya, who had become prime minister in July 1967, and a sheik of the Shammar, a major northern tribe, angering several officers in the guards' tank battalion who were closely related to the Shammar sheik. They decided to throw their lot in with the plotters. One officer later boasted that he had sat with his four tanks, deployed, armed, and ready, while he watched thirty Baathists, including Saddam, arrive at the guards' barracks before dawn the morning of the coup. "I could have blown them to smithereens with my tanks," he said. "But I could not let Tahir Yahya's insult to my tribe pass."

The Republican Guard was the key to the coup's success. It was an elite force, personally picked by Arif—he considered its commander, Colonel Ibrahim al-Daud, to be a loyal subordinate. The guard's main responsibility was to protect the president against coups and assassinations and to keep order in Baghdad. The young officers, who held the key to the success or failure of the coup, believed that they were masters of the situation. They thought that they would form the government, with the Baath participating only in a subordinate role. They were mistaken.

The Baath had learned important lessons from the events of 1963, and they were careful not to repeat the errors which had cost them power then. While Bakr became Iraq's new president, the Baath's allies, Nayif and Daud, became prime minister and defense minister, respectively. But neither was destined to remain in the government for long. A key lesson from 1963 was that it was necessary to remove one's coalition partners quickly. This the Baath did.

Thirteen days after the coup, on July 30, when the Baath had arranged for Daud to be abroad, Bakr invited Nayif to lunch at the presidential palace. After the meal Bakr took him to a lounge elsewhere in the building to have tea. The president then excused himself and left Nayif alone in the room. But Bakr never returned. Instead, Saddam and an armed companion entered the room. Saddam pulled out his pistol and began to abuse Nayif, calling him a "son of a whore" and other obscenities. Then he pistol-whipped the prime minister on the face. Nayif broke down and pleaded that his life be spared. Saddam ridiculed him and bundled him to the airport, shipping him off to Morocco. His civilian associates were swept from the cabinet. Thus ended Nayif's thirteen days. The Baath were back in power. (A decade later, Nayif would be killed in London on Saddam's orders; Daud never returned to Iraq and currently lives in exile in Saudi Arabia.)

That the Baath had taken power in a military coup was simply one more testament to the party's lack of support in the country as a whole. According to the party's own estimates, the Baath had no more than 5,000 members in 1968. That the Baath always attempted their coups in coalition with non-Baathist officers testified to their lack of strength even in the more limited circles of the military. The return of the Baath was regarded with near universal dread by the Iraqi population, which remembered clearly the excesses of 1963. But then, as before, there was little that the people could do.

The initial composition of the Baath government after the purge of July 30 reflected the preeminence of military officers within the party then. Compared to the younger civilian element, dominated by Saddam, the officers were older, more established, and not quite so ruthless. The ruling Revolutionary Command Council that took over with the ouster of Nayif and Daud, consisted, at least publicly, of five men—Bakr, the president, who was also promoted to field marshal; General Hardan al-Takriti, deputy prime minister and defense minister; General Saleh Mahdi Ammash, deputy prime minister and interior minister, and once military attaché in Washington under the monarchy; General Sadun Ghaydan, commander of the Republican Guards; and General Hamad Shihab, chief of staff and a cousin of Bakr.

Significantly, Saddam Hussein chose to be anonymous. Although deputy secretary-general of the party, his membership in the council was not announced until November 1969. He feared that the Baath would be ousted again, as had happened in 1963, and in that event he preferred to be unknown.

Saddam had the clearest vision of all the Baath leaders. With Bakr's patronage, Saddam built his base in the party through the intelligence apparatus. He defined his aim as the total control of Iraq and its people, and he proceeded to pursue this goal through party control of the country and, behind that, through his control of the party. The original party terror and intimidation organization, the Jihaz Haneen, was developed and organized as the Mukhabarat, and it reported to Saddam.

Knowing that its ascension had not been welcomed by the people, the Baath was quick to demonstrate that "we came to stay," as the party's new slogan went. Saddam was responsible for arranging the display of the Baath's power and determination through a public spectacle. Qassim's spectacle, the Mahdawi court, had been for the most part bloodless. Saddam's spectacle focused on blood.

In October 1968, three months after taking power, the regime claimed that it had broken up a major Zionist spy ring. In reality, the regime had laid a trap. An agent, Sadiq Jafer, was employed to deliver letters to prominent people in Baghdad and Basra, letters which were written as if addressed to agents of an Israeli spy ring. Soon after Jafer delivered each letter, a security agent would appear and pretend to discover it. Dozens of prominent people were arrested, including former prime minister Bazzaz (whose death in 1973 would come as a result of his maltreatment in prison).

Saddam put Salah Omar Ali al-Takriti, a member of the party's regional command, in charge of the investigation. The experience of one of the accused, Abdul Hadi al-Batchari, a former member of parliament, was typical. When savage torture failed to elicit from him a confession fingering others as spies, as his interrogators demanded, he was threatened with the rape of his wife. He signed the confession—and was hanged.

The regime also arrested Iraqi Jews. Among the first fourteen Iraqis to be publicly hanged, eleven were Jews. The executions, on January 27, 1969, were deemed the occasion for a public festival. Although Iraq's bourgeoisie was appalled, some 200,000 people attended the event, many of them Baghdad's workers and peasants from the surrounding countryside, some with their small children in tow. The accused were strung up in rows of gallows in Baghdad's "Liberation Square." The proceedings continued for twenty-four hours. Bakr, Salah Omar, and others made haranguing speeches condemning Zionism and imperialism, against the backdrop of bodies dangling from the gallows.

Although the object of the regime's fury seemed to be those associated with Zionism and imperialism, particularly the dwindling Jewish community of Iraq, the real target was Iraq's political elite, the potential opposition to the regime. By raising the ghosts of Zionism and imperialism, entirely irrelevant to the problem at hand—how to secure the Baath in power—the regime was able to mobilize some elements within society to give enthusiastic support to the murder of other elements. The Iraqi elite quickly realized that the same tactics could be turned against them, as was already happening. In fact they were expected to recognize that. A former official of the regime recalled sitting with Saddam one day when Saddam suddenly began talking about spy satellites. The satellites, Saddam asserted, were so powerful that they could even read what was written on the paper in his hand. "Then why," asked the official, "did we hang the Jews?" "To teach the people a lesson," replied Saddam. That lesson was that the regime would not hesitate to resort to brutality, even a brutality unprecedented in Iraq's modern history.

More executions followed. But the regime also found other ways to instill fear and terror in the population. Government-sponsored assassinations and kidnappings began. The first prominent victim was Nasser al-Hani, a former foreign minister who had once been a lecturer at London's School of Oriental and African Studies and Iraq's ambassador to Washington. In November 1968 a group of young Baathists called at his house and asked Hani to accompany them to the palace to see President Bakr. He went with them, never to return. His body was discovered in a ditch outside Baghdad a few days later. Hani's wife, an Irishwoman, discovered the identity of his kidnapper when a picture of a Baathist "martyr" was published in the Baghdad papers a few years later. The man had been killed in an automobile "accident," a classic case of the murderer having been murdered in turn. Abdul Karim al-Sheikhli, another former foreign minister and an important Baath party member and rival to Saddam, likewise met his end in a car accident a decade later. Many other lives ended in the same way.

The Baath also resorted to a novel method of terrorizing the well-to-do segments of the population. In the early 1970s, a gang began breaking into homes in affluent Baghdad neighborhoods and murdering whole families with an axe. People were terrified by the leader of the gang, who became known as the axeman of Baghdad; they stayed up nights to stand guard over their homes. After many grisly murders the axeman was apprehended. Samir al-Khalil reports that the axeman's gang had expert knowledge of secret radio frequencies to help them elude the police. According to persons familiar with the case, the axeman was a security agent, under orders to commit the random murders.

The regime pursued a deliberate policy of humiliating respected personalities in Iraq to demonstrate that its authority was total. Seyyid Muhsin al-Hakim, the leading spiritual figure for the world's Shiites, was publicly humiliated in September 1969 when he traveled from Najaf to visit Baghdad. Thousands of people came to visit him in the city over a week's period. The regime grew disturbed by this display of popular loyalty, a loyalty which it could never command. One week later, a man appeared on Iraqi television, confessing to the fact that Hakim's son and representative, Seyyid Mahdi, was a spy and a conspirator. The government took steps to prevent people from visiting Seyyid Muhsin or accompanying him. He was obliged to return to Najaf in one car, alone with his aides, an indignity he was obliged to bear in silence. His son Mahdi went underground and was subsequently sentenced to death in absentia. He remained active in opposition to the regime, and Saddam had him assassinated nearly twenty years later, in 1988, in the lobby of the Hilton Hotel in Khartoum.

While much of the Baath's violence was preemptive, designed to intimidate and cow the population, real threats to the regime also existed, and it dealt ruthlessly with them as well. On January 21, 1970, the government announced the discovery of a plot to overthrow the regime. This one was genuine: Iran had backed some Iraqi elements, led by Nayif and a former deputy prime minister from the second Arif government, in an effort to oust the Baath. Once the plot was exposed, a revolutionary court was constituted, which tried and sentenced forty-four people to death in thirty-six hours. Many of the condemned had had nothing to do with the plot, as they had been in prison for some time. But the regime took the opportunity to settle many scores.

The condemned were shot outside the court, as soon as the sentences were passed. Among the people executed was a young army officer, who (it was discovered later) had been executed by mistake. The regime had not even wanted to kill him. The Baath offered his father, a senior civil servant, 5,000 dinars compensation for the life of his son. He was obliged to accept.

In addition to consolidating the regime's hold on power vis-à-vis the population, the party's leaders also sought to consolidate power within the regime itself. Essentially the same methods were used. Although he was number two in the party Saddam had powerful rivals, older than he was, who enjoyed significant support in the military. He gradually had them eliminated. General Hardan al-Takriti had continued to serve in Arif's government after the November 1963 split, making him particularly suspect to Saddam. At his urging, Bakr elevated Hardan from defense minister to the meaningless post of vice president in April 1970, before dismissing him altogether in October and sending him out of the country. The following February, while on a visit to Kuwait and in the company of the Iraqi ambassador, Hardan was murdered. The Kuwaiti government neither arrested the assassin nor prevented him from leaving Kuwait for Iraq. Another rival, General Salih Mahdi Ammash, was also "elevated" to a vice presidency in April 1970 (he had been minister of the interior) before he was dropped from the Revolutionary Command Council in September 1971 and sent out of the country as ambassador to Moscow.

The rest of Saddam's rivals disappeared in the course

of the Kzar coup. General Nadhim Kzar, a long-time Baathist of Shiite origin, had been appointed director of the internal security forces in 1969. In 1973 he contrived a plot whereby Bakr would be assassinated at the Baghdad airport upon his return from Eastern Europe on June 30. Earlier in the day, he had taken hostage General Hamad Shihab and Sadun Ghaydan, the defense and interior ministers.

Bakr's plane was delayed two hours, and Kzar's plans miscarried. He fled for the Iranian border with his two hostages. Near the border he shot Shihab before he himself was seized. Saddam personally led the suppression of Kzar's coup. He gathered an armed band and took them to the barracks of General Security, where Kzar's supporters were. Saddam led the arrest and the shooting of several men there.

A week later, Kzar, seven security officers, and thirteen army officers were tried and executed. The next day thirty-six civilians were tried, with thirteen sentenced to death. Abdul Khaliq al-Samarrai, a member of the Revolutionary Command Council, was among those sentenced to prison, where he remained until Saddam had him shot in 1979 after the infamous July party meeting. Although Kzar had implicated Samarrai—at one point in his escape, he offered to negotiate at Samarrai's house—he denied any knowledge of the plot. Many people believed that Saddam had used the incident to remove a powerful rival.

Indeed, the result of the Kzar coup was to remove all of Saddam's remaining rivals. Moreover, Saddam's personal role in suppressing the coup cowed many other officers. After 1973, the so-called military faction of the party, which just five years before had been dominant, was eliminated. Bakr was the only officer who remained in a key post, while Saddam became the undisputed strongman of the regime.

In addition to the power struggles conducted largely within Iraq's Arab community, the Kurds presented yet another pressing problem. Even before the Baath seized power, the settlement that Prime Minister Bazzaz had reached with the Kurds in 1966 had begun to unravel. By the spring of 1969, the Kurdish war was once again in full swing. The Shiite Kurds of Iraq were being deported to Iran by the tens of thousands.

The Kurdish war became a serious threat to the Baath regime when the Soviet Union sent an envoy to the Kurdish leader Mustafa Barzani, who had spent eleven years in exile in Moscow before returning to Iraq in 1958. The Soviets asked Barzani to make peace with the Iraqi regime. Saddam in turn adopted a seemingly accommodating position toward the Kurds, and in 1970 he himself went to see Barzani in Kurdistan. Saddam offered the Kurdish leader a sheet of blank paper with his signature at the bottom and asked Barzani to fill in his terms. Those talks soon produced a fifteen-point agreement detailing the terms for Kurdish autonomy. But Saddam's subsequent conduct showed that he had little intention of abiding by the accord. Not only did he fail to engage in meaningful discussions about implementing the agreement, but shortly thereafter he tried to kill Barzani's son, Idris, whose car was machine-gunned in Baghdad in September 1970.

A year later, Saddam even tried to assassinate Barzani. A group of religious sheiks went to talk to Barzani at Kzar's request, on Saddam's orders. The sheiks returned to report to Kzar, who asked them to meet with Barzani again, giving the men two machines, which he said were tape recorders. Kzar asked them to turn the machines on while Barzani was not looking and to record his exact words, as he wanted to hear them for himself. Kzar then sent them north. They arrived at Barzani's headquarters in Hajj Omran, and sat with him. One sheik took the opportunity of the serving of tea to push the button on the machine as Kzar had instructed, since the tea server blocked him from Barzani's view. When he pushed the button, the machine exploded. The sheik and the tea servant were killed. There was little for Barzani to talk to Saddam about after that.

Although the Baath in 1963 had reasonably cordial relations with the United States and otherwise pursued what has been called a "moderate" foreign policy, the Baath behaved quite differently the second time around. It was radical in every respect, though in many instances, beneath the ideological rhetoric there was either no action or the reverse of what seemed to be the case.

Among the Arab states, Iraq was the most virulent in its refusal to countenance any agreement with Israel. Baghdad's extremism was so great that it was virtually isolated within the Arab world. It is possible that isolation is what the regime genuinely wanted so that it could focus its attention on establishing control at home.

After 1968 Iraq supported the most radical factions of the PLO and was more actively involved than any other Arab state in promoting Palestinian terrorism. According to the Israeli journalist Yossi Melman, the most notorious of terrorist chieftains, Abu Nidal, was originally a Baathist. When he began to establish his organization in the early 1970s, Abu Nidal received the support of Iraqi intelligence, and he maintained close ties with Baghdad throughout the decade. In that time, Abu Nidal's primary targets were other Arabs, particularly Yasir Arafat's Fatah, with which the Baath also had a dispute then.

The extremism of the Iraqi Baath was due in part to the fact that Iraq does not border Israel, and its posture was ordinarily without much cost. However, in September 1970, during a bloody Jordanian-PLO clash, Iraq's virulence created a dilemma for the regime. Iraq had had troops stationed in Jordan since the 1967 war, but as tensions between King Hussein and the PLO erupted into open fighting, Iraq was publicly committed to the PLO. The United States feared that Iraqi troops would tip the balance by supporting the Palestinians. Despite its public posture, however, Iraqi troops in Jordan sat in their barracks throughout the conflict.

Within the party's ranks, the Baath leadership was accused of not living up to the party's commitments to the Palestinians. When the 1973 Arab-Israeli war broke out, Saddam wanted to remove doubts about the army's passivity in 1970. He therefore decided, over Bakr's hesitations, to send a large contingent of the Iraqi army to fight on the Golan Heights. Saddam condemned the Egyptian and Syrian decision to accept a cease-fire with Israel and immediately withdrew his troops, leaving the Syrians exposed if the cease-fire should break down. Despite his radical posture, Saddam's fundamental concern was that Iraqi forces not remain where they might be obliged to act in ways contrary to the regime's judgment of Iraqi interests. Once the postwar negotiations between Israel and the Arab states began, Saddam attacked the agreements. It cost him little to do so, and he hoped to embarrass his principal rival, Syrian President Hafez al-Assad. The propaganda war between Syria and Iraq would continue unabated for five years.

In the initial years of Baathist rule, Iraq was closely aligned with Moscow. Iraq supported the Soviet invasion of Czechoslovakia in August 1968, one month after the Baathist coup. As Phebe Marr explained, this pro-Soviet alignment was largely due to Iraq's own internal problems.

Two months after Saddam visited Moscow in February 1972, the two nations signed a "Friendship Treaty," which provided the Baathists with some backing against external enemies and helped them deal with internal problems as well. Moreover, the pact was further assurance that the Baath's rival, the Communist party, would not become a danger. The Soviets pushed for the creation of a National Progressive Front, which would include the Communists, but after all that they had suffered at the hands of the Baath, the Communists were understandably reluctant to enter into any such agreement. After considerable pressure from Moscow, however, they agreed, and the Front was formed in 1974. Perhaps the Iraqi Communists should have trusted their instincts, because in 1978 the regime again began a brutal crackdown on the party.

The Friendship Treaty also allowed Iraq to assume a militant position regarding oil. In June 1972, Saddam nationalized the Iraq Petroleum Company. The oil nationalization brought Iraq no advantage beyond what other Gulf oil-producing countries obtained through negotiations with the oil companies. In fact, it cost Iraq heavily. Income dropped by some 25 percent as its oil became subject to international embargo led by the Western oil companies, and Iraq lost much of its market. Though Baghdad had to cut expenditures drastically, the nationalization nonetheless served to enhance the image of the Baath as a fearless party bravely confronting the forces of imperialist monopolies.

But the Soviet-Iraqi treaty also created problems for Saddam. It caused the United States and Iran to agree upon a plan to destabilize Iraq through covert action in Kurdistan. Barzani was willing to participate in such a plan, but only after he had first secured specific American assurances that assistance would continue until the Baath regime was overthrown. Fighting in Kurdistan escalated throughout 1973 and early 1974, breaking into open warfare in March. Saddam personally took charge of the operations, approving massive bombings of civilian targets throughout the campaign. In the bombing of one town, Qala Dizeh, over 200 people were killed. By the autumn, however, the campaign had stalemated, and the army, which was taking heavy casualties, was growing restive at the lack of progress.

In a move that reflects the pragmatic and opportunistic side of his rule, Saddam attempted to reach an agreement with the shah, enlisting the help of Egyptian President Anwar el-Sadat and Algerian President Houari Boumedeine. Their efforts bore fruit at an OPEC summit in Algiers on March 5, 1975. Saddam and the shah reached a surprise accord in which the shah agreed to withdraw support from the Kurds in exchange for Iraq's recognition of Iran's claim to half the Shatt al-Arab waterway. Even before the accord was signed, Iraq had begun a ferocious and ultimately decisive drive against the Kurds. Barzani left Iraq, never to return. He later expressed his bitterness, affirming that while he would never have taken the shah's word, he had trusted that the United States would not betray him.

The Algiers agreement was linked to a broader shift in Iraq's position. Iraq's extremism began to wane. Saddam, it seems, had judged that, with the suppression of the Kurdish rebellion, his position at home had become secure enough to allow Iraq a more normal posture in world affairs. Besides, if the radicalism had had any purpose beyond isolating Iraq so the regime could better establish its control, the Baath's extremism had brought no profit. After 1975 Iraq began to ease tensions with a number of Arab states, including Egypt, Saudi Arabia, and Jordan. Ultimately, Saddam realized that he could better pursue his ambitions if his country's relations with others were less tense.

The big shift in Saddam's policy was facilitated by the fourfold increase in oil prices that followed the 1973 Arab-Israeli war, as well as the recovery of markets that it had lost after the 1972 nationalization, regained through Iraq's nonadherence to Arab production cutbacks during the war. The government raised production, even as it called for a total ban on exports to "imperialist states that insist on backing Israeli aggression." By staking out such an extreme position, which Iraq knew would not be endorsed by the other Arab states, it avoided observance of the punitive measures that the Arab states had adopted.

After 1973, the cash crunch that Iraq had faced because of the oil nationalization disappeared. Iraq's 1974 oil revenues were ten times the 1972 level. The government spent money on the improvement of living standards through a program of massive imports of consumer goods. The levels of government allocations for industry increased twelve times; funds for transportation rose eleven times; for building and housing nine times. Most important, this windfall provided the regime some hope that even if it could not win the people's support, then at least it could gain their toleration of Baathist rule.

Iraq's new wealth also led to a change in its dealings with the superpowers. Looking to the superior technological products of the West and no longer so reliant on Soviet aid, Baghdad grew increasingly independent of Moscow. Economic ties with the United States grew, even though diplomatic relations had been broken off ever since the 1967 Arab-Israeli war. By 1980 Iraq was importing $700 million in American goods. The U.S. interests section in the Belgian embassy in Baghdad expanded accordingly, but Iraq was not then interested in restoring diplomatic relations with Washington. It twice rebuffed offers from the Carter administration to renew relations, even as it grew increasingly hostile to Moscow. Iraq, in fact, was one of the most vociferous Arab states in condemning the 1979 Soviet invasion of Afghanistan.

Lurking behind the shift in Iraq's policy after the Algiers agreement, including the criticism of Moscow and the aloofness toward Washington, was Saddam's ambition. This motive first became apparent in the Iraqi-orchestrated ostracism of Egypt after the September 1978 Camp David accords. Saddam was now seeking a major role on the Middle Eastern stage, and toward that end, he felt, Iraq could be tied to no one.

VI

War Without End

On assuming the presidency of Iraq in the summer of 1979, Saddam Hussein set his nation on a new course, motivated by both ambition and fear. Saddam's ambition was to make Iraq the dominant power in the Persian Gulf and in the Arab world. His fear was that Iraq's Shiite majority would be stirred to revolt by the fiery rhetoric of the Ayatollah Khomeini, who had returned triumphant to Iran on February 1, 1979, after fifteen long years of exile.

Iran's erratic politics had a decisive impact on Iraq and the region as a whole. Secular figures headed Iran's first two revolutionary governments, but they were engaged in a ceaseless power struggle with radical clerics. From the start, Iran's secular governments had sought stability in relations with their neighbors. But elements around Khomeini soon began to call for exporting Iran's Islamic revolution, while championing the rights of the disadvantaged Shiite communities in the Gulf region.

As authority in Iran fragmented, a propaganda war developed between Tehran and Baghdad. In June, four months after Khomeini's return, tensions escalated into border clashes as elements in each country incited sectarian strife within the other's boundaries. Baghdad began assisting non-Persian separatist groups in Iran, sending money and arms to Kurdish rebels in the north and supporting Arab elements in Iran's oil-rich, and predominantly Arab-inhabited, province of Khuzistan, which before 1924 had been an autonomous Arab principality. Toward this end, Saddam activated cells of the Baath party and recruited the sons of an Arab Shiite cleric in Khuzistan. He sent them money and arms through Iraq's consulate in Khorramshar, a major city in southern Khuzistan and Iran's main port on the Shatt al-Arab. For their part, Iranian clerics called on Iraqi Shiites to overthrow their government, while also supporting a Kurdish rebellion in northern Iraq.

On November 4, 1979, radical elements in Tehran, with Khomeini's backing, seized the U.S. embassy and took its staff hostage. The embassy seizure precipitated the resignation of the Iranian government, and the French-educated Marxist economist Abolhassan Bani-Sadr became president. At the same time, the clerics continued to undermine the legitimate government with their agitation for radical action.

All the Gulf Arab states felt threatened by Iran. Saddam responded by seeking to exploit the political and ideological threat from Iran to establish Iraq's primacy. He offered to assume the role of protector of the weak Arab monarchies. The Gulf states, however, had little desire for his "protection." And Saddam's efforts to create a new role for Baghdad in the Gulf brought him into rivalry with the United States. After the Soviets invaded Afghanistan in late December, President Jimmy Carter announced that the United States would defend Saudi Arabia and the Gulf states against foreign aggression. The new policy came to be known as the Carter Doctrine. Two weeks later, Saddam Hussein proclaimed that he would do the same. On February 8—the seventeenth anniversary of the 1963 Baathist coup—Saddam issued the "Pan-Arab Charter." Dubbed the "Hussein Doctrine," the charter called for collective Arab defense and rejected any foreign presence in the Gulf. It also prohibited "any Arab state from resorting to armed force against any other Arab state."

The events of April 1980 were to lead Saddam to decide on implementing the Hussein Doctrine. On April 1, the revolutionary Shiite Islamic party, al-Daawa, tried to assassinate Tariq Aziz, Iraq's deputy prime minister, and significantly, a Christian. Aziz survived, but others present at the time died. Four days later the Daawa launched another assault at the funeral procession for the victims of the first attack.

Saddam responded ruthlessly. Membership in the Daawa party was made punishable by death. Saddam deported some 15,000 Shiite Kurds and also began to deport en masse the middle-class Shiite population of Iraq's major cities. By the summer, some 35,000 Arab Shiites had been expelled from Iraq, but this proved to be only the beginning.

Ayatollah Mohammad Baqr al-Sadr was the Arabs' leading Shiite religious figure. He was sympathetic to Khomeini. Saddam arrested Sadr and his sister, Amina bint al-Huda, both of whom were taken to Baghdad, where they were brutally tortured by Saddam's half brother Barzan Ibrahim, then head of the General Intelligence Department (Mukhabarat). Bint al-Huda was assaulted in the presence of her brother, who was in turn killed by burning his beard and driving nails through his head. His body was delivered to his family for burial in Najaf, with instructions not to open the coffin. But a pious Muslim is buried in a shroud, not a coffin. In accord with religious law, the coffin was opened, and the evidence of torture revealed.

In the spring of 1980, Iran's official secular government still hoped to calm tensions with Iraq, despite the belligerence of the increasingly powerful revolutionary elements led by Khomeini. Toward that end, Iran's foreign minister toured the Gulf sheikdoms, in late April, but at his first stop in Kuwait, Iraqi agents tried to assassinate him. Saddam had decided on war.

The exiled generals and politicians of the shah's regime had gathered in Baghdad. They told Saddam that Iran was an easy target. They claimed that many Iranian air force pilots would defect with their planes as soon as they were permitted to fly. They reported that Iranian armored units, especially in Khuzistan, were in complete confusion. They spoke of the army's resentment toward the newly formed popular militia, the Revolutionary Guards, who acted as a political police, while trying to take over the army's function and equipment. The émigrés convinced Saddam that surgical air strikes against selected targets, in conjunction with a massive armored attack, would suffice to rout the Iranian army and even cause the collapse of the revolutionary government. By and large Saddam accepted this view, buoyed further by the hostility of the international community toward Iran, particularly for its seizure of the American embassy. It thus appeared unlikely that there would be any effective international opposition or even much dismay if Iraq attacked Iran.

Saddam expected a quick, easy victory, within two or three weeks—as did key agencies in the American government. Iraq's war plans were drawn up, at least in part, on the basis of a staff exercise conducted by British military instructors at the Baghdad War College in 1941. Saddam thus did not seek or want help from other Arab states, believing that Iraq could easily achieve its aims alone. Those aims were threefold. Saddam's minimal aim was to capture and secure for Iraq the eastern shore of the Shatt al-Arab. His second aim was to induce the secession of Arab-inhabited Khuzistan from Iran, perhaps also triggering the revolt of other non-Persian ethnic groups. His maximal aim was to precipitate the collapse of the Tehran government. Appearing on Iraqi television on September 15, Saddam tore up the 1975 Algiers agreement in which he had ceded half the Shatt al-Arab to Iran. Seven days later, he invaded.

Despite his lack of military experience, Saddam directed the war himself. He decided the timing of attacks and their objectives. He went to the front and conducted military operations from forward headquarters. Often his activities with the army were shown on Iraqi television.

Saddam tried to repeat the success of Israel's dramatic opening move in the 1967 Six-Day War. He began by attacking ten Iranian airfields on the first day of the war. But these attacks achieved little. The Iranian air force remained intact and quickly retaliated with strikes on Iraq. Iraqi air defenses, in turn, proved to be completely inadequate, obliging Baghdad to seek an effective air defense system from France.

As Iraqi planes attacked Iranian airfields, Iraqi armored units launched a thrust across the Shatt al-Arab toward Khorramshar. Although Iran's army was in no position to fight, the local population put up fierce resistance. It took a month of unexpectedly heavy fighting before the city was captured on October 24. Iraq then tried to push toward the city of Abadan, ten miles to the south, but despite several assaults, Iraqi forces failed to capture it.

Once it became clear that the Iranian regime was not about to collapse—indeed, the Iraqi attack did much to consolidate the revolution—there really was nowhere for Saddam to go. Iraq's failure to take Abadan meant that it could not achieve even its minimal aim of occupying the eastern shore of the Shatt al-Arab. Thus, soon after consolidating its hold on Khorramshar, the Iraqi army began to dig in, despite having penetrated only 45 miles into Iran. The conflict settled into a war of trenches and earthworks.

As the war dragged on, Saddam began to learn what strategic depth truly means, as he tried to subdue an enemy whose land mass is three times the size of Iraq's. Except for installations in Khuzistan, Iraq's air force had to penetrate hundreds of miles into Iran to hit major targets. The Iranian air force had to travel less than a hundred miles to reach all major targets in Iraq. "Geography is our enemy," Saddam said publicly barely six months into the war.

Iran, moreover, has thousands of miles of coastline on the Persian Gulf and on the Indian Ocean, while Iraq became essentially landlocked once its access to the open sea was cut at the outbreak of war. In the first days of fighting, disabled commercial shipping, along with the debris of war, rendered the Shatt al-Arab unnavigable, paralyzing Iraq's only significant commercial port, Basra, which lay fifty miles upriver.

Iraq's small navy was quickly bottled up in the Khor Abdullah, a small channel that forms part of the Iraqi-Kuwaiti border. Iraq's military port, Umm Qasr, is located on the Khor Abdullah. Fearing Iran's wrath, Kuwait refused Iraq permission to use a channel leading south between the islands of Warba and Bubiyan, in Kuwaiti coastal waters, which would have given Iraq access to the open sea. The inadequacy of Iraq's ports and coastlines was amply illustrated. And Iraq's problem of access was compounded by the overwhelming superiority of the Iranian navy.

Iraq thus had to rely on pipelines to export its oil. At the war's start it had one pipeline across Turkey and another across Syria. But they soon proved inadequate, and over the course of the war, Iraq built a second pipeline through Turkey and another through Saudi Arabia. Iraq also became dependent on other nations for the overland transport of critical imports. Jordan, Kuwait and Turkey became the principal conduits for the transshipment of goods as a huge transport infrastructure involving tens of thousands of trucks and maintenance installations sprung up in those countries. Saddam also ordered the construction of modern fourlane highways to handle Iraq's wartime transportation needs. One road ran from Baghdad south along the war front to the Kuwaiti border; another, from Baghdad due east to the Jordanian border.

Saddam received another rude lesson about Iraq's vulnerability when the Soviet Union cut off arms supplies soon after his invasion of Iran. To get ammunition, spare parts and new arms for his largely Soviet-supplied forces, Saddam turned to Eastern Europe, China, and Egypt. Anwar el-Sadat had seen in Iraq's predicament a way out of the isolation in which Egypt had been cast—largely at Saddam's initiative—for its peace treaty with Israel. Yet Iraq chose to treat the weapons trade strictly as a business deal, maintaining a harsh ideological posture toward the "Camp David regime" and the "traitor" Sadat. During the war, Iraq also developed an indigenous weapons-manufacturing industry to alleviate some of the vulnerabilities in foreign supply of critical military items.

Other political and military tremors, moreover, would soon cause the ground to shift in Baghdad. On June 7, 1981, in a daring suprise attack, Israeli warplanes bombed the Osirak nuclear reactor near Baghdad, destroying Saddam's capability to develop atomic weapons. Meanwhile, in Iran frustration mounted at the unpreparedness of the nation's armed forces and their inability to launch an effective counterattack against Iraq. President Bani-Sadr became a scapegoat; when Khomeini dismissed him from office on June 17, he immediately fled the country. Bani-Sadr's dismissal intensified violent resistance to clerical rule in Iran. The bombing of the Islamic Republican party headquarters on June 28 killed scores of top clerical leaders, touching off two months of bloody internal strife. But the clerics prevailed. In the martyrdom of its leaders, the revolution found new fervor.

Beginning in the fall of 1981, Iranian forces began a series of offensives, which soon pushed the Iraqi army back to the border. In September, the Iranians launched their first major successful offensive in Khuzistan. In its next offensive in November, Iran employed a devastating new strategy. Hundreds of thousands of ill-trained and lightly armed Revolutionary Guard volunteers, filled with intense religious fervor, joined the fighting. Led into battle by their clerics, the guards showed little fear of dying, for the regime had taught them that heaven was a martyr's reward. The new Iranian tactic had a terrifying effect on Iraqi soldiers. Stories of the horrors of facing such an attack circulated in Iraqi cities. As one Iraqi officer told the British military historian Edgar O'Ballance, "They came at us like a crowd coming out of a mosque on Friday. Soon we were firing into dead men, some draped over the barbed-wire fences, and others in piles on the ground, having stepped on mines."

More Iranian offensives followed. In December Iran succeeded in capturing a key crossroads, the only road linking the entire southern sector. A month-long Iraqi effort in February to recapture the junction failed, even though Saddam went to the front himself to lead the counterattack.

At the end of March, the Iranians achieved yet another, more dramatic victory, pushing the Iraqi army back thirty miles and taking 15,000 Iraqi prisoners. After that offensive, Syria threw its lot in with Iran, severing Iraq's pipeline to the Mediterranean, which cost Baghdad some $30 million a day in lost revenues. Syria would remain Iran's close ally for the duration of the war.

It soon became well-known in Baghdad that Saddam was nearly captured during the March offensive. While driving around the rear of the fighting, near the Iraqi border, Saddam's convoy was besieged by Iranian troops, unaware of Saddam's presence. The only Iraqi force close enough to relieve Saddam was commanded by General Maher Abdul Rashid, a Takriti general who was not on speaking terms with him. Many years earlier, Saddam had arranged for his clan to murder Rashid's uncle. When Saddam asked for help, Rashid insisted that he request the aid, swearing by the name of the murdered man. Under heavy bombardment, and with his bodyguards piled on top of him to protect him, Saddam agreed to Rashid's demand. Rashid promptly relieved the besieged president, and even though his daughter later married Saddam's son, the two men never overcame their mutual antipathy. Even before the war ended Rashid would be placed under house arrest.

Iran achieved its greatest success in May 1982. In a month-long campaign, Iranian forces drove the Iraqis from their remaining positions and recaptured the city of Khorramshar, along with 22,000 Iraqi troops.

Saddam responded to the mounting setbacks with a surprise announcement. On June 10 he declared a unilateral cease-fire and ordered the withdrawal of Iraqi forces from the small pockets of Iranian territory they held. Saddam proposed that Iran and Iraq use the cease-fire to confront Israel, which had invaded Lebanon four days before.

Israel's attack on Lebanon was not, from Iraq's perspective, merely a fortuitous coincidence, for Saddam had triggered the Israeli invasion. It was widely known throughout the Middle East that Israeli Prime Minister Menachem Begin and Defense Minister Ariel Sharon wanted to drive the Palestine Liberation Organization from Lebanon. But an excuse was needed. Yasir Arafat, fearful of the consequences, was trying desperately not to give Israel any pretext. However, the near-fatal shooting of Israel's ambassador to London on June 3 set the Israelis in motion. The British arrested and tried the man who organized the assassination attempt, who turned out to be a colonel in Iraqi intelligence. Two Israeli journalists, Zeev Schiff and Ehud Yaari, further reported that weapons for the operation came from the military attaché's office of the Iraqi embassy in London. Schiff and Yaari, as well as a *New York Times* account, concluded that Iraq had sought to precipitate an Israeli attack on Lebanon, which would perhaps provide the occasion for a cease-fire with Iran, and at the very least would tie up Syria and prevent Damascus from aiding Iran in Baghdad's desperate moments.

Yet Khomeini rejected Saddam's cease-fire proposal. On July 14 Iran launched another offensive, for the first time attacking Iraq itself. The war's unpredictability was again shown by the effective resistance of Iraqi troops, when defending their own land. For the first time since September 1981, a determined Iranian offensive failed to break Iraqi lines. Now Tehran was the party suffering disappointments, absorbing heavy casualties and failing to inspire Iraq's Shiites to rise in support of Khomeini, as the Ayatollah had expected.

But even as Baghdad withstood Iran's assault, it was the beginning of very hard times for Iraq. Saddam's dreams of glory had dissipated. Iraq had been slated to host the September 1982 summit of nonaligned states, and the regime had expended great efforts to prepare for that event. All of Baghdad's first-class hotels were built in preparation for this summit, including those hotels in which Iraq would detain foreigners following its invasion of Kuwait in 1990. However, the hotels never served their intended purpose, as the 1982 summit was moved to India because of the Gulf war.

As the war settled into a long-term stalemate after 1982, the mood in Baghdad grew somber, and a sense of hopelessness set in. People shared a grave concern about the casualties, which increasingly affected every home, many households suffering multiple losses. A feeling of malaise and bitterness against the regime spread among the population for having dragged Iraq into a war against its much larger, more populous neighbor. There seemed no way out of the dying, no light at the end of the tunnel. The frustration was especially great among Iraq's youth. Many of them were drafted for the entire duration of the war. Young women could not get married. The war seemed endless.

Among Iraq's army officers a willingness existed to accept the abuses and terrors of Saddam's rule in order to continue to stave off the Iranian threat from without and the Kurdish and Shiite threats from within. The Sunni Arab population generally shared the sentiments of the officers.

But the Shiite population was terrorized by their more active fear of Saddam. Deportations of the Shiite community, which had begun in 1979, escalated during the war years, peaking in 1981, 1983 and 1985. Eventually some 300,000 were forced out of Iraq into Iran. The deportations were particularly harsh because the deportees were rounded up on short notice, or sometimes lured under false pretenses, to a point of concentration, transported to the Iranian border and dumped there, even in the midst of fighting. In the winter of 1981, for example, some 700 leading Shiite businessmen received telephone calls from the Chamber of Commerce inviting them to attend a session in Baghdad where they would meet officials of the Ministry of Trade in order to obtain coveted import licenses. When they arrived, they were herded into buses, taken to a security office and told to stay there overnight. At dawn they were forcibly put in trucks, driven to the border, and told to make their way on foot to the Iranian lines.

Yet despite their anger at Saddam, the overwhelming majority of Iraq's Shiites had no desire to live under a fundamentalist government like Khomeini's. Rather, they were bitter at Khomeini for continuing the war. The Shiites, particularly the poor, constituted the bulk of Iraq's infantry. They were the cannon fodder who absorbed the first and deadliest blows of Iran's human wave assaults.

It was not surprising, then, that assassination attempts on Saddam increased with the dismal course of the war. In July 1982 Saddam's motorcade was attacked by men with machine guns in a mixed Sunni-Shiite rural area. The attackers missed Saddam's car, and he drove on. Four hours later, the village was attacked by helicopters dropping napalm. Every house was burnt and razed. Bulldozers plowed the houses under and turned the village into agricultural land.

In an incident in Takrit in 1985, a car packed with explosives was parked along Saddam's motorcade route, but the car bomb went off before he entered the city. Saddam's bodyguard, Sabah Mirza, who was with him, later reported that the president's eyes filled with tears as he realized that the opposition to him had reached even to his native city. Other attempts on Saddam's life occurred in 1984 and 1987. Before 1982, Saddam had paid frequent visits to various parts of the country, but he no longer did so. Instead, the anniversaries of his previous visits to various places were celebrated in his absence.

Such celebrations reflected the cult of personality around Saddam that had emerged with the passage of time and the strains of the war. In April 1983, his birthday was made a national holiday; 2,500 candles were thrown into the Tigris to mark the occasion. According to the Israeli scholar, Ofra Bengio, the growing cult indicated two somewhat contradictory aspects of Saddam's rule, the precariousness of his position and his ability to impose his control.

After 1982, the regime's resources were increasingly devoted to the war effort. In the war's first two years, Iraq was able to supply both guns and butter, supported by some $10 billion in aid from the Gulf states. Saddam had sought to alleviate the war's hardships, particularly the discontent that mounting casualties generated, by making available an ample supply of imported consumer goods and providing generous compensation for families of the war dead, who received an automobile, 7,000 dinars, and a grant of land and money to build a house, if they did not have one.

Although the day of reckoning was long postponed, the accumulating economic difficulties had to be acknowledged. An austerity program was introduced in November 1982, including a ban on foreign travel. The next year no budget was published. Sporadic, sometimes severe shortages of foodstuffs began to appear, particularly of meat and vegetables. Inflation eroded incomes, and almost every family came to rely on two or more salaries simply to make ends meet.

The pressures of war produced changes in the party's ideology. The new line was laid down at a high-level party meeting in June 1982, after Saddam had withdrawn Iraqi forces from Iranian territory. As Bengio explains, "The commitment to socialism was significantly reduced; Iraqi nationalism was given precedence over Arab nationalism; the issue of liberating Palestine was not even mentioned." Although these changes were ambiguous and shrouded in obfuscating rhetoric, they constituted the general thrust of Iraqi policy for the duration of the war.

The changes in the party line occurred because Iraq was in desperate straits. Michel Aflaq's adolescent fantasies now haunted Iraq. Baathism posited the unity of the Arabs in an unending struggle with Zionism and Western imperialism. But the Arabs were not united (Syria, for one, supported Iran), and Iran, the enemy, was neither Zionist nor imperialist. It was, in fact, the fanatically self-professed enemy of both. Iraq was thus perversely compelled to turn to the Zionists, the imperialists and those associated with them to try to secure their help against Iran.

Saddam's first step was to develop much closer ties with Egypt. In January 1983 he dispatched Tariq Aziz to Cairo. It was the first trip to Egypt by a ranking Iraqi official since the condemnation of Sadat at the 1978 Baghdad summit, initiating what was to become a far-reaching rapprochement. Saddam's friendship with Jordan's King Hussein also grew stronger as Iraq established cordial relations with all the Arab monarchies, from Morocco to Saudi Arabia, governments that orthodox Baathism damned as feudal and reactionary. Iraqi-American ties also began to evolve at this time.

Beginning in 1983 the war assumed a pattern that was to prevail nearly until its end. Iran usually launched one major offensive in the winter or spring of each year, when the rainy season gave tactical advantage to Iran's largely infantry force. Iraq assumed a strictly defensive position, in part because the Iraqi regime had become very sensitive to casualties. In the fall of 1982, in fact, Iraq stopped publishing casualty figures. The war was thus extended, but most of the time there was no major combat.

In the spring of 1983 Iran's offensives in the south resulted in heavy Iranian casualties, but these did not seriously threaten Iraq, whose difficulties appeared in the north. In alliance with Massoud Barzani, son of the renowned Kurdish leader, Mustafa Barzani, Iranian forces in July 1983 captured the town of Hajj Omran, Mustafa's old headquarters. This victory enabled the younger Barzani to establish a base for much larger operations against the regime later in the war.

As the fighting continued, year upon year, the Iraqi army became increasingly unable to withstand Iran's superior numbers. In the autumn of 1983, Saddam warned Iran that Iraq had a secret modern weapon. The meaning of this warning became clear the following February, when Iran, using human wave attacks, launched a massive offensive in the marshes of southern Iraq. The Iraqis were surprised by the Iranian assault, having considered the marsh area impassable to large forces. Iran took very heavy casualties (some 20,000 dead), but it succeeded in capturing and holding the oil-rich Majnoon islands, while Iranian forces briefly cut the strategic Baghdad–Basra highway at several points. The Iranian offensive seemed so threatening that Saddam ordered the use of chemical weapons.

After 1984 Saddam began to deal somewhat differently with the army. For the first time he began to allow the public mention of army commanders' names, previously kept anonymous. Apparently, such a step came to seem necessary to provide the incentives for effective command. It also made it easier to blame someone in the event of failure. Moreover, the criteria for promotion became less political. Non-Baathist officers began to rise in the ranks.

When Tehran launched its March 1985 offensive, it again did so in the southern marshlands. For a while, Iraqi forces were hard pressed. Egypt airlifted badly needed ammunition to Iraq. Iranian troops again threatened the Baghdad–Basra road. But this time they failed to cut the highway. After heavy fighting, Iraqi troops managed to hold off the Iranians, again using chemical weapons. King Hussein of Jordan and Egyptian President Hosni Mubarak flew to Baghdad in a show of solidarity in the middle of the offensive. It was the first time an Egyptian president had gone to Iraq since the Baghdad summit.

The offensive a year later, in February 1986, proved to be Iran's most successful since the May 1982 campaign that drove Iraq out of Iranian territory. On the night of February 9, taking advantage of wet and foggy weather, a force of 100,000 Iranian troops, mostly lightly armed volunteers, staged an attack in the extreme south. They succeeded in taking the Fao Peninsula in less than twenty-four hours. The peninsula was not far from Umm Qasr, Iraq's military port, but Iraqi forces succeeded in containing the Iranians within the peninsula. The heavy Iraqi casualties, estimated to be between 10,000 and 15,000, were devastating to Iraq's small and dispirited population. Over the next two months, Saddam tried to recapture Fao through heavy counterattacks, in which elite units of the Republican Guards participated. But he failed to dislodge the Iranians from the peninsula.

Unable to recover Fao, Saddam ordered the capture of an Iranian town in the central sector in May. But a month later Iranian forces succeeded in recapturing the town. The situation looked grave—the Iraqis were not accustomed to failures of defense—and Saddam made what must have been an extremely hard decision for him: he gave more authority to his military commanders in the conduct of the war.

The loss of Fao, moreover, made Iraq sufficiently desperate as to approach Israel for assistance. In the spring of 1986, independent sources confirm, Iraqi and Israeli military intelligence officers met under Egyptian auspices in Europe. A follow-up meeting was scheduled for July, but it is unclear whether the Iraqis showed up.

Iraq's next move, in July 1986, was aggressively to attack Iranian shipping, in an effort to deprive Tehran of oil revenues and to generate international pressure to stop the war. As Baghdad had no shipping in the Gulf, Iran responded to Iraq's new policy with attacks on the shipping of Iraq's allies, particularly Kuwait. A Kuwaiti diplomat explained his country's perspective. "Fao," he said, "had intoxicated the Iranians. They wanted to impose a siege on Kuwait which would lead to a domestic uprising against Kuwait's support for Iraq."

Then, in early November, it was suddenly revealed that the United States and Israel had been secretly selling arms to Iran and funneling the profits to support the contra rebels in Nicaragua. As American policy fell into disarray, Baghdad's bitter charges about the conspiracies of Zionism and imperialism seemed grounded, this time, in a strange reality.

But before the debates over Washington's tangled Persian Gulf policy could be resolved, Iran launched its 1987 offensive against Iraq. Iran's January 6 thrust toward Basra brought Iranian troops within artillery range of the city. In a three-month campaign, Iranian forces (armed with American Hawk anti-aircraft missiles and Tow anti-tank missiles) succeeded in penetrating four out of Iraq's five defensive lines. Many Basra residents fled the city. For Iraq it was the most difficult offensive of the entire war; not until late March did the danger of an Iranian breakthrough at Basra abate.

By then, Washington had worked out a new policy in the Gulf. Kuwait had asked the superpowers to help protect its oil exports, but Washington had been in no hurry to meet Kuwait's request until the Kuwaitis raised the prospect that Moscow might assume this responsibility. (One wonders whether Saddam assumed in

1990 that with the end of the Cold War and in the absence of a Soviet threat, the United States would have little interest in protecting Kuwait in and of itself.) The Reagan administration agreed to protect Kuwaiti tankers, and sought approval for an effective United Nations resolution to bring the Gulf war to an end. The U.S. Navy began escorting Kuwaiti tankers through the Gulf on July 20, 1987. And in August the U.N. Security Council passed Resolution 598, which called for a cease-fire on the basis of the status quo ante and threatened an arms embargo on either party that rejected the resolution. Iraq accepted it. Iran avoided giving a clear answer, and the fighting continued.

Although it became apparent only in hindsight, a variety of factors had begun to erode Iranian morale. With the American and European navies in the Gulf, Iran was increasingly isolated and under international pressure. Iran understood from the American deployment that Washington would not countenance an Iranian victory in the Gulf. The Iranians thus decided to focus their attention further north, in Kurdistan. They developed a strategy in the autumn and winter of 1987–88 aimed at the capture of a province in the north, so that Iranian forces would be in a position to threaten the Kirkuk oil fields. Iran worked closely with the Kurdish leaders on the strategy. The furthest point of the Iranian advance occurred in March, when they reached Halabja. Iraq's retaliation with chemical weapons in that village destroyed Iran's will to pursue this strategy further.

After six years of being on the defensive, Iraqi troops suddenly launched an assault of their own on April 15, recapturing the Fao peninsula in thirty-six hours. On May 25 they retook the town of Salamjeh, which restored the eastern approachs to Basra to Iraqi control.

The two consecutive successful offensives suggested that momentum had shifted to Baghdad.

Saddam resumed his dealings with Israel, broken off in 1986. Again, the Egyptians mediated between Israel and Iraq. The two sides exchanged signals. In late May, Saddam broke off in the middle of a speech decorating soldiers to say, "I believe that the Zionists and Israelis [*sic*] have come to regret their role in continuing this war." That was Iraq's signal to Israel, and Saddam himself had given it. The speech, broadcast over Iraqi radio, was easily monitored in Jerusalem. The next month, Israeli Defense Minister Yitzhak Rabin announced, "I've changed my mind. The continuation of the Iran-Iraq war no longer serves Israel's interests because of the arms race it generates." As the Israeli newspaper *Ha'aretz* reported, Rabin's statement was a response "to messages from Baghdad." Most likely, Israeli-Iraqi talks were to be held again.

But the long Gulf war soon took a surprise turn—it ended. On July 18, 1988, Khomeini suddenly accepted a United Nations–sponsored cease-fire. Iranian morale, it seems, had collapsed, turning the tide with great speed. The war, which many Iraqis believed would never end, was finally over. Many commentators compared the war, in its devastating and senseless fury, to the Great War of 1914–18 which so traumatized an entire European generation. Iraq's war was one of monstrous proportions, in which the mobilization of whole peoples, and not merely their respective armies, were organized and pitted against each other. The casualties that resulted were greater than all of the Arab-Israeli wars that have taken place over the past forty years, including the slaughters that have occurred during the past decade of Lebanon's internecine civil strife. The cost to both nations in blood and treasure was hideous and, on its face, incomprehensible. And yet perhaps there was something deeply cynical at work. George Orwell, in *Nineteen Eighty-four,* observed that "the consequences of being at war, and therefore in danger, makes the handing-over of all power to a small caste seem the natural, unavoidable condition of survival. . . . [Every] Party member is expected to be competent, industrious, and even intelligent within narrow limits, but it is also necessary that he should be a credulous and ignorant fanatic whose prevailing moods are fear, hatred, adulation, and orgiastic triumph."

Iraq began the war in this spirit. However, the conflict's long and terrible course ultimately raised questions about the small caste that ruled Iraq, questions that were to haunt Saddam once the war ended.

VII

No Victory, No Peace

When Iraq agreed to the cease-fire with Iran on the eighth day of the eighth month of 1988, Baghdad erupted in joy. Unlike Tehran, where the mood was glum, millions of Baghdadis spilled into the streets, dancing and chanting, by night and by day. They set off fireworks, shot rifles in the air, sprayed water at passersby. Iraq's fortunes had reversed with stunning speed. Just four months before, Iraq seemed to be losing in a long-drawn-out war of attrition. But suddenly it was all over. One Iraqi described the feeling in Baghdad as one of "delirium mixed with sadness in memory of the losses that came suddenly to mind."

The celebrations went on for over fifteen days. The government, normally in tight control, could not stop them. It was, according to one Iraqi, the first time in the entire period of Baathist rule that such spontaneity on the part of ordinary people had existed. With the cease-fire, Iraqis looked forward to enjoying life after eight years of terrible war. Iraqis expected prosperity. Without much reflection on their county's economic situation—Iraq had incurred a debt of more than $70 billion, half to other Arab states and half to the West—people believed that the war's end would somehow restore the prosperity that had existed before the war. So too did Gulf businessmen who briefly drove up the black-market value of the Iraqi currency, in anticipation of a postwar reconstruction boom. As an Iraqi explained in Baghdad one month after the cease-fire, "For now, people have stopped buying imported goods. We're waiting for the dinar to rise when the treaty is signed, and everything will be cheaper."

He meant the treaty with Iran. Even though Ayatollah Khomeini had declared that accepting the cease-fire "was more lethal for me than poison," Iraqis expected a quick signing of an accord. Such a treaty also meant the return of the 65,000 Iraqi POWs held in Iran. The POWs were the population's number one concern.

Many people also hoped for a loosening of the wartime restrictions, especially the lifting of the ban on foreign travel imposed seven years before. Not only was Baghdad terribly hot in the summer, travel provided a release from the tension of life in a police state, tension even the privileged elite felt. The war made the regime's repression less acceptable, and some Iraqis thought that the war's end might bring "more democracy." They said, "We gave our lives for Iraq. We showed our loyalty. Saddam should trust us more."

None of these expectations—peace, prosperity and democracy—which the population took as a natural consequence of the war's end, could be realized easily. Such expectations, however inchoate, nevertheless exerted some pressure on the regime. To be sure, the Iraqi government does not believe in making policy by public opinion. But no government can long afford to ignore its people. A sense of the public pulse is necessary to stay in power, and some minimal accommodation of it may be prudent.

The Iraqi government faced great problems after the war. Although the regime made much of its "victory" over Iran, the country had paid a terrible price (120,000 killed; 300,000 wounded; an astronomical foreign debt). It had got little from the war. Iraq had laid claim to the entire Shatt al-Arab, its riverine border with Iran, but Iraq did not actually possess it, and the waterway remained closed.

At the war's end, Iraq's army numbered a million. Almost all able-bodied men had served some time in the army, many for the war's entire duration. Soldiers do not return easily to civilian life. Men carry the habits they learned at the front back with them. Having faced death so often, they become less willing than before to obey the representatives of civilian authority. Fighting brutalizes, making men less afraid of violence or the threat of it, and more prone to take violent action themselves.

Tens of thousands of soldiers had deserted the army during the war. If caught, they risked being shot. They could not work legally, and they became an outlaw group, concentrated in the marshes of southern Iraq, much of which is inaccessible by land transport and therefore difficult to police. Many deserters turned to crime in order to survive, committing robberies and breaking into homes.

Beneath the surface calm of Baghdad, a turbulent current ran whose source was the long and exhausting war with Iran. Such wars, entailing mass military mobilization and general sacrifice, usually cause major social changes. Merely fighting such a war creates change, as society's resources are mobilized more intensively to meet the demands of the war effort. Women, for example, are brought out of the home and into the labor force. Moreover, as the population is asked to make ever more difficult sacrifices, people develop expectations of what is due them in return.

The regime was aware of all this. Senior Iraqi officials were far more sober than the general public in their expectations for Iraq after the cease-fire. They cautioned that although people were looking to an improvement in Iraq's economic situation, the hard currency problem would remain. Officials explained that there would be problems in "rehabilitating men who spent eight years at the front, with all the killing." And already in August 1988, when the population was still giddy over the cease-fire, Foreign Minister Tariq Aziz told a visiting delegation of Arab professors that there would have to be political change in Iraq or there would be political turmoil.

Yet it took some time for the population to realize that its expectations were unrealistic. Disillusionment began to set in during the late autumn of 1988. *The Wall Street Journal* described the situation well: "Returning to the Iraqi capital three months after the Gulf war cease-fire is like arriving at a party just as the hangovers are setting in."

The peace itself was proving elusive. The Iranian foreign minister refused to talk to the Iraqi foreign minister. The U.N.-sponsored peace negotiations were stalemated. And the exchange of POWs was suspended.

It was apparent that the cease-fire had not brought prosperity. Instead, a two-track economy had developed. A small private sector, which had emerged during the war, became immensely rich. The public sector, which employed the bulk of the labor force, was poor. In 1988 the average public sector wage was 125 Iraqi dinars a month. A university professor made 400 dinars. But the owner of a small vegetable store made 1,000, a bar girl in Basra 1,500, and even a taxi driver earned more money than a professor. Public-sector employees had not had a raise in the eight years since the war began, while inflation ran over 40 percent annually.

The dinar's official exchange rate—three dollars—was more than six times its value on the black market, more aptly called the free market, because the government had made that market semi-legal to bring more hard currency and imports into the country. While goods made by Iraq's public-sector industries were not expensive, they were in short supply. Goods imported by the private sector were readily available, but sold at the dinar's free-market price, far beyond the purchasing power of public-sector workers. Thus, a roll of film cost 7 dinars or $21; a man's shirt 30 dinars or $90; a bottle of Jordanian shampoo 4 dinars or $12. The Baath party rank and file worked in the public sector. They grumbled along with everyone else.

In late November, as the Iraq-Iran peace talks faltered, Saddam Hussein suddenly announced to a Baghdad conference of Arab lawyers that there would be a new program of democracy for Iraq, including freedom of speech, constitutional reform and "pluralism," permitting the formation of political parties besides the Baath. Three high-level committees were established to study the three issues. Each foreign embassy in Baghdad was asked for a copy of its country's constitution, and "democracy in Iraq" became a prominent theme of government propaganda.

It was in the context of the democracy campaign that Saddam complained about the media to Latif Nusayif Jassim, his minister of information, who headed the committee on press freedom. Saddam told Jassim that the press was "boring." Jassim passed along Saddam's complaint to the editors of the country's government-owned newspapers. In small, very limited ways, of note only relative to the previous absolute sterility of the Iraqi press, it became more open. All the newspapers introduced a page for readers' letters of complaint. A statement by Saddam Hussein appeared at the top of the page: "Write what you like without fear." Syrian newspapers had long carried such a page with a similar injunction at the top by Hafez al-Assad. Perhaps Saddam was looking to his rival in Damascus for ideas on how to curb some of the problems of governing a police state.

Letters poured in, almost all complaining of administrative problems and police abuse. For example, in the March 9, 1989, issue of *al-Jumhurriyah,* one man wrote a letter detailing how his car had been stolen, strongly implying that the local police had cooperated with the thieves. A widow with two children wrote a similar story in *al-Iraq* about the theft of furniture from her house, in which she too hinted that the thieves were in league with the police.

The complaint page quickly became the most popular page in the newspapers, more popular even than the sports page. But the letters never touched on political questions. However, one article in *al-Iraq* on March 7 by an Iraqi journalist, Sabah al-Lami, entitled "How the People Are Made Quiet about the Crimes of Public Corruption in the Name of Fear of Troubles," was astonishingly bold. Written in the allusive style made necessary by the constraints imposed by dictatorship, it began and ended with praise of Saddam. But Iraqis, accustomed to reading between the lines, were startled by Lami's daring. "My colleagues challenged me to write this article," wrote Lami. "They said you would lose your head and your freedom. I said if someone believes in God, he should not be frightened by someone whom Almighty God has created." Lami then proceeded to ask a series of allegorical questions about prominent personalities close to the regime, his meaning readily understood by educated Iraqis.

Did you hear of the *zarzour* [pesky bird] whose ancestors were *zarzours,* who, between night and day, became a falcon living in the palace of Kawarnak [a rich man's or ruler's dwelling]? My colleagues answered, probably they were merchants.

But I replied that a merchant is a clever man. I can't remember a "clod" becoming a millionaire merchant. Well, my colleagues, do you remember the football player with the pearl shoes, who became a millionaire with one kick. . . . Did you hear of an orchard owner who was a Mr. Nobody and now owns all the orchards of the country? . . . How about the man they tell me is a poet?"

Even Saddam could be seen as a *zarzour.* The first query suggested a damning question—where did the regime and its elite come from, and by what right did it monopolize power and wealth? The second question referred to a soccer player, Adnan Dirga, made wealthy on a whim of Saddam's. The third referred to Khayrallah Tulfah, Saddam's uncle and foster father. The fourth to Abd al-Razzaq Wahhab, a poet favored by Saddam, who had won first prize at Iraq's poetry festival the year before.

The public expression of complaint in the Iraqi press was matched by an equally unaccustomed private expression of complaint. Sensing the underlying discontent in the country, the regime encouraged people to let off steam, and they did. Kuwaitis who visited Iraq then were astounded to hear Iraqis so openly voice their frustrations. Saddam is in trouble, perhaps the regime will fall, some Kuwaitis thought. Egyptians had a different view, colored by their own historical experience. They believed that Iraq was going through the sorts of changes that had occurred in Egypt after the 1973 Arab-Israeli conflict. Between 1967 and 1973 Egypt was in a state of war. The seven years of wartime austerity created a pent-up consumer demand. Once the state of emergency passed with Egypt's qualified success in the October 1973 war, people were less willing to accept heavy-handed political control. In Egypt, a gradual economic and political liberalization followed the 1973 war. Perhaps Iraq was passing through the same stage for the same reasons after the end of its war.

The results of Iraq's National Assembly elections in April 1989 added to the Egyptians' sense that Saddam was following in Anwar el-Sadat's footsteps. The elections were held against the background of the regime's democracy campaign, and they proved more open than any previously held. Although the candidates were well screened for their loyalty to Saddam, a fairly honest process followed. Foreign observers, including British M.P.s, were invited to supervise the elections.

Party members won only 40 percent of the assembly seats, considerably fewer than the 75 percent they had won in the last elections in 1984. Some prominent Baathists lost, while some winners proved to be unorthodox figures. The sister of a well-known renegade Baathist, for example, won election in a Baghdad constituency with 90 percent of the vote against a high-ranking party member.

Iraq's National Assembly meets for two months, twice a year. It is not an important body. Yet the unusual election results eroded some of the skepticism with which Iraqis had greeted Saddam's announcement of political reform. Many people began to believe that the newly elected National Assembly would approve a new constitution before its spring session closed at the end of May. Then the assembly would dissolve itself to pave the way for new elections under a liberalized regime. Assembly members did not expect to remain in office through the term.

But nothing happened. No new constitution appeared, and no new elections were scheduled. Two weeks after the assembly session ended, the government announced a 25 dinar pay hike for public-sector employees, thus raising average public-sector wages 20 percent. But the wage hike, the first in nine years, only amounted to half the annual inflation rate. It was of little significance. The regime seemed willing to address popular expectations for peace, prosperity and more democracy only in a desultory fashion. The result was motion without much movement. Saddam was either unable or unwilling to do more.

By July frustration had set in. One Iraqi explained the regime's dilemma: "You Westerners don't see the pressure. Everything looks under control. But you don't see beneath the surface. People are fed up. The regime worries that one day there will be an explosion." He then told of a riot the week before at the central bus station. Soldiers had been returning to their units after a major Muslim holiday. Something happened. Either there was not enough transportation, or drivers were exploiting the situation to charge exorbitant rates. There was a riot and a shoot-out by the hard-pressed soldiers, who faced severe punishment for returning late to their bases. "That," he explained, "is what the regime fears and why it looks for change. But it doesn't know how to do it, and the party is still debating. It is debating between democracy and stability. Some claim that for the past twenty years Iraq has had stability so it doesn't need democracy. Others say the opposite, stability requires more democracy."

Serious problems in Iraq continued to arise. On August 17, 1989, a mysterious explosion occurred at the Qaaqaa munitions factory, thirty miles south of Baghdad, one of Iraq's two main arms-manufacturing plants. The Western press reported 700 people killed. Iraq's Foreign Ministry claimed that the "high temperature of the day" had caused the accident, but the explosion's cause was never satisfactorily explained. Was it sabotage? By whom? How much did it rattle Saddam? Farzad Bazoft, a British-based journalist who sought answers to those questions, was arrested and hanged six months later.

The slow-paced demobilization of the Iraqi army gathered momentum in late September when the government announced the decision to disband five army divisions. That decision reflected the regime's growing awareness of its overwhelming supremacy over Iran. That had not been entirely apparent at first. In the first few months after the cease-fire, senior officials expressed skepticism about Iranian intentions, while it was not until after Khomeini's death in June that the Iraqi population became more confident that the fighting with Iran was genuinely over.

Whether caused by the accelerated demobilization of the Iraqi army or merely coincident with it, tragedy soon followed for Egyptian laborers in Iraq. Some two million Egyptians had been working in the country, but suddenly Iraqis began murdering Egyptians, and the Iraqi government began returning an ever-increasing number of bodies to Cairo. In a three-week period in late October and early November more than 1,000 Egyptian bodies were flown back to Cairo. Although the Egyptian and Iraqi governments worked to contain the crisis, the Iraqi government's role was never entirely clear. No investigation was announced in Iraq and no one was ever brought to account for the murders.

Some 300,000 soldiers, one-third of the army, were demobilized in the eighteen months after the cease-fire. But there was no work for them. As a Western diplomat remarked in early 1989, Saddam needed the equivalent of a GI Bill. He had to jump-start his economy through massive foreign investment to create jobs for returning soldiers. But Iraq was so indebted, its repayment of debts so haphazard, that little investment came into the country. By the end of 1989 increasing numbers of idle young men could be seen hanging around Baghdad and other towns and villages across Iraq.

On January 5, 1990, the official Iraq News Agency reported that Saddam's automobile had had an accident while the president was escorting Jordan's King Hussein around Baghdad. The streets of the capital, however, are routinely cleared when the presidential motorcade moves, making a collision most unlikely. Far more credible is the claim of Iraqi dissidents that four officers tried to assassinate Saddam with machine guns and rocket-propelled grenades.

The annual army day parade was scheduled for the next day in the "Grand Festivities Square" beneath the Victory Arch. Large numbers of the public were invited. At the last minute, however, their invitations were canceled, and the Iraqi army marched under Saddam's oversize forearms before a restricted audience made up largely of foreign diplomats.

The problems that Saddam faced in the first eighteen months after the cease-fire were severe. Developments elsewhere were ominous. In October 1988 price riots erupted in Algeria. The Western press estimated that between 150 and 300 civilians, mostly teenagers, were killed as the Algerian army suppressed the riots. Five months later, in March 1989, price riots broke again, this time in neighboring Jordan. The leaders of both countries addressed the popular anger with promises of far-reaching political reform. In both Algeria and Jordan, elections were soon held, elections that were meaningful and open. They constituted a genuine exploration of what democratic reform among the Arab states might entail. Nothing similar took place in Iraq.

Moreover, the collapse of the Communist governments of Eastern Europe in the fall of 1989 did not go unnoticed in Baghdad. Between mid-October, when the government of Hungary fell, and the end of Decem-

ber, when Nicolae Ceausescu was overthrown and shot,
three other Communist regimes collapsed. Around the
world, astonishment and wonder greeted the fall of
these seemingly well-entrenched regimes. Iraq, to be
sure, was not Eastern Europe, but like the governments
there, it was a repressive one-party state. Comparisons
with Romania seemed particularly apt, because, like
Saddam, Ceausescu had developed a stupendous cult of
personality and police state run for his family's benefit.

There is evidence that the fall of the Eastern European governments worried Saddam. In an interview, he
told ABC's Diane Sawyer three times, "I am not Ceausescu." He repeated it to the U.S. Ambassador April
Glaspie on the eve of Iraq's invasion of Kuwait. *The
Observer* reported that after the fall of the Romanian
government, Saddam ordered Baath party officers to
watch videotapes of Ceausescu's overthrow in order to
analyze what went wrong with crowd control and how
coordination among the security services broke down.
Yet the strange exercise had unanticipated consequence. It demoralized Iraqi apparatchiks, who suddenly realized that overnight they too could become as
vulnerable as Romania's Securitate.

In February a prominent Arab lawyer, who had
heard Saddam first announce his program of democracy
for Iraq in November 1988, asked the president what
had happened to those promises. Saddam told him, "As
you saw in Eastern Europe, democracy may not be the
best thing. We have to be careful on how to proceed."
Eastern Europe showed beyond doubt that any reform
program could easily get out of hand and cause governments to fall. The lawyer left with the impression that
Saddam did not intend to do anything more about democracy in Iraq.

Yet Ceausescu's fall, and the attempt on his life only
a few days later, finally spurred Saddam to make the

first genuine gesture to the popular expectations that arose after the cease-fire. On January 17 the wartime travel ban was lifted. At about the same time, Saddam made an ostentatious shopping trip through Baghdad as imported goods were released from government stores and poured into the local markets. Yet Iraq did not have the hard currency to pay for consumer imports or foreign travel. In fact, the economic situation had continued to deteriorate after the cease-fire. The debt rose another $10 billion, while the dinar fell even further.

More than most leaders, Saddam needs money to stay in power. Money is necessary to keep his people quiescent, to placate any simmering restlessness. Money is necessary for the huge, wasteful prestige projects, including Saddam's exotic weapons program, that convey to his people the image of his unassailable might. For Saddam there is little room between restless motion and collapse. He is like a bicycle rider. Sitting on a very narrow base, Saddam either moves forward or he falls.

VIII

The Special Relationship

On the seventh floor of the State Department, inside the Command Center at the Pentagon, in the wood-paneled offices of the National Security Council, American policymakers had watched Saddam's agile balancing act for years. At first there was relief that he was taking on America's Great Satan, Iran. Unlike the Ayatollah Khomeini, Saddam, for all his ruthlessness, seemed to be a man with whom Washington could deal, and despite its distaste for the Iraqi leader, the U.S. government welcomed his survival. But appreciation turned to consternation as the bicyclist began to lose his grip. Thus one of the more peculiar relationships in American diplomacy was born.

The problem with the relationship eventually came to be known in Washington as the "mindset." The phenomenon was rooted in the mercurial forty-year history of U.S.-Iraqi relations, which have been marked by periods of hostility, thaw, cordiality, disappointment, support, and unrealistic expectations on both sides. A key turning point was Saddam Hussein's seduction of the United States and fellow Arab leaders that began in earnest in the early 1980s during the Iraq-Iran war when his military campaign was badly faltering. It was then that Washington initiated its famous "tilt" toward Baghdad, in an effort to stave off an Iraqi defeat, and in the hope that better relations might eventually have a moderating effect on the dictator and make even closer cooperation with this key regional power possible.

The Iraq-Iran war, however, was not the first time that Washington had nurtured such hopes for its relationship with Baghdad. America had similar diplomatic fantasies just after World War II. In the 1930s, the U.S. government had not been particularly involved in the region. The Middle East was the traditional imperial domain of Britain, and to a lesser extent, France. American presence in the region was largely economic; American interests were represented by the oil companies, and were seen as virtually synonymous.

The postwar years were heady for the United States, elevated by virtue of its victory and the concomitant collapse of Europe as the world's undisputed center of power. The nation could afford in some ways to be magnanimous in spirit and deed. The Marshall Plan to rebuild Europe was underway. But in the East, the Cold War struggle with "godless Communism" was taking firm hold. American policy toward the Middle East after the war thus became an expression of both idealism and anti-Communism. Some American officials, of course, sympathized with young Arab opposition groups who were seeking to end European privilege and demanded the right of self-determination. And some accepted the Arab dissidents' argument that overthrowing the feudal Arab monarchies and other bastions of privilege not only would create governments led by individuals who identified with American values, but would also be the best possible bulwark against Communism in the Arab Middle East.

Many State Department officials at Foggy Bottom, as the agency has long been known (both for its location and decision-making processes), saw the young Arab army officers who were staging narrowly based military coups in the name of "revolution" as a new middle class that would serve as the agent of modernization in their backward societies. Intelligence agencies, too, sometimes contrived to help bring these men to power. In his book *The Game of Nations,* Miles Copeland, a former U.S. intelligence officer, described how the United States planned the Arab world's first postwar coup—the 1949 overthrow of Syria's parliamentary government. The CIA developed contacts in Egypt's Free Officers movement shortly before their coup in July 1952. But for the most part, the American government continued to favor the monarchies.

There had always been dreadful economic and social inequities within Arab states, including pre-oil Iraq; much of the population lived in ignorance and squalor. The monarchies sat atop long-impoverished societies. Before World War I, Mesopotamia was synonymous with epidemic disease. A commander of the British forces there died of cholera. Baghdad was a filthy town that was routinely flooded by waters from the Tigris River. King Faisal, installed by the British in 1921, made great strides in development. The monarchy built the dams that finally stemmed the waters of the Tigris. It dramatically improved public health and education. And best of all, from Washington's standpoint, the monarchy was firmly pro-Western.

In 1954, Iraq accepted military aid from the United States and in February 1955, joined the American-sponsored Baghdad Pact, a mutual defense and cooperation agreement among Turkey, Iran, Pakistan and the United Kingdom, which was roundly criticized by other Arab states.

When a secret organization of army officers overthrew King Faisal in a coup in Baghdad in 1958, the U.S. government was dismayed. The new leader, General Abdul Karim Qassim, soon developed close ties with the Iraqi Communists and withdrew from the Baghdad

Pact in 1959, cancelling military assistance from the United States. The Soviet Union welcomed the new regime's attempts to craft an independent policy of nonalignment with the West. Baghdad and Moscow restored diplomatic relations in 1958; Soviet money and arms were soon pouring into Iraq. But Qassim was unable to deliver on his promises. His regime grew more repressive and unstable, having to fend off, among other things, a CIA effort to kill him by sending him a poisoned handkerchief. One unsuccessful coup succeeded another with wearying regularity until the Baathists briefly came to power in 1963, also with CIA help, according to Jordan's King Hussein. The agency, it is said, provided lists of Communists, whom the Baath then hunted down, tortured and killed.

In 1967, the Six-Day War resulted in a complete break of diplomatic relations with Washington. After the Baath came back to stay in 1968, Iraq became one of the main "rejectionist" states, eschewing talks with either Israel or the United States. In 1972, Baghdad signed a fifteen-year Treaty of Friendship and Cooperation with Moscow, which formalized its friendly relationship.

But in 1975, strains developed between Iraq and the Soviet Union. Moscow cut off arms shipments to Iraq after the Iraqi army moved against the Kurds. The United States, sensing an opening yet again, indicated its desire to restore normal relations with Iraq. The offer went unheeded.

Both Washington and Baghdad were alarmed in 1979, however, when the Ayatollah Ruhollah Khomeini assumed power in Iran. Richard M. Preece, a Middle East specialist in the Congressional Research Service, has noted that contacts between Iraqi and American diplomats increased markedly after Iranian students seized more than fifty hostages at the U.S. embassy in

Tehran in November. And on April 12, 1981, Preece recounted, "Deputy Assistant Secretary of State Morris Draper met in Baghdad with Iraqi officials to discuss future U.S.-Iraqi relations, economic ties, and Secretary of State Alexander Haig's plan to develop a 'strategic consensus' to counter Soviet expansionism in the region." Once again, hopes emerged of better ties to Baghdad. Contacts continued despite Israel's raid in June 1981 (in American-built planes carrying American munitions) on Iraq's prized nuclear facility.

But true rapprochement began only after Saddam invaded Iran in 1980 and the war began to go badly. In late 1981 and 1982, as his military position deteriorated, Saddam repeatedly expressed his desire to expand diplomatic contacts with the United States. By 1982, Iran had leveled Iraq's major oil facilities at Fao and had crossed into Iraqi territory to lay siege to Iraq's second largest city, the southern port of Basra. Then Damascus cut off Iraq's oil pipeline through Syria, which meant that Iraq's only source of revenue was what it could ship through Turkey. "The memory of the hostages was quite fresh; the Ayatollah was still calling us the Great Satan and attempting to undermine governments throughout the Gulf states," said Geoffrey Kemp, then the head of the National Security Council's Middle East section under President Reagan. "It wasn't that we wanted Iraq to win the war, we did not want Iraq to lose. We really weren't naive. We knew he was an S.O.B., but he was our S.O.B."

The United States was eager to lend assistance for which Saddam Hussein assured he would be grateful. But there was a major obstacle. The terrorist Abu Nidal, who was to stage the horrific airport raids on Rome and Vienna in 1985, was one of several known terrorists in residence in Baghdad. And American law precluded credits, loans and extensive ties with countries on the terrorism list.

After further consultations between Iraqi and American officials, Abu Nidal left Baghdad, leaving some men and materiel in place, and shifted his headquarters to Damascus. In March 1982, Iraq was removed from the terrorism list, without consultation with Congress. Noel C. Koch, then the Defense Department's director for counterterrorism, told *The Washington Post* that Iraq had not been removed from the list because it was any less of a haven for terrorists. "No one had any doubts about [the Iraqis'] continued involvement with terrorism," Koch said. "The real reason was to help them succeed in the war against Iran."

Abu Nidal was gone, but others were not. Radical fringe groups from the Palestine Liberation Organization which had been pushed out of Lebanon found refuge in Baghdad in the early 1980s; in 1985, Iraq helped Abul Abbas, the planner of the hijacking of the cruise ship *Achille Lauro,* to escape arrest and prosecution by receiving him in Baghdad.

Striking Baghdad from the list made Saddam eligible for help he desperately needed. In December 1982, the Department of Agriculture's Commodity Credit Corporation (CCC) agreed for the first time to guarantee about $300 million in credits for the sale of rice and wheat to Baghdad. The CCC credits were important to an increasingly cash-starved country. Under the program, Baghdad had three years to repay the loans, and if Iraq defaulted, the U.S. government would be obligated to pay off the debt itself.

The seduction of Saddam continued. Meeting in 1982 with Representative Stephen Solarz of New York, an activist member of the House Foreign Affairs Committee and an avid supporter of Israel, Saddam accepted in principle Israel's right to exist. Just in case Solarz decided not to pass the word along to the administration and the Jewish community, Iraq published through its news service a transcript of the meeting Solarz had considered private. Subsequent meetings were held with Secretary of State George Shultz in May 1983; and in October, Iraq's deputy foreign minister came to Washington.

Geoffrey Kemp said that when the Reagan administration came into office, they did high-level studies of what America's policy should be, but that the policy adopted was basically that of the Carter administration. Then, as Iraq's position deteriorated in the war, the administration decided that the policy should be reevaluated. According to Preece, a study done by the National Security Council in October 1983 concluded that American interests in the region would be seriously harmed if Iraq were to collapse. But it also noted that there was little the United States could do to aid Iraq directly, since Washington was officially neutral in the dispute. Indirect aid, however, could be provided, and soon was. At the Reagan administration's urging, the Gulf states attempted to increase their support for Iraq.

In November 1984, just after President Reagan was reelected, the United States restored full diplomatic relations with Iraq. Cooperation increased, including a relationship between the two countries' intelligence agencies. A State Department official said that most of what Baghdad provided the CIA—information about Soviet weapons in its arsenal and about terrorists—proved virtually worthless. But Bob Woodward of *The Washington Post* reported in 1986 that Iraq, for its part, was given information gleaned from satellite photos of Iranian troop positions that helped it plan and wage its campaigns. Meanwhile, "Operation Staunch," aimed at persuading foreign countries to cut off weapons sales to

Iran (which refused to negotiate an end to the dispute), was beginning to bite.

In 1986, Iraq opened another pipeline for its oil through Saudi Arabia, but by that time the nation's financial situation was precarious. Baghdad had missed payments at least once on loans from every country except the United States. Although the international banking community favored a collective meeting to work out a rescheduling of the debt, Iraq insisted on renegotiating each loan separately with different banks and countries. Foreign banks imposed lending limits to Iraq, but American banks did not follow suit.

By 1987, Iraq's participation in the CCC program had increased dramatically to $567 million, up from $215 million four years earlier. Private banks also helped, especially the Atlanta branch of the Italian-owned Banca Nazionale de Lavoro, which between 1983 and 1990 arranged about $3 billion in loans. Not all of these funds went for wheat and rice, though Iraq did become the fifth largest importer of American wheat and the largest importer of rice. *The Financial Times* wrote earlier this year that some of the letters of credit were used to finance highly questionable transactions of "dual use" equipment that seemed to be destined for military purposes. By mid-September, a grand jury was weighing charges against the Banca Nazionale.

In a relationship that has traditionally been characterized by ups and downs, November 1986 was a nadir for Iraq and the United States. News of the Iran-Contra affair, the Reagan administration's secret sales of weapons to Tehran, shocked Saddam. "Damage control," as it is known in government, began with a series of heartfelt apologies that were reinforced by a risky commitment undertaken the next year. After Iran threatened to attack oil tankers from Kuwait, which was transporting much of Iraq's oil, Washington announced that it would "reflag" Kuwaiti ships and ensure their protection by escorting them through the Gulf. The highly controversial reflagging program touched off an intense debate in Washington, but it assuaged an angry Saddam Hussein.

In 1987, another incident threatened the relationship: A French-made Exocet missile fired by an Iraqi jet hit the U.S.S. *Stark*, killing thirty-seven sailors. But Saddam moved fast. An effusive apology for the "accident" was followed by payments of $27 million to the victims' families.

In August 1988, the Iraq-Iran war ended with a cease-fire. Because Iran had vowed to fight until Saddam had been removed from office, the cease-fire was interpreted by many as a victory, of sorts, for Iraq. Most analysts in Washington expected Saddam to retrench, demobilize, and begin rebuilding his shattered economy. But this was not to be. Almost immediately, Saddam attacked his country's Kurdish minority with poison gas.

Secretary of State Shultz assailed the action in the strongest terms, demanding a pledge that Iraq would not use such a weapon again, a pledge he secured from Baghdad. But now that the war was over, opposition was growing in Congress to what many perceived as an inappropriate "cozying up" to a tyrant.

Peter Galbraith, a staff member of the Senate Foreign Relations Committee, had been appalled by what he had seen during a 1987 visit to the Kurdish areas of Iraq. "Village after village had been destroyed," Galbraith said. "The place had a kind of eerie silence and beauty, but what had once been an area filled with villages and life and some 2 million people was suddenly empty. The Kurdish villages that had been there almost since the beginning of time were gone. Their inhabitants had been moved to concentration camps erected hastily around a few major towns."

Then came the Iraqi gas attacks. Senator Claiborne Pell of Rhode Island, the liberal patrician chairman of the Senate Foreign Relations Committee, teamed up with Jesse Helms, the arch-conservative of North Carolina—the supreme political "odd couple"—to support Pell's Prevention of Genocide Act of 1988. The bill would have imposed a trade embargo on Iraq that could be lifted only if the president certified that Iraq was not committing genocide and Iraq pledged that it would not use poison gas again. The Reagan administration opposed the bill, and after passing the Senate unanimously, the legislation became mired in procedural politics and died.

Meanwhile, the presidential election campaign had taken center stage, leaving the Reagan administration as the lamest of lame ducks. After George Bush was elected, jockeying began over posts in the new administration. "So it took a while to get its feet on the ground," said a State Deparment official. "There was a long period of time where there was no substantive focus on the Gulf. I guess in retrospect, the absence of either a clearly articulated policy or even any emphasis on the Gulf was unfortunate."

A review of America's policy options in the Persian Gulf was finally launched in the spring of 1989, almost a year after the Iraq-Iran cease-fire had taken effect. John Kelly, the assistant secretary of state for Near Eastern and South Asian affairs, who would normally have supervised the drafting of so crucial a policy paper, had not yet even been confirmed in his job. A new policy paper, known as a National Security Directive, was eventually approved in the summer. "The policy was, essentially, more of the same," one administration official recounted. "Wean the Iraqis away from nuclear and chemical proliferation; tie them economically closer to the U.S. and the Western world; try to use carrots, rather than sticks, in moderating their behavior."

Most analysts in Washington did not quarrel with the policy toward Iraq when it seemed that Baghdad might be overrun by Iran. "There was a huge consensus that Saddam was the lesser of two evils on Capitol Hill, at State, DoD, and throughout the government," said a House staffer. But maintaining that policy after the cease-fire made little sense to many of its critics, who saw Iraq engaging in consistent and even growing human-rights abuses, nuclear development, and the proliferation of chemical warfare agents. "It wasn't really a new policy paper that the Bush administration drafted," said Representative Solarz. "It was more of the same under a new number."

It was, in short, a policy on "automatic pilot."

Some on Capitol Hill and within the administration argue that the policy review should have come even before the cease-fire in the Iraq-Iran war. According to a knowledgeable source in the House of Representatives, the Defense Intelligence Agency had decided by late 1986 that Iraq was not going to lose the war.

Although the policy was subjected to an occasional review in 1989 and 1990, the Persian Gulf simply had no priority in the Bush administration, according to several policymakers. "Jim Baker was absorbed last year by the momentous events in the Soviet Union and the collapse of communism in Eastern Europe," said one official. "To the extent that he worried about the Middle East at all, it was about how you could get peace talks going between Israel and the Palestinians," government sources said. In another administration, more junior officials might have been able to seize control of the issue and force the Secretary of State to concentrate on it. But that was not possible in Baker's State Department.

"Everybody's blaming John Kelly for the statements he made just before the invasion on Capitol Hill," said another State Deparment official. "But in the Baker State Department, neither John Kelly nor any other assistant secretary makes policy. It's Jim Baker and a few pals on the seventh floor who make policy. They don't talk a lot outside their inner circle. It would have been very hard to get their attention on something that most analysts in and outside of government thought would never happen."

As evidence of Iraq's misdeeds mounted in mid-1989 and early 1990—the execution of a British journalist charged with spying, the confiscation of components for a "supergun" and triggers for nuclear devices, allegations of bribery in connection with loans from the branch of the Lavoro bank in Atlanta—pressure built on Capitol Hill to impose economic sanctions against Saddam. The administration opposed such legislation. Though White House officials said that economic considerations did not affect the decision to lobby against sanctions, many companies and farmers had a considerable stake in defeating the various measures being debated on Capitol Hill.

By 1990, 486 licenses for shipments of some $730 million worth of sensitive technology to Iraq had been granted, following assurances that the items would not be used for military purposes, according to *The Washington Post;* about 160 more were pending when Iraq moved into Kuwait. Iraqi loans from the CCC had grown from $547 million in 1987 to $1.045 billion. Between 1983 and 1989, annual trade between Iraq and the United States had grown sevenfold, from $571 million to $3.6 billion. The United States, over that span, had bought $5.5 billion in Iraqi oil. Some seventy companies were members of the U.S.-Iraq Business Forum.

The White House, however, discounted money as a

motive for the policy. During the Bush administration's first eighteen months, a White House official said, the policy could best be characterized as a "limited détente," a policy somewhat akin in spirit to the détente in U.S.-Soviet relations in the early 1970s. In the last few months before the invasion, he continued, the relationship, which "was never buddy-buddy," became far more strained. "If the policy before had been balanced between 70 percent sanction and 30 percent incentive, that proportion shifted to 90 percent sanction–10 percent incentive in the weeks before the invasion."

This official went on to say that there had been a strong consensus within the administration, as well as among America's allies in Europe and in the Arab world, that this was the right policy. Iraq did seem to have emerged from the war more moderate, more pro-American and pro-Western. It had entered into a cooperation agreement with Egypt, Jordan, and Yemen—all countries friendly to the United States. "It would have been crazy not to try to continue to move Iraq toward us. I firmly believe the strategy was right," the official said. "There was never an intense debate about it, ever," he added.

He also disputed the notion that Iraq had been able to buy or get whatever it needed here. "We never threw open the cupboard," he said. "And toward the end, the cupboard was open only a crack." There was no military relationship to speak of; the United States did not sell weapons to Iraq; in 1990 the White House suspended some $500 million (half of Iraq's yearly allotment in the CCC guarantees) after questions were raised about possible Iraqi kickbacks and malfeasance; the administration confiscated shipments of supergun components and other "dual use" technologies that deeply embarrassed Baghdad; it denounced the execution of the British journalist accused of spying.

At one point, he maintained, Iraq was so disturbed by the barrage of unfavorable publicity coming out of the United States that Saddam had suggested to fellow Iraqis and diplomats that there might well be a conspiracy against Iraq. The same point was made by Milton Viorst in an article in *The New Yorker* in late September. Viorst, who had accompanied Jesse Jackson to Baghdad, quoted with only a trace of skepticism Iraqi Foreign Minister Tariq Aziz's bizarre assertion that Kuwait and the United States had entered into a strange conspiracy to destroy Baghdad following the American effort to protect Iraqi oil by reflagging Kuwaiti vessels.

Moreover, after Saddam had threatened both the United Arab Emirates and Kuwait, the administration had approved a Defense Department recommendation to stage emergency maneuvers in the Gulf. The U.A.E., which had sought the show of support, was nevertheless so fearful of provoking Iraq that it publicly denied participating in them. "There was a limit on what we could have said and done before the invasion and retained Arab support," the White House official asserted.

While the strategy was defensible, he said, perhaps the tactics were not. The White House never issued a clear warning that the use of military force to solve an economic or territorial dispute was unacceptable to the United States. The Defense Department sent a tougher set of signals. "Perhaps the rhetoric could have been explicit," he conceded.

This line of reasoning is not persuasive on Capitol Hill. For while the administration was dangling its 30 percent carrot, a growing number of legislators, alarmed by Saddam's behavior, wanted to wield the 70 percent stick. The administration was battling the effort to impose sanctions against Iraq almost until the day before the invasion.

Giving Iraq the benefit of the doubt has been the

result of a curious blend of cynicism and naivete on Washington's part. Administration after administration has looked for an opening to this closed, xenophobic regime. In its zeal to effect a more positive relationship, Washington overlooked human rights and other abuses and persuaded itself that what for Saddam was a temporary and tactical political repositioning was, in effect, a basic shift in his orientation and objectives. Saddam Hussein needed the United States, Western Europe and even some of the moderate Arabs first to fight his war against Iran and then to rebuild his battered state. But even in the midst of the war, he quietly pursued another agenda.

IX

The Manufacture of Death

It was all over in less than a minute. At dusk on Sunday, June 7, 1981, eight Israeli F-16 jet fighters and six F-15 fighter interceptors zoomed out of the setting sun and obliterated Iraq's most prized possession, the French-built nuclear reactor, Osirak, named after Osiris, the Egyptian god of the dead.

Although the nuclear facility on the outskirts of Baghdad was protected with French-made Roland ground-to-air missiles, the Iraqi soldiers on the ground never fired them. The only resistance came from a small battery of antiaircraft guns which sprayed the air haplessly with fire as the fighters dived down on their target again and again. The planes covered the nuclear reactor's sandy-brown concrete dome with bombs bearing delayed action fuses, designed to explode when they hit the base of the dome, so that the reactor core, buried deep in the ground, would be destroyed. In less than a minute, Osirak was history, and so was the raid.

"It's gone like a Swiss watch," a relieved Israeli Prime Minister Menachem Begin was told, according to Steve Weissman and Herbert Krosney's dramatic account of the mission. "Better than a Swiss watch."

The announcement from the prime minister's office on the afternoon of the attack was more subdued. "On Sunday, June 7, 1981, the Israel Air Force launched a raid on the atomic reactor Osirak, near Baghdad," the communiqué stated. "Our pilots carried out their mission fully. The reactor was destroyed. All our aircraft returned safely to base."

The attack, of course, was to have profound diplomatic and political consequences. The United States would spend the next months working with Iraq on various United Nations resolutions condemning Israel. Even more vehement was France, which deplored the attack and the killing of a French engineer at the site. But France's outrage was in part theatrics. According to an authoritative source, Israel had told the newly elected and friendly Socialist government of President François Mitterrand that it intended to stage such an attack. And President Mitterrand—the only foreign leader to be informed before the raid—had not objected.

Most governments professed shock and disapproval. But among many of their nuclear experts, there was a sense of relief. The French had supplied technology that was far too sophisticated for Iraq's nascent nuclear energy program. Baghdad's steady stream of acquisitions in the late 1970s, some of which could only be explained if Iraq was planning to build a bomb, had raised concern in capitals throughout the West. Although Iraq, unlike Israel, did not have a weapon and was a signatory in good standing to the Nuclear Nonproliferation Treaty, most nuclear experts eventually concluded, as did Leonard S. Spector, a respected analyst in Washington, that "the hidden objective behind Iraq's expansion of its nuclear sector in the mid-1970s was the gradual acquisition of a nuclear weapons capability."

Iraq, of course, was humiliated by the Israeli attack. The ground-to-air missiles had been installed specifically to prevent an attack on the precious reactor. In September 1980, eight days after Iraq had invaded Iran, another reactor had been damaged in an air attack, this time by the Iranians, not the Israelis.

As deputy president in 1976, Saddam Hussein had personally negotiated the purchase of the French reactor during a visit to Paris—a rare foray to the West. According to Weissman and Krosney, Saddam had told a Beirut newspaper in 1975 that his hunt for a supposedly peaceful reactor was part of "the first Arab attempt at nuclear arming."

After the Israeli raid, his visions of an Iraqi bomb were as shattered as the blocks and shards of concrete that littered the Osirak site. President since 1979, Saddam called upon the world to defend Iraq against Israel's overwhelming military and nuclear capabilities. "Peace-loving nations should now help the Arabs to acquire atomic bombs as a counterbalance to those already possessed by Israel," he declared. His plea went unheeded. Despite numerous press reports that the French had agreed to rebuild the reactor with Saudi financing, Osirak was not reconstructed.

But Saddam did not abandon his quest. Quite the contrary, judging from his country's activities since the raid. The attack helped persuade Saddam that Iraq must never again be dependent on any one country for one kind of military technology. Iraq would build wide-ranging, highly protected military capabilities in chemical, biological and nuclear armaments, which no single foreign enemy would easily be able to destroy. In the aftermath of the devastating Israeli raid, Iraq launched an ambitious long-term program not just for buying arms but also for obtaining the material and technology needed to construct its own weapons of mass destruction. Dummy corporations and phony trading agents were created. European companies that produced components for weapons plants were secretly acquired. Huge "shopping lists" of desired materials and compo-

nents were assembled and distributed. In the midst of
the Iraq-Iran war, Baghdad was already working hard
on assembling what it would need for the next confrontation. Iraq would never again be humiliated.

Since the Israeli raid less than a decade ago, Iraq has
done much to achieve its goals. The Iraq-Iran war, of
course, generated enormous demand for weapons on
both sides. The Stockholm International Peace Institute
estimated that in 1984 alone, Iraq spent $14 billion—
about half of its gross domestic product—on arms and
defense. According to Anthony H. Cordesman, a defense expert on the staff of Senator John McCain of
Arizona, Iraq imported $42.8 billion worth of arms between 1982 and 1989, $27.3 billion of that between 1982
and 1985, and $15.5 billion between 1986 and 1989.
Though these figures represent an enormous investment, Cordesman noted, overall defense spending was
probably 10 to 30 percent higher than the figures listed,
since some of what was clearly military infrastructure
was reported in the civilian budget.

Baghdad's decision to continue this prodigious
spending indicated that despite the cease-fire with Iran
in August 1988, there would be no peace dividend for
Iraq. The spending spree for arms continued even after
the immediate justification for it disappeared. During
the past five years, Iraq was the world's largest importer
of weapons; alone, it accounted for more than 9 percent
of the world's arms purchases. Forty percent of those
arms transfer agreements, Cordesman reported, came
from the Soviet Union; 13 percent came from China;
and Western European countries provided 15 percent.

As the war dragged on, the nations of Western
Europe became huge suppliers, and not just of weapons. France, for example, sold Iraq about $12 billion
worth of military equipment between 1981 and 1988.

And according to figures from the office of North Carolina Senator Jesse Helms, French companies also sold equipment and components that could be used to make weapons. Only when Saddam fell behind in paying for his purchases, several months before the invasion of Kuwait, did France stop selling to Iraq. All this activity, of course, was quietly sanctioned by the U.S. government. Washington had concluded that the purchases were essential to keep Iraq from losing the war, and did not alter its policy after the cease-fire took effect. Such untrammeled growth of the military sector meant that by the war's end, Iraq had emerged, in Cordesman's words, not just as the victor, but as "a significant military power in the Gulf."

Part of Iraq's strength lay in oil: unlike other ambitious developing nations, Baghdad had the oil resources to buy what it needed. But the Iraqis also became adept at modifying and significantly improving what they had purchased. Cordesman noted that in February 1988 alone, Iraq launched five new extended-range missiles. One of these new missiles, the al-Abbas, a Soviet Scud missile variation, supposedly has a range of 530 miles—more than twice the range of the Scud. Cordesman said it was tested in April 1988. Israeli military sources said they had seen no evidence of a test, but that they are sufficiently impressed with the al-Hussein, another Scud variation that was first tested in 1987. The al-Hussein has an estimated range of 400 miles, more than enough to hit Tel Aviv from the western part of Iraq. More than 200 of these missiles were used against Iran.

In December 1989, Iraq tested a new missile booster, known as the al-Abid, or Worshipper, with a range of nearly 1,500 nautical miles. Two days later, Baghdad announced it had developed two more new missiles; the Tamuz I, a three-stage liquid-fueled 48-ton missile; and a new solid-fuel missile known as the Condor, built with Egyptian and Argentinian assistance.

Israeli military officials said they first suspected that Saddam was planning some new adventure almost a year before the Kuwaiti invasion, when Iraq deployed more than a dozen al-Hussein missiles at three fixed sites, one in the western part of the country. This site, located near the road connecting Jordan and Iraq, had six launchers aimed at targets in Israel or Syria. The Israelis were puzzled: why would Saddam make such an obvious move, one which every spy satellite and defense attaché would see, if he were planning a move against Israel? When Israeli Defense Minister Moshe Arens visited U.S. Defense Secretary Richard Cheney in July, Iraq was the focus of his discussions. Near the top of his agenda was Iraq's mysterious deployment of this new missile cluster. But Israel, obviously, was focused on the threat to its own borders; it did not predict the threat to Kuwait.

By the end of the Iraq-Iran war, Saddam had made large strides toward achieving his goal of freeing himself from the need to import finished weapons systems. True, he still had to buy planes and air defense systems abroad, but he had demonstrated that Iraq could develop a major research and development capability without buying key components like finished boosters. As Cordesman observed, "Iraq is proof that a rich buyer can always find a third party, or new method of purchasing a given technology or components, as long as only a few nations adhere to a permissive arms control regime."

Many of Iraq's missile modifications were carried out at a facility known as Saad 16, a state-of-the-art plant with high-speed wind tunnels, motor test ramps, a missile launch range, and chemical and electronics laboratories. Located near Mosul in the northern part of the country, the plant reportedly cost more than $200 million. In addition to developing and modifying missiles, scientists at the plant also reportedly develop chemical weapons there, and possibly even experiment with making high-speed centrifuges to enrich uranium that can be used in a nuclear bomb.

The chief contractor for supplying the Saad 16 facility was the Consen Group, a Swiss-based consortium which acquired foreign technology and expertise for Iraq's missile program though far-flung subsidiaries in Argentina, Monaco, Switzerland and West Germany, according to Michael Eisenstadt, an analyst at the Washington Institute for Near East Policy. "Consen closed down operation in early 1989," Eizenstadt states, "having found that as a result of adverse publicity, it could no longer conduct business." That function was reportedly taken over by another Swiss firm, Vufvalturn und Financierung AG (VUFAG), Eizenstadt said.

Christopher Crowley, a British engineer who worked at Saad 16 in 1988 and 1989 (and is now facing charges for his alleged part in helping Iraq acquire a "supergun"), was interviewed by the BBC for a recent documentary on Iraq's weapons arsenal. He called the plant "absolutely brilliant. . . . I've never seen anything in Europe that compared with that particular research facility [or] that had such superb equipment."

While Saad 16 is Iraq's major ballistic missile research and development facility, it is not the only one. Other facilities, Eizenstat reported, include engineering workshops near Falluja, a rocket propellant production facility near Mahmudiya, and a missile test area for static testing of rocket motors and missiles trials near Karbala. Construction for these projects was completed in early 1989, Eizenstadt said, reportedly at a cost of $400 million. Cordesman said that the scale of Iraq's program was illustrated by an explosion about a year ago at a chemical and fuel facility named al-Hillal, about thirty miles south of Baghdad. That mysterious explosion killed up to 700 people, but still did not cause a long halt in production.

Unlike Osirak, virtually all of Saddam's new facilities are now well protected, at least theoretically. Saad 16, for example, is surrounded by an air defense system; it also has dummy buildings intended to deceive spy satellite cameras and serve as decoys in event of a raid.

An early and unusually outspoken critic of the spread of ballistic missiles and chemical weapons has been William H. Webster, the director of central intelligence. In an unusual speech in March 1989, he warned that the development by some fifteen countries of their own ballistic missile systems by the year 2000 was part of a "disturbing trend" that included increasing development of nuclear, chemical and biological weapons by Third World countries. Though he did not identify the countries, administration officials put Iraq high on his list of concerns, long before the invasion of Kuwait.

In what is surely among the most public campaigns ever waged by a director of the agency responsible for secrets, Webster warned that as many as twenty countries might be developing chemical weapons, what Churchill referred to as "that hellish poison," and that "the moral barrier to biological warfare has been breached." There is no doubt that he was referring, among other countries, to Iraq.

W. Seth Carus of the Washington Institute for Near East Policy concluded in a report last year that "Iraq now has the largest and possibly most sophisticated chemical weapons program in the Third World." Significantly, he noted, Iraq has continued, and even expanded, its ability to build chemical weapons since the end of its war with Iran. Although Iraq signed the Geneva Protocol of 1925, forbidding the use of chemical agents, except in retaliation against another country that uses them first, Baghdad used chemical weapons repeatedly during the war (beginning in 1983 and 1984), and even after the cease-fire the regime used them to help put down Kurdish unrest.

Carus said that Iraq probably launched its chemical weapons program in the 1960s, long before Saddam came to power. In a meticulous article documenting the history of Iraq's chemical weapons program, David Ignatius of *The Washington Post* reported that Iraq initially approached the Pfaudler Company of Rochester, New York, as early as 1975 to help them build a "pesticide" blending plant. Pfaudler stalled, and tried to persuade Iraq to build a more modest facility, to no avail. Baghdad eventually broke off the talks, and undaunted, turned to a British concern, Imperial Chemical Industries. ICI also rapidly understood what Iraq was planning and backed out of the negotions. The second rebuff, however, did not "discourage Iraq," Cordesman said. "The Iraqis turned to West German, Swiss, French, Dutch, Belgian and Italian firms," and eventually obtained what they needed. In the chemical weapons business, it seems, persistence matters.

Carus argued that a "high-level decision" was made—almost surely by Saddam himself—to build plants to manufacture chemical agents for weapons and that this goal was fully accomplished by 1985. At that time, he wrote, "Iraq was producing a number of chemical agents, including mustard gas and two different types of nerve agents—tabun and sarin." Based on information provided by Webster, Carus concluded that Iraq now has plants that can produce between 3,300 and 13,200 tons a year of several different chemical agents—that is, five to twenty times more than previously estimated. The stocks are scattered throughout the country, and even those who have enormous respect for air power say that destroying all of them through bombing would be extremely difficult.

Another indication of the importance of the chemical weapons sector is the fact that it has been placed under the stewardship of Hussein Kamal, Saddam's son-in-law, a rising star within the family. Hussein Kamal runs the Ministry of Industry and Military Industries, or MIMI, which oversees all sensitive military procurement. Chemical warfare, which was rarely used since World War I, is back in vogue, thanks in large measure to Saddam Hussein.

The main chemical weapons site is a complex near the town of Samarra, about seventy miles northwest of Baghdad. In addition, Webster said, there are several other facilities, whose locations he did not identify. But Carus said Iraq might be producing other chemical agents as well, such as phosgene, arsenic compounds and cyanide compounds.

Chemical weapons are a natural extension of Baathist tradition. Baath party leaders have long been enamored of heavy metal poisons and chemical agents that kill dissidents silently. In his book *Republic of Fear,* Samir al-Khalil wrote that it became a favored practice in the late 1970s to give unsuspecting enemies long-term poisons, like thallium and lead, in soft drinks offered during interrogations. In 1981, Amnesty International published statements by British doctors concluding that at least two such individuals suffered from thallium poisoning, and that fifteen Iraqis had been killed in this way. In 1981, *New Scientist* published a report on the repression of Iraqi scientists, containing interviews with victims and descriptions of individual cases. "Shawkat A. Akrawi, a consulting industrial chemist who graduated from Leeds University, managed to 'smuggle' a telephone call from a Baghdad hospital to a *New Scientist* contact," the report said.

"Speaking in Kurdish, he said, 'The accident they arranged didn't kill me, so they gave me thallium in the hospital where I am being treated. Say goodbye to everybody.' The line was then cut off."

Now Iraq has the capability to poison on a grand scale. But manufacturing the gases and nerve agents in bulk has proved challenging. The process has not changed much since it was used in the Great War. To make mustard gas, for example, Iraq first needed to obtain a "precursor" called thiodiglycol, a chemical most commonly used in making dyes and inks. When thiodiglycol is mixed with hydrochloric acid, a readily available chemical with wide-ranging applications, the mixture produces mustard gas. But thiodiglycol was regulated, and Iraq was unable to make it in the early 1980s. An American company in Belgium apparently was the first to oblige, according to Carus.

"In the future, however, it should be possible for Iraq to avoid export controls by making its own thiodiglycol," he concluded. In fact, Iraq should be able to produce "thousands of tons of mustard gas per year, should it so desire." And while the production of nerve agents is far more complicated than making mustard gas, West German companies built two plants at the Samarra complex in the early 1980s capable of making a maximum of forty-eight tons a year of sarin and tabun. Once again, Carus stressed, Iraq was able to turn to European companies and other foreign suppliers to buy the raw ingredients it required.

Israeli military sources say that while Iraq has some relatively crude air bombs and thousands of artillery pieces to deliver chemical weapons, there is no evidence that it has succeeded in developing highly accurate missiles with chemical warheads. Should it accomplish this, however, Iraq would have added yet another lethal capability to its already impressive arsenal. One Israeli military source noted that a warhead loaded with conventional explosives aimed at Tel Aviv would result in an estimated five to ten casualties per warhead. A missile loaded with chemicals would kill fifty people per warhead, but the estimate assumes that the population has gas masks and rudimentary training in using them. Another analyst points out that chemicals also serve as a terror weapon; and as already seen from Iraq's previous use of them, they have a devastating psychological effect.

An even more terrifying, if more primitive, program is Iraq's research and development in the field of biological weapons. Although Iraq has denied that it is trying to develop such a program, the main Iraqi biological warfare research facility is at Salman Pak, according to Carus. Iraqi scientists are believed to be investigating several well-known diseases for possible use—typhoid, cholera, anthrax, tularemia and equine encephalitis. Neither Carus nor several Israeli sources, who understandably closely monitor Iraqi weapons programs, think that Iraq has yet managed to "weaponize" these diseases—that is, to find the means to deliver them accurately to a targeted population, a process which is scientifically complex. But there is little doubt, Carus concluded, that the Iraqis "have acquired much of the equipment needed to produce biological agents on a substantial scale."

While most of this technology and equipment has come from West Germany, the United States may have also unwittingly lent assistance. The Centers for Disease Control in Atlanta routinely transports potentially deadly cultures for scientific research—on planes, trains and even through the mail and Federal Express. Senator John Glenn and his staff, who have long followed proliferation issues, note that it is very difficult to ensure that a culture ostensibly shipped for genuine medical and scientific research is not being used for military research. The problem of controlling the export of these "dual use" materials plagues not only efforts to control biological agents and toxins but missile and chemical-related technologies as well.

According to records of outgoing shipments published in recent committee hearings, the CDC in Atlanta made three separate shipments of West Nile Fever virus to a research facility in Basra in 1985. That same year, according to documents provided to NBC News under the Freedom of Information Act, scientists who specialize in biological warfare agents at Fort Detrick, Maryland, were working on a vaccine for this disease. And in 1989, the West German press carried reports that Iraq had bought from a German company a small amount of mycotoxins—toxins produced by fungi found on wheat and grass, some of which kill humans and animals by inhibiting the ability of cells to synthesize proteins.

An aide to Senator Glenn cautions that "just because a country has obtained a culture doesn't necessarily mean that they are experimenting with biological warfare." But this "dual use" problem, coupled with advances in the field of biotechnology, has led administration officials to conclude that it is enormously difficult to stop the spread of biological weapons. H. Allen Holmes, a State Department official charged with monitoring the proliferation of biological warfare agents, told Congress in testimony last year that it would be impractical to impose a system of international export controls on such agents, even though he acknowledged that their spread was a threat to American security and that "it may only be a matter of time before terrorists do acquire and use these weapons."

"There are no precursor chemicals or equipment that can be used only for the production of biological warfare agents," CIA director Webster said last year. "Actually, any nation with a modestly developed pharmaceutical industry can produce biological warfare agents if it so chooses."

Webster said last year that at least ten countries were trying to produce existing or new types of biological weapons. Though he did not mention any by name, administration officials have repeatedly listed Iraq among them.

More than 110 countries, including the United States and the Soviet Union, are members of a 1972 convention banning the development and stockpiling of biological weapons. But even though both countries have signed and ratified the convention, a loophole in American criminal law allows private individuals and concerns to make such weapons. Moreover, Iraq has signed the convention, but it has not ratified it, which means that it is not legally binding. But even if it were, Iraq's flagrant disregard for treaties and rules of law would offer the world little reassurance.

Despite its advances in chemical and biological warfare research and development, however, Iraq's nuclear program remains the single most pressing of his threats to the region, Israeli and American arms control specialists agree. Once again, the pattern is clear: Iraq embarked on a well-planned, well-financed quest to buy the technology and the components it needed to make atomic weapons many years ago. Only recently have the fruits of that labor become apparent.

According to Leonard Spector, Iraq could acquire a bomb in two ways. First, it could use the enriched uranium it has stored under international safeguards to make a single crude weapon that would be used in extremis. France provided some twenty-seven pounds of enriched uranium (enough fissionable material for such a weapon) for the Osirak reactor. This scenario is unlikely, in Spector's view. "First of all, they could only make a single bomb, which wouldn't help them very much," said Spector, who noted that nuclear experts believe that Israel now has an unacknowledged stockpile of more than 200 bombs. The second, and more likely alternative, is that Iraq will continue trying to buy the components it needs to build a plant in which it can enrich its own uranium to weapons-grade.

Spector notes in his book *Nuclear Ambitions* that in 1980 and 1981 Iraq bought "inexplicably large amounts of natural uranium from Brazil, Portugal, Niger and Italy." None of this material could be used in the old Osirak reactor, which required enriched uranium fuel. Spector also points to at least four sites where nuclear-related work is believed to be taking place: Tuwaitha, the site of the old Osirak reactor; Saad-16, near Mosul University; Irbil, near the Kuridish border; and al-Qaim, the site of a phosphate plant that may be producing hexafluoride gases, essential for building a weapon. Israeli military sources said there are at least five other locations where work is underway, but declined to specify the nature of the work or their location.

The seizure within the past two years of components for a plant that could manufacture centrifuges, in which uranium can be enriched, was among the first incidents to spark alarm among nuclear analysts. In February 1989, the Commerce Department blocked Iraq's attempt to buy specialized vacuum pumps. Although such pumps can be used for many non-nuclear purposes, they can also be used in an enrichment plant. In December 1989, the West German magazine *Der Spiegel* reported that a West German company was under investigation for having supplied Iraq between 1987 and 1989 with special rolling machines for manufacturing enrichment centrifuges. Also in late 1989, *The Financial Times* reported that Iraq was attempting to buy in Western Europe special magnets made of samarium cobalt, which Spector said are used to hold enrichment centrifuges in place while they spin at high speed. Interestingly, the article noted that since Iraq had failed to make the purchase, there was evidence suggesting that it had decided to make the magnets itself with the help of the Chinese government. Last March, a large shipment of military-grade capacitors, which can be used to trigger nuclear weapons, were seized in a well-publicized sting operation before they could be shipped to Iraq. *NuclearFuel,* a respected trade publication, reported in August that the Swiss government was investigating companies that may have sent to Iraq end caps for centrifuge tubes, equipment that can be used in an enrichment plant. That same month, *The Washington Post* reported that West German officials seized a Swiss shipment of metals to Iraq to determine whether the shipment contained maraging steel, a particularly strong metal used in uranium enrichment centifuges.

Most of this technology was supplied by European companies, a few of which had been purchased by Iraqi-owned front companies to handle the transactions more efficiently. Military sources estimate that Iraq has spent literally millions of dollars bribing officials and setting up dummy corporations to acquire equipment that will enable it to construct a plant that will manufacture nuclear components.

One of the more interesting cases that demonstrates how bureaucratic infighting in the U.S. government has sometimes hampered the already complicated effort to stop the export of "dual use" technology involves the Consarc Corporation USA, which is located in Rancocas, New Jersey. The month before Iraq's invasion of Kuwait, the Defense Department waged a fierce campaign to persuade the Commerce Department to rescind its approval of a $7.6 million sale to Iraq of special furnaces for melting titanium. Baghdad had clamed that it needed the furnaces to melt metals to be used in prostheses for its many soldiers disabled during the war. But Defense argued that the skull furnaces, as they were called, could also be used to make parts for nuclear weapons and missiles.

According to a Customs Office memorandum, originally reported in *The Washington Post*, an overzealous Commerce Department official, Michael Manning, tried to stop the Defense Department investigation and to go forward with the sale, which he had signed off on in 1989. Manning called the customs agent handling the investigation, demanding to know why the sale was being held up. "His reputation was at stake," the memo said, "since Consarc acted on his advice" in negotiating the contract. After making several calls to the Defense office that had blocked the sale, Manning called the customs agent again, demanding more information on the investigation—this time from inside Consarc's offices. The customs agent informed him that this could be misconstrued by the company and the investigators scrutinizing the transaction. But Manning pressed on. In yet another call, he expressed concern about the detention of the furnaces because of the "potential loss of money" to the company, which was, he noted, "a major employer in the South Jersey area."

Manning did not respond to calls about his role, but subsequent press reports indicated that several officials at Commerce, including Manning, had known that the titanium had potential nuclear use yet had chosen to ignore that fact. In the wake of press reports about the prospective sale less than a month before Iraq's invasion of Kuwait, the White House announced that it would not permit the sale as licensed by Commerce to proceed.

Secretary of Commerce Robert Mossbacher said he

was not troubled by the incident. "The bottom line is that it did not go through," he said. Commerce Department officials, he said, were just fulfilling their mandate to help promote the sale of American goods and services abroad. Perhaps the nuclear potential of the equipment should have been flagged sooner. Perhaps it shouldn't have been necessary for the sale to have been vetoed only by the highest authority—in this case the National Security Council. "But once it got kicked upstairs, the sale was quickly killed," Mossbacher said.

The crackdown on "dual use" exports has created something of an anomaly according to Les Aspin, the chairman of the House Armed Services Committee, for it has coincided with a desire in Congress to increase trade with the Soviet Union and the former East Bloc countries. "Commerce was traditionally more favorably disposed toward such sales than Defense. So for the past two years, Congress has been shifting the leading role in export approval over to Commerce," he said. And, in light of its mandate, Commerce has been less interested in blocking "dual use" exports.

Under the current system, the State Department is normally responsible for reviewing all items contained on a list of munitions, but in cases of "dual use" exports to Iraq, the Commerce Department has the final say. The Pentagon can register objections to the sale, but Commerce can choose to ignore them. Even if primary responsibility for such sales were transferred to the Pentagon, as some in Congress are now advocating, some "dual use" equipment might well slip through, for the Defense Department has occasionally been divided as well over such transactions.

The major impetus for blocking such deals has come from a relatively tiny unit within the Pentagon known as the Office of Technology Security Operations. With a ten-person staff, Michael Maloof, its director, and

Steve Bryen, who headed the unit between 1985 and 1988, have managed to prevent many such sales to Iraq from being approved. But not always.

Alan Friedman of *The Financial Times* reported in mid-September that as many as fourteen times between 1985 and 1990 Commerce brushed aside the office's objections and approved export shipments to Iraq that "directly helped Baghdad's development of nuclear, chemical and ballistic missile capabilities." In some cases, Friedman reported, Commerce had not even informed the Defense Department of the sale. The most recent missile-related export license, approved by Commerce last February, allowed a California company called International Imaging Systems to ship a computer and related equipment that is designed for infrared imaging enhancement, which can be used for real-time tracking of missiles.

One sale that did not take place was plans by West Homestead Engineering, of Homestead, Pennsylvania, to export forges and a related computer that Bryen says could be used to manufacture sixteen-inch gun barrels. "The good news," said Bryen, "was that we stopped Iraq from buying the guns. The bad news was that they almost bought the plant to make those guns."

Commerce approved the sale in the summer of 1989. The forge was being purchased supposedly to make containers for petrochemical products. The Defense Department had looked only at the small electronics that were to accompany the forge; Maloof's office saw no problem with the electronics but was eager to examine the specifications for the forge, which Commerce refused to let them see. On July 13, Commerce wrote Defense that it was "willing to listen to any suggestions you may have . . . however, the development of biological and chemical weapons, as well as the missile technology regime, are part of the foreign-policy controls and are beyond the preview [*sic*] of DoD." Since foreign-policy controls applied only to missile and nuclear technology, and not to forges, furnaces and low-level computers, Defense had little choice but to recommend that the sale be approved, provided Commerce checked with other government agencies.

In a letter to the Commerce Department dated July 30, 1990, West Homestead described a meeting its president, Bill Cook, had had with two State Department officials on July 24, long after his license was approved, but soon after press reports disclosed the suspension of the skull furnace sale. The letter stated that Cook had informed the officials—Joseph McGhee, deputy director of the Office of Northern Gulf Affairs, and Edward J. Marcott, deputy director of the Office of East-West Trade—that the forge "could be used to make a wide variety of large forgings, including large gun barrels." This statement should have set off alarm bells inside State. It was well known that Iraq had engaged the services of Gerald Bull, a visionary munitions maker who had long been trying to build the world's largest cannon—a "supergun." Only a few months before, the U.S. government had stopped the shipment to Iraq of materials needed to construct such a weapon. And the previous March, Bull had been murdered under mysterious circumstances in Brussels. But the State Department officials told Cook that despite the forge's potential application, they "did not foresee any potential problem with the proposed export." But just to be sure, they added, they recommended that he seek reconfirmation from the Commerce Department.

It was not the government that stopped this export but Cook's discomfort with the potential misuse of his company's own product that led him to raise the issue again and, ultimately, to cancel the more than $15 million order. A week later, though, Saddam had made the issue moot.

Yet another structural problem in stopping the export of "dual use" technology has been identified by Gary Milhollin of the Wisconsin Project on Nuclear Arms Control, which has doggedly tracked nonproliferation issues. In recent months, Milhollin observed, COCOM—the group set up by the United States and its allies after World War II to control technology—has been removing restrictions on high technology exports to the Warsaw Pact and other communist countries. Among the items decontrolled in June, he said, "were the very nuclear weapon triggers that Iraq tried to smuggle out of the United States in March." Also on the decontrol list were the machines that Iraq needs to make the bodies for its uranium enrichment centrifuges, known as spin-forming and flow-forming machines. Milhollin warned, and others agree, that the effect of COCOM's decontrol will probably be to decontrol them for Iraq, too. Any COCOM country can now sell such items to Poland, Hungary, Czechoslovakia, as if they were "a bag of onions," he said. There will not even be a record of their shipment. "So Iraq might well be able to order U.S. bomb triggers through front companies in Eastern Europe without breaking any laws," he concluded. Moreover, since the COCOM list for most of America's Western European allies is the only basis for export control, removing them from that list means that they can be sold without record throughout Europe. Unlike the United States, most European nations do not maintain a separate control list for stopping nuclear arms proliferation or the spread of ballistic missiles.

Whatever the failings of the export system, however, the United States has won high marks in general for its emphasis on stopping the spread of such technology. In

1987, the United States and six other weapons-producing allies set up the Missile Technology Control Regime to curb dangerous technology transfers to regimes like Iraq's. They restricted government sales of rockets, but did not always require their own private companies to abide by the accord. And as *The New York Times* noted in a recent editorial, companies in France, Sweden, West Germany and Belgium helped Brazil to develop an engine capable of sending a missile across continents and to improve its missile guidance system. The regime, it seems, does not include Brazil or other arms sellers in the Soviet Union, China, Eastern Europe. It was Brazil that helped Iraq build its long-range and potentially deadly Condor missile.

Nevertheless, the small but devoted group of experts, House and Senate aides, administration officials and journalists who have pursued these questions tend to agree with Leonard Spector's assessment that the Bush administration's sensitivity to the consequences of the problem has been growing. Furthermore, concern among the more free-wheeling European nations about the spread of chemical, biological and nuclear-related technology is also slowly intensifying. Too slowly, some critics say. Senator Helms's office issued a list this summer of what it labeled "Saddam's Foreign Legion," which enumerated the confirmed and reported instances of military-related sales to Iraq by foreign companies. Fourteen nations were listed as sellers, with West Germany at the top with seventy companies so named. Tiny Austria was not even a close second, with sixteen companies having been identified as sellers. The United States and the United Kingdom tied for third, each with eleven companies listed.

Here, too, the administration has set a new tone. Richard Perle, a former assistant secretary of defense in the Reagan administration, once referred to the demarches (the protests made by the U.S. government over sales of sensitive equipment to suspect states) as "demarshmallows." But increasingly tough messages from Washington, coupled with growing concern abroad about the spread of such technology among European states, has led to greater scrutiny of such transfers.

In the long run, though, the experts see little alternative but to continue trying to tighten export laws, draw up new treaties, and close loopholes in existing ones to ban weapons of such awesome destruction. But with an "outlaw state" like Iraq, as Jim Hoagland of *The Washington Post* so aptly called it, there is a limit to what can be done.

April Glaspie, the U.S. ambassador to Baghdad, probably does not need to be persuaded that Iraq's adherence to international agreements is unlikely. On the day she left Baghdad for vacation, having been given assurances by Saddam that he would not strike out at Kuwait as long as his neighbor was reasonable, she was summoned to another impromptu meeting. Hussein Kamal, the Minister of Industry and Military Industries, wanted to see her before she left. He said he knew that she had been told much about the skull furnaces that Iraq was trying to purchase. It wasn't he who had ordered them, he assured her, but the former Minister of Industry. And yes, he continued, they really were for peaceful purposes. "You have seen all the young men without limbs on our streets," he told her, pleading for her help in ensuring that the sale would continue. "You above all people know how much we need prostheses."

But in Washington, the Bush administration was hearing from its very unsentimental group of nuclear experts. The furnaces, they argued, were much more sophisticated than anything needed for Iraq's stated purpose. The only likely use, they agreed, was military. The sale was denied.

X

Black Gold

Oil is the modern world's heroin. The pleasure it provides fuels a way of life no other energy source can satisfy so plentifully and so cheaply. Efforts to kick the habit have proven halfhearted, painful, and unsuccessful. Today the trade in petroleum, like the traffic in drugs, is so much in the veins of nations that most countries, whether rich or poor, find their economies held hostage to this remarkable substance. How this state of affairs arose is a tale of greed, rivalry and collusion. Against the tapestry of Middle East passions, the struggle over the control of oil is the one thread that unites the region's combustible admixture of historical rancor, nationalist sentiment and religious fervor. That struggle is at the heart of the confrontation now unfolding in the Persian Gulf.

When Winston Churchill persuaded the British Admiralty to abandon coal in 1911 and adopt oil as the basic energy propellant for the Royal Navy, the line between government and private enterprise in the oil industry was forever muddled. This was particularly so in the Middle East. Churchill's decision led to the formation of the Anglo-Iranian Oil Company, in which the British government had an ownership interest, for the express purpose of exploiting the crude oil reserves of Iran. The Persian Gulf was vital to Britain in the early twentieth century as a fueling station for the British fleet in protecting the Empire's routes to India.

Britain's supremacy would not last. At the end of World War II, the United States supplanted it as the most powerful nation in the world. For Standard Oil of New Jersey, now Exxon, this was a most welcome turn of events; for decades, the oil company had found its international ventures stymied by the Europeans, primarily the British. After World War I, for example, the company had been barred from drilling for oil in Burma; it tried to get into Libya and was refused; it was blocked from getting into northern Iran; and it was excluded from Iraq. Only in Mexico and Venezuela was it partially successful.

Standard had complained to the U.S. State Department about this European "closed door" policy. The State Department addressed a series of strong notes in the early 1920s to the British Foreign Office, objecting to the exclusion of the American companies. The department insisted that the territory of the former Ottoman Empire should be open for oil development to all of the nations of the world on an equal basis. The American position was to extend the "open door" policy first enunciated with respect to China to the Ottoman territory, which included Iraq, Arabia and Bahrain, but not Kuwait.

In Iraq, however, the Iraq Petroleum Company had an exclusive right to explore for and produce petroleum. This company had been set up before World War I as the Turkish Petroleum Company (it would change its name in 1929) by Calouste Sarkis Gulbenkian, the son of an Armenian oil trader who had been a close friend of the sultan of the Ottoman Empire. Gulbenkian had organized the Iraq Petroleum Company with the assistance of German interests and British banks in Iraq, along with the Royal Dutch Shell Company. Shortly before the outbreak of war in 1914, the British government succeeded in ousting Gulbenkian as the dominant interest in the company, installing the Anglo-Iranian Oil Company in his place. But after the war, Gulbenkian reemerged as an adviser to the French government in postwar oil negotiations with the British.

Under the terms of the Treaty of San Remo (1920), which divided Germany's overseas assets among the Allied victors, the German interest in Iraq's petroleum passed to the French. The French interest was represented by the government-owned Compagnie Française des Petroles. Gulbenkian also retained his financial interest in the Iraq Petroleum Company. Competition in the oil trade was anathema to Gulbenkian; therefore, when the State Department insisted upon American access to oil development in Iraq, he counseled: "Let the American groups in or they will break in and then we will really have a mess." Rather than have the "mess," the European partners acceded to the American demands. Standard and its American partners, principally Socony-Vacuum (now Mobil), obtained a nearly 24 percent share in the Iraq company.

The State Department had supported Standard's complaints on the understanding that it was opening the door for all American companies on an equal basis. But this was not what the European members of the Iraq Petroleum Company had in mind. By 1927, it was clear that the Iraqi concession was a potential bonanza. One of the first wells drilled, at Baba Gurgur, came in at 100,000 to 200,000 barrels a day. The entire area of the former territory of the Ottoman Empire looked like a potential "black" gold mine. Gulbenkian drew a red line on a map of the Ottoman Empire, and all the members of the company agreed that they would each share in any concession which any of them obtained within the "Red Line" area.

The existence of the Red Line Agreement impelled other oil companies to pursue more aggressively the petroleum concessions of Bahrain and Saudi Arabia, where they would not have to share their interests with partners. This was the strategy adopted by the Standard Oil Company of California (now Chevron). Socal, as it was known, first obtained a concession in Bahrain; then, convinced that oil must also exist on the Arabian peninsula, the company opened negotiations with Ibn Saud, the Saudi Arabian ruler. Eventually, Socal gained the exclusive concession to explore for oil in Saudi Arabia; it sold a part of its interest to the Texas Company (now Texaco), in order to share the capital cost of developing the Saudi concession and to take advantage of the Texas Company's wider marketing apparatus.

Standard Oil of New Jersey, by contrast, appeared to be in a highly vulnerable position in its overseas operations. Although it had been one of the first and most aggressive American companies to go abroad, Standard had expanded primarily by buying into existing concessions. In Iraq, it was therefore subject to the Red Line Agreement with its original European partners. If it obtained new concessions in the Red Line area, it was obliged to share such concessions with its partners in the Iraq Petroleum Company. Similar arrangements constrained their opportunities elsewhere.

Recognizing this fact, Standard and Socony-Vacuum proposed that they buy into the Arabian American Oil Company (Aramco), which was owned by Socal and Texas. Gulbenkian and his fellow Iraq Petroleum Company partners, particularly the French, objected to this gambit, but they ultimately recognized that Standard and Socony, backed by the State Department, would not be deterred from going ahead.

The Aramco deal was sealed in 1947, leaving the four American companies—Texas, Socal, Standard of New

Jersey, and Socony—firmly in control of the Arabian oil concession. Standard had solved its competitive dilemma: it had obtained an ownership interest in the Arabian concession; and it had freed itself (and Socony-Vacuum) of the Red Line Agreement so that it was able to invest in Aramco without carrying its European partners with it. Yet at the same time it had retained its position as a partner in the Iraq Petroleum Company. More important, it had maintained its cooperative relationship with the European oil companies, Shell and Anglo-Iranian, by means of long-term agreements to purchase substantial amounts of crude oil from their other oil-producing territories in the Middle East. The Aramco consortium became the jewel in the crown of the four partner companies—Exxon, Texaco, Mobil, and Chevron. The interests of the other Persian Gulf oil-producing states would in the future be subordinated to this preeminent concern with the Arabian concession. The result would be a running sore of resentment in Iraq and Iran as these more populous states witnessed their oil production limited to no more than that of the sparsely populated Arabian peninsula.

At the same time as the Aramco consortium was consolidated in Saudi Arabia, the other oil-producing countries, especially Iran, became increasingly assertive in demanding changes in the terms of the original oil concessions that gave exclusive rights to the Western oil companies. The Iranian concession dated to 1901. The onerous terms of that concession and of its subsequent amendments were the principal symbol of Western exploitation. Iranian leaders demanded radical changes in the concession, and in March 1951, the Iranian parliament defiantly nationalized Anglo-Iranian's holdings in Iran. Two months later, Mohammed Mossadegh, a radical non-Communist nationalist, was elected prime minister. The British, after nearly half a century of dominating Iran's oil industry, had been expelled from the country.

The American government was alarmed. If Iran was permitted to nationalize Anglo-Iranian's properties, then other governments in the region might well follow its example. The issue was debated in January 1953 in the National Security Council, and a paper was jointly issued by the departments of State, Defense and Interior. This paper concluded that since oil was the principal source of wealth and income in the Middle Eastern oil-producing countries, "their economic and political existence depends upon the rate and terms on which oil is produced." The operations of the American companies in these countries—how much oil they produced and marketed and the price they paid for it—are "for all practical purposes instruments of our foreign policy toward those countries. . . . What they do and how they do it determine the strength of our ties with the Middle Eastern countries and our ability to resist Soviet expansion and influence in the area." The bugaboo of Bolshevism was a convenient rationale for the American government's refusal to consider that the peoples of these countries might share a legitimate antipathy toward the reassertion of imperial privilege, whether of the East or of the West.

The fundamental premise of American oil policy, the paper went on, rested on the presumption that the interests of the oil companies and the U.S. government were parallel; the companies were reliable instruments to achieve the goals of American foreign policy. It was in the national interest of the United States to preserve the international oil industry in its existing form—dominated by a small group of companies, seven or eight in number, five of which were American, that had had the experience of working together. No settlement with Iran of the Anglo-Iranian dispute was possible. The U.S.

resolve was demonstrated unequivocally in August 1953, as CIA-financed street mobs set off a coup that toppled Mossadegh and restored the shah (who had recently fled the country) to the Peacock Throne.

The following year, a new Iranian consortium agreement was struck. Anglo-Iranian was the largest shareholder with a 40 percent interest; the five major American oil companies—Standard of New Jersey, Texas, Socal, Socony and Gulf—each had 7 percent (or 35 percent as a group); Royal Dutch Shell owned 14 percent; and Compagnie Francaise des Petroles, the French company, had 6 percent. The remaining 5 percent was in the hands of a group of American independent oil companies. The American major companies were now the dominant force in the Middle East. Whereas before World War II, the British-owned Anglo-Iranian had held an exclusive concession in Iran, that concession was now shared with the American majors; likewise, the British had been the political mentors of the Arab oil-producing sheikdoms before the war, but in the postwar era, American political influence would increasingly predominate. And Saudi Arabia, the premier oil-producing concession with the largest potential known reserves, rested securely in the hands of four American companies.

Yet the primary market for Middle East oil production was to be Western Europe and Japan, not the United States. In explaining to congressional leaders the National Security Council's approval in January 1954 of the American companies' participation in the Iranian consortium, the Secretary of the Treasury Robert Anderson assured them that the sale of oil from Iran would be in the Eastern and not the Western Hemisphere. This understanding was subsequently confirmed in correspondence between Senator Lyndon B. Johnson and Secretary of State John Foster Dulles. Two years later, in 1956, the U.S. domestic oil industry was protected against the importation of cheap Middle East crude oil by a voluntary system of crude oil import quotas, which was subsequently made mandatory. The U.S. market was effectively closed to oil produced in the Middle East. The outlet for that oil thus had to be the markets of Western Europe and Japan. And by virtue of their strong position in the Middle East oil-producing concessions, the American majors were well positioned to take advantage of the conversion of that energy market from coal to oil.

Joe Stork of the Washington-based Middle East Research and Information Project calls these years between 1948 and the founding of the Organization of Petroleum Exporting Countries (OPEC) in 1960 "bonanza years" for the oil companies. Over that span, the Middle East proved a gusher of gargantuan profits, $22.2 billion to be exact, split between the local governments and the oil companies. The locals got $9.4 billion, while the oil companies took home a whopping $12.8 billion. Finally, significant amounts of money came to the oil-producing states. Before then, the Gulf states, including Iraq, had been relatively poor. Collective bargaining through OPEC allowed them to eventually grab a larger share of the black gold beneath their sands, but as the 1970s began, the rulers of the Arab countries sought to exert more control over production and price, even while leaving distribution and selling in the hands of the companies. The key questions became: Who would control oil? And who would profit from that control?

Then came the oil embargo of 1973, imposed on the United States and other Western nations in the aftermath of the October Arab-Israeli war. The embargo was directed primarily against the United States and the Netherlands, with the British and French having been declared "friendly" nations by the Arab ministers coordinating the embargo policy. The British and the French initially tried to take advantage of the discrimination against the United States and the Dutch to maximize the Saudi oil supply for their consumers. Moreover, Arab oil provided potential leverage for the British government in dealing with a threatened strike by the miners' union; and for the French, the embargo offered an opportunity to penetrate the American monopoly in Saudi Arabia.

Not only did the British and French governments put pressure on their oil companies to cash in on the status accorded them by the Arabs as friendly governments, but the Arab countries also sought to enlist the help of the oil companies in their campaign to compel Western governments to pressure Israel to withdraw from territories occupied in the 1967 Six-Day War. This the companies did not do; rather, they mitigated the effects of the Arab oil embargo on the United States and the Netherlands, allocating the shortage on a rough pro rata basis, changing cargo destinations on the high seas. In the event, the companies were neither completely nor primarily instruments of the foreign policy of any particular nation. They were balancing interests for their own account. The companies thus showed themselves to be no longer reliable instruments through which national foreign-policy interests could be implemented.

Two major consequences occurred. First, the United States realized that it could no longer manage its relationship with the Persian Gulf states through the oil companies. It was forced into a more direct role in negotiating with the Gulf states. Oil production and price decisions became more overtly linked to decisions with respect to arms and politics. In 1972 and 1973, Saudi King Faisal had used the Aramco parent companies as intermediaries to convey a sense of urgency about the need for a change in U.S. policy in the region if the Americans were not "to lose everything." These communications were largely ignored by American policymakers in the spring of 1973; in the aftermath of the oil embargo, the Saudis had no need for intermediaries. They were heard directly by policymakers who were only too eager to accommodate their demands, particularly for sophisticated arms sales.

Second, the U.S. government felt a more compelling need to inject itself directly into negotiations between Arabs and Israelis in order to bring about a settlement, or at least a lessening of tensions to assure a steady flow of Middle East oil, not only to America but to America's allies in Western Europe and Japan as well.

As the direct involvement of the U.S. government became more overt, what had been only implicit became increasingly explicit: that the United States was now committed to maintaining the oil reserves of the Persian Gulf in hands friendly to the United States and its allies. The Nixon Doctrine tried to limit the American commitment through the promotion of a shared hegemony of the two major powers in the Gulf—Iran and Saudia Arabia. These "twin pillars of stability" were to assure continued access to Persian Gulf oil for the industrial West. In return, the arsenal of the United States was opened virtually without limits to both states. A 1972 directive by National Security Adviser Henry A. Kissinger ordered that Iran be allowed to purchase without restriction the most sophisticated American weapons systems. And the Congress was cajoled, threatened, and enticed to acquiesce in arms sale after arms sale to the Saudis, not on the basis of any analysis of the threat that Saudi Arabia faced, but as a show of "good faith" on the part of the United States.

There were severe problems with this strategy. First,

there was no guarantee that the "twin pillars" would not use these weapons in pursuit of their own interests—interests that might well diverge from those of the United States. Indeed, this is precisely what the shah of Iran did with the price of oil. In the 1970s, the shah led the fight within OPEC to demand higher oil prices. (In the three-month period from October to December 1973, oil prices rose nearly 400 percent, from three to almost twelve dollars per barrel.) Each of the "pillars" had a mind of its own—and their objectives did not necessarily coincide with those of the United States.

Second, the "pillars" were not inherently stable. The huge increase in resources that flowed into Iran and Saudi Arabia, if not carefully controlled and managed, could be destabilizing when combined with the relatively primitive social conditions in both countries. This was especially so in Iran, which did not have the political cohesion of the Saudi royal family to absorb the dislocations resulting from rapid development. The arms buildup in Iran was accompanied by spectacular corruption and conspicuous consumption: inflation hit disproportionately hard at the lower classes; and the displacement of large numbers of people from their rural settings left them susceptible to messianic appeals for a return to traditional values and ways. An effective and charismatic exiled opposition religious leader gave expression to that discontent, through modern cassette recordings played in the mosques.

In 1979, the shah of Iran was deposed by a revolution which the Iranian military was unable or unwilling to suppress. He was replaced by a government headed by a religious establishment of mullahs virtually unknown in the West. It was as if the shah, having finally achieved the riches he craved to make Iran a power among the nations, was being punished for his greed, arrogance and pride. In the process, American strategy was revealed to have been built on a pillar of sand. The mullahs repudiated not only the shah but also the very idea of modernization; instead of emulating the West, they rejected it. And they proclaimed their intent to spread their gospel beyond their nation's borders.

The disaster in Iran deepened the American commitment to Saudi Arabia. President Jimmy Carter guaranteed Saudi Arabia's security against external aggression. President Ronald Reagan extended the promise to support the continued rule of the House of Saud. In the course of a decade U.S. policy in the Persian Gulf had evolved from indirectly managing the region through the oil companies, to enlisting the two most important states as local gendarmes, to assuming direct responsibility to protect the largest oil producer, Saudi Arabia, from both internal and external challenge.

Yet another consequence of the Arab oil embargo was that France achieved its long-term objective of breaking the American monopoly in Saudi Arabia. Ever since the formation of the Aramco consortium in 1947, the French had considered it intolerable that Europe, and particularly France—so much more dependent than the United States on Middle East and especially Saudi Arabian oil—should have had to rely on American multinational oil companies to assure its access to such oil.

In 1967, after the Six-Day War, France obtained a large concession in Iraq, which was hailed throughout the Middle East as a great victory over Anglo-American imperialism. The reaction in France was equally euphoric. The respected French daily *Le Monde* wrote: "Because of France, the Anglo-Americans [lose] any chance of expansion into the hitherto unexplored parts of the country. They have been outmaneuvered; they cannot block France from a place in the untouched zones of Iraq without provoking a grave political crisis.

This is their just reward because on the morrow of the last war they would not let France into the game in this region."

After the October War, the French saw the opportunity to undo the quarter-century-old American monopoly in Saudi Arabia. France increased its arms sales to the Saudis, and to other Arab states. The French national oil company entered into long-term supply contracts with the Saudi authorities for the import of Saudi crude oil. And in 1979, when a small band of fanatical dissidents seized the Kaba Mosque in Mecca, the most holy place in all of Islam, the Saudis turned not to the United States, but to the French for expert counterinsurgency advice in rooting out the rebels. These developments did not go unnoticed across the Atlantic. Indeed, each turn of the historical screw deepened direct American political and military involvement in the tumultuous politics of the region.

At the same time, Saudi Arabia had its own ideas about maintaining its independence and security. The nation sits atop what is probably the world's greatest existing pool of known oil reserves, but with a population of barely seven million (and that may be a high estimate; the Saudis have never permitted a public census), the armed forces of Saudi Arabia have not been, are not now and will never be an effective barrier to a determined invader from any of the its more populous neighbors. Hence, the Saudis have pursued a strategy of balancing regional interests by buying off each of their neighbors. Direct subsidies have variously been paid to Egypt, Iraq and Syria. With regard to Iraq this approach backfired.

By financing the arming of Iraq to check Iran, Saudi Arabia (and the other sheikdoms, including Kuwait) helped to create a Frankenstein. Armed to the teeth, politically confident but financially bankrupt, the Iraqi leadership was convinced that the regional balance of power had shifted in its favor. As 1990 began, Iran was defeated and exhausted; Syria bogged down in Lebanon; Egypt seemingly paralyzed by a conflict with the International Monetary Fund over domestic economic reform and by the perennial problem of staying one step ahead of social unrest in an economy of grinding poverty; and Israel preoccupied with the absorption of Russian immigrants and an increasingly tense confrontation with the United States over the Palestinian question.

With an apparent American attempt to gain favor with Baghdad, and assurances that the United States had no security commitment to Kuwait, Saddam Hussein concluded that the way was clear for Iraq to assume the mantle of regional superpower status, to assert its historical claim to Kuwait, and above all to cut the Gordian knot of debt and simmering discontent left by the war with Iran. It would reverse the territorial settlement imposed by Great Britain in the Gulf; it would finally gain secure access to the sea; and it would give vent to the widespread resentment in Iraq that the Gulf Arabs had lived in luxury throughout the war while Iraqis had bled and died to protect them.

Whatever the motivation which led Saddam Hussein to invade Kuwait and whatever the local tragedy for the Kuwaitis, the invasion, by itself, constituted no immediate threat to any vital interest of the United States. Control of Kuwait's oil reserves will not give Iraq decisive leverage over the oil price market. It is not in Iraq's economic interest to withhold such production from the world market. The issue is price, and as the oil shock of 1973 conclusively demonstrated, dramatic increases in the price of oil stimulates exploration and exploitation of higher-cost reserves, and prompts much stronger conservation efforts in the consuming states, all of which diminishes the reliance upon the lower-cost but politically uncertain Persian Gulf producers. The perennial battle within OPEC has been between those like the Saudis who wish to maintain the dependence of the consuming states and therefore urge price moderation, and those like Iraq with an urgent need for immediate revenues who want to limit production in pursuit of higher prices. But this is basically an argument within a relatively narrow margin.

Non-OPEC production has increased; new producers in Mexico, Angola, the North Sea and elsewhere have forced OPEC to collaborate with these new producers. The fight within OPEC over price and production is constrained by the existence of these additional producers. Should Baghdad be successful in melding Kuwaiti production with that of Iraq, this equation will not fundamentally change.

What is at issue is not so much the invasion of Kuwait, terrible though it is, but rather the potential Iraqi invasion or domination of Saudi Arabia. Together, Saudi Arabia, Kuwait and Iraq contain about 40 percent of the world's known petroleum reserves. Although it is true that the world's share of oil consumption satisfied by imports is higher today (45 percent) than before the shocks in the 1970s (35 percent in 1973 and 43 percent in 1979), the global economy is significantly less reliant today on both energy in general and on oil in particular, due to declines in the ratio of energy use to Gross National Product and of oil to overall energy use. Still, dependence on Persian Gulf oil by America's principal allies remains high: In 1989, it accounted for 35 percent of France's oil, 32 percent of Italy's, and 64 percent of Japan's.

Secretary of State James A. Baker 3d, in testimony on September 4 before the House Foreign Affairs Committee, noted that "perhaps, most obviously what is at stake economically is the dependence of the world on access to the energy resources of the Persian Gulf. . . . It is not just a narrow question of the flow of oil from Kuwait and Iraq. It is rather about a dictator who, acting alone, could strangle the global economic order, determining by fiat whether we all enter a recession or even the darkness of a depression." For this nightmare to come true, however, Iraq would have to achieve what it has not threatened: the takeover of Saudi Arabia.

Bush administration officials admit that neither the Central Intelligence Agency nor the Defense Intelligence Agency thought it probable that Iraq would invade Saudi Arabia. Prior to the invasion of both Iran and Kuwait, Baghdad mounted noisy propaganda campaigns, emphasizing its historical claims against its future targets. This has not been the case with regard to Saudi Arabia. In fact, Iraq in 1989 signed a nonaggression treaty with Saudi Arabia. The Iraqi threat, administration officials argue, is that Baghdad will be able to somehow control Saudi oil policy through "intimidation." If Iraq, through the shadow effect of its huge army and arsenal of mass destruction, can also determine the oil policies of Saudi Arabia, as well as the policies of the smaller oil-producing United Arab Emirates, then Iraq, it is argued, would exert significant influence over nearly half the world's oil supply. Not Kuwait, but the Arabian side of the Persian Gulf is the administration's concern. An American military presence is necessary, say these officials, in order to bolster perceptions of strength and will to deter aggression. Weakness in the face of such a challenge would be tantamount to accepting the impermanence of the territorial settlement at the close of the colonial era in the Persian Gulf. It would also imply an understanding that in this region stability is as elusive as a desert mirage.

XI

The Lion and the Lamb

In 1986, two years before the end of the Iraq-Iran war, Mazher A. Hameed, an Arab analyst, pondered events in the Gulf from faraway Washington. "Should a peace finally arrive on the front with Iran through whatever means," he mused, "how certain can anyone be that Iraq, with essentially the same political leadership in place as during more aggressive interventionist years, will not again turn its attention toward the smaller Gulf states? The border conflict with Kuwait, for example, remains unresolved. Will Baghdad not use its extraordinarily large, well-equipped and now experienced army to extort or even force a settlement on its terms?"

In fact, as Hameed was writing, the war that Saddam Hussein had launched in 1980 was going badly. There was no reason at the time to think that Baghdad would be victorious. Most Arab, European and American analysts were "white with fear," recalled Richard L. Armitage, a senior Defense Department official in the Reagan administration, that Iraq would be overwhelmed by Iran. Things were so desperate at one point that Saddam had finally been persuaded—exactly how or by whom is not really known—to relinquish his personal stewardship of the war to professional military officers and strategists.

Yet, as Hameed and a few other analysts noted early

on, a future conflict between Iraq and Kuwait seemed likely, if not inevitable. For despite the Baathist rhetorical devotion to Arab nationalism and Kuwait's multi-billion-dollar assistance to Baghdad during the war with Tehran, Iraq had long been contemptuous of its weak and soft neighbor, who in its view held territory that Baghdad had long considered its own.

Tensions between Kuwait and Iraq are deeply rooted in history, geography and ideology, not to mention dramatic differences in culture and style. In the weeks since the invasion of Kuwait, *The Baghdad Observer*, the regime's English-language newspaper, has run almost daily articles on the historical underpinnings of Iraq's claim to Kuwait. One report in August, for example, dated an Iraqi presence there to the second millennium B.C., thanks to the discovery of a clay statue on the Kuwaiti island of Feilaka that bears a resemblance to the Assyrian kings. A second "proof," the paper argued, was the fact that Kuwait is listed on eighth-century maps as one of the Arab army headquarters of the Iraqi city of Basra.

While Iraq traces its origins back 5,000 years to ancient Mesopotamia, Kuwait has been more modest. Sometime in the early eighteenth century, the Sabah family, a member of the Utub clan, migrated from the Najd region of central Arabia, probably in search of water. They came to what is today Kuwait City, where they built a small fort. The name Kuwait is the diminutive of *kut*, the common word in the Gulf for fort. The town that grew up around the fort lived on fishing, pearling and trade. Its small sailing vessels, known as dhows—the distinctive, brightly painted boats that used to dot the harbor—once traveled as far as East Africa, laden with precious cargo.

Until World War I, Kuwait was under the nominal control of the Ottoman Empire. Specifically, it was considered part of the *wilaya*, or administrative district, of Basra. The Sabahs, who had ruled Kuwait since 1752, had secured a degree of independence for themselves by skillfully playing off the bullies of the region against one another, be they Turks, Wahabis (the future Saudis), or the British.

The historian Jacob Goldberg notes, for example, that when the Ottoman governor in Baghdad sought to assert control over Kuwait in 1897, Sheik Mubarak al-Sabah sought British protection to countervail the Turks. When the British demurred, Sheik Mubarak publicly mused about giving their rivals, the Russians, a coaling station in Kuwait. The British reversed course. In 1899, Mubarak signed an agreement pledging himself and his heirs neither to cede any territory nor to receive any foreign agents or representatives without British consent. In exchange, the British gave him 15,000 rupees, the currency of British India, and a letter assuring him of the "good offices of Her Majesty's Government towards you, your heirs and successors," as long as the agreement was scrupulously observed, an informal agreement to protect Kuwait. Sheik Mubarak's appeal to the British for protection was the first of many such calls. For Kuwait has always sensed, correctly in retrospect, the need for a powerful protector.

The Sabahs pretty much ran things inside Kuwait, while after 1899 the emirate's foreign policy was determined by Great Britain. But jockeying for influence continued among the Turks, the British, and the ever-maneuvering Mubarak. In July 1913, as war fever built in Europe, the British and the Turks reached an agreement recognizing Kuwait as an autonomous district of the Ottoman empire, and the sheikdom's frontiers were formally defined. But the Ottomans, soon to be allied with Germany, deferred ratifying the accord. Britain, in turn, intent on shoring up its interests in the Gulf on the eve of the war, recognized Kuwait as independent of the Ottomans. In exchange, Mubarak was to cooperate with Britain against the Ottomans in Iraq in the coming war.

Mubarak, however, continued smuggling and trading with all sides, despite his pledge. There was money to be made, after all, and Kuwait was still a poor tribal country. After the war, though, Britain exacted a price for Mubarak's double dealing. In 1922, Britain convened a conference at the Gulf port of Uqair that included Saudi Arabia, Iraq and Kuwait. Presiding was Sir Percy Cox, the British high commissioner in Baghdad. To compensate the Saudi ruler Ibn Saud for the territory he was forced to cede to Iraq, Kuwait's rights to the coastal hinterland south of the 1913 frontier were abrogated; this area became the Neutral Zone, which both countries' tribes could use. Iraq's border with Kuwait was also decided in a flick of Sir Percy's pen.

As a result of such imperial cartography, Iraq was left virtually landlocked. Its coastline on the Gulf was a mere twenty-six miles long, with its only passage to the Gulf through the Shatt al-Arab waterway, which can be easily blocked by a hostile power. Kuwait, by contrast, possessed 120 miles of Gulf shoreline, as well as the largest natural harbor in the region. Small wonder that Iraq coveted its tiny neighbor to the south.

The Kuwait-Iraq borders were confirmed upon Iraq's independence in 1932. But soon after that, Baghdad began pressing for the right to lease some of the islands off Kuwait's coast—islands, it claimed, that properly belonged to Iraq. With the death of Iraq's King Faisal in 1933, moreover, relations with Kuwait worsened as Baghdad stepped up its agitation against Kuwait's Sabahs. Opposition groups emerged in Kuwait, aided by growing tension between the Sabahs and other merchant families that wanted to limit the ruling family's power, and by the absence of serious development schemes as the prospect of oil wealth became apparent. Arab nationalism was on the rise among younger members of the Kuwaiti intelligentsia and the sheikdom became fraught with political intrigue.

In 1937, King Ghazi began broadcasting diatribes against Kuwait from a private radio station in his palace. The historian Phebe Marr writes that the young Iraqi leader, an ardent but inexperienced Arab nationalist, also denounced French rule in Syria, Zionist claims in Palestine, and British influence in the Gulf. As for Kuwait, he advocated its absorption by Iraq, the first time this specific claim was made. Ghazi depicted the emir of Kuwait as an outdated feudal monarch maintained in power by the British, a early variation of the theme that Saddam would echo more than fifty years later. His words struck a nerve in Kuwait. In 1938, some of the Kuwaiti merchant families forced the emir to relinquish some of his power; the Sabahs were saved from total disaster, though, by British intervention and a bit of good luck. In April 1939, Ghazi, stone drunk, drove his car at high speed into a power pole. The Sabahs held on.

On June 19, 1961, Britain granted Kuwait full independence. Sheik Abdullah al-Sabah, then Kuwait's ruler, moved quickly to establish a National Assembly and to write a constitution, according to Marr, partly to legitimize the status of his state as separate from Iraq and sovereign. Six days after Kuwait's independence, Iraqi leader Abdul Karim Qassim claimed the emirate as an integral part of Iraq. At a press conference, he asserted that Kuwait belonged to Iraq because it had been a district of Basra province under the Ottoman Empire. Although Qassim said he did not intend to use force to reunite Kuwait with its motherland, he refused to rule out the possibility. There were even rumors of troop movements on the Iraq-Kuwait border. But no troops were ever sent, nor could they have been, as virtually all of Iraq's forces were busy suppressing a Kurdish rebellion in the north. Barely a brigade was left in the south.

But the day after Qassim's press conference, Emir Abdullah sent cables to all the Arab kings and presidents requesting support, citing the threat to his new country. Only Saudi Arabia pledged help. So Abdullah sought, yet again, British protection; in July, British forces moved in. Later that month, the Arab League admitted Kuwait as a member, outraging Iraq, which abruptly resigned from the league and withdrew its representatives and ambassadors from all countries that had recognized Kuwait. The first contingent of Arab League forces arrived to defend Kuwait in September, including troops sent by King Hussein of Jordan, who apparently was more persuaded in 1961 than he would be in 1990 of Kuwait's legitimacy. The crisis soon passed, and by 1963 the Arab League forces were gone. Kuwait had survived its first major confrontation with Iraq.

Qassim's failed bid for Kuwait embarrassed and weakened him internally. In 1963, the Baath party overthrew him and seized control of Iraq. Socialist in rhetoric but opportunistic in spirit, the Baath put forward a moderate foreign policy, despite its ruthless repression of enemies at home. The party quickly reversed Qassim's policy toward Kuwait, and in October 1963, it recognized Kuwait's independence, apparently settling the long-standing border dispute in exchange for a substantial payment. In a separate agreement, Iraq agreed to supply Kuwait with 120 million gallons of water daily from the Shatt al-Arab. In November, Iraq and Kuwait signed an economic agreement which virtually abolished customs duties on trade between them.

This newfound harmony, however, did not last long.

The Baath was ousted nine months after coming to power in 1963, but managed to regain it through another coup in 1968. This leaner, far meaner Baath regime renewed old quarrels. In March 1973, tensions escalated as Iraqi troops occupied Al-Samitah, a border post in northeastern Kuwait. This time the dispute centered on Bubiyan and Warbah, two Kuwaiti islands that control access to Umm Qasr, Iraq's military Gulf port. Only in 1977 did both sides withdraw their forces.

By this time, moreover, Iraq's deteriorating relations with Iran had begun to divert its attention from Kuwait. And when Iraq invaded Iran in September 1980, the Kuwaitis felt that at last the threat from Baghdad had receded.

It is hard to imagine two societies more different than Iraq and Kuwait. Iraq, as a consequence of geography and history, is inward-looking and suspicious, filled with dogma and fear. Kuwait, by contrast, is a merchant society, outward-looking, cosmopolitan, and above all, unapologetically consumer-oriented.

After the Iraqi invasion, articles quickly appeared in the Western press critical of Kuwait. Reporters and Arab analysts described Kuwait, and by implication the other Gulf sheikdoms, as a "company with a flag," an "air-conditioned Eden," or in one account, "the world's largest shopping mall." Criticizing the victim of Iraqi aggression was suddenly in vogue.

But while Iraq was opening weapons plants and amassing chemical-weapons stockpiles in the 1980s, Kuwait was unveiling the Suq al-Manakh, the Arab world's first stock exchange, and Kuwaitis were flocking to the opening of Al-Khaleejia, Kuwait's first department store of international standing. While the Iraqis were fighting the long war with Iran and setting up dummy corporations throughout the world to buy, or steal, components for nuclear bombs or advanced missiles, the Kuwaitis were waterskiing and shopping.

While Baghdad was awash in rumors of coups and purges, Kuwaitis were hurling insults at one another in the National Assembly, which until it became too obstreperous for the emir in 1986, was the Gulf's only elected parliament and one of the few such institutions in the Arab world.

While Iraq lacked the money to pay a large host of foreign laborers, Kuwait had no such limitation, and hence accepted them in mind-boggling numbers. Though population estimates in Kuwait and the Gulf states have always been unreliable, it is generally agreed that about two-thirds of the 1.9 million people who lived in Kuwait before the Iraqi invasion were non-Kuwaitis, among them 350,000 Palestinians, the largest concentration in the Gulf.

While Baghdad was virtually closed to foreign journalists except by special visas that required weeks, often months, of groveling to acquire, Kuwait gave visas on a forty-eight-hour notice. During the Iraq-Iran war, it was a favored Gulf listening post for the foreign press.

On paper, Iraq was the more "progressive" of the two societies—socialist and secular. Kuwait, by contrast, was the feudal monarchy, a religious state in which alcohol and other Western vices were supposedly taboo, and whose women could not vote. In practice, however, Iraq ruled mainly through arbitrary terror and intimidation; Kuwait, by contrast, was relatively open and tolerant, a place where authorities tended to wink at regulations, or look the other way when it pleased them.

What kind of place was Kuwait before the invasion? By almost any standard, a quite remarkable one. In the Arab world, it was known as the "Beirut of the Gulf," whose liberal atmosphere, free press and independent spirit were reminiscent of Lebanon before its tragic civil war. Kuwait was in many respects a city-state, as more than half of its inhabitants lived in Kuwait City. Without doubt, Kuwait was the most enlightened state in the Gulf, its small population (about the same as Philadelphia's) supporting thirteen newspapers—seven dailies (five Arabic, two English) and six weeklies. Seventeen thousand students attended the University of Kuwait, which was coeducational and used the American college-credit system. According to Youssef Ibrahim of *The New York Times,* Kuwait's comprehensive education, medical and welfare systems also made it "the Arab world's ultimate welfare state." And the *Area Handbook for the Peripheral States of Arabian Peninsula,* a standard reference work for U.S. officials, concluded, "Kuwait's broad range of public services had few rivals even among the world's most developed nations."

Early in this century Kuwait was an intensely poor and backward country of scarcely 50,000 people; in the mid-1980s, its citizens enjoyed the world's highest per capita income, $15,000 a year. By 1971, its car-to-population ratio was already among the world's highest, as was its number of videocassette recorders per capita. Kuwaitis paid no taxes, received generous land and housing allowances, and could study anywhere in the world on the government's tab. Some 1,500 were studying in the United States at the time of the Iraqi invasion.

Kuwait's 6,178 square miles, slightly smaller than Connecticut, consist mostly of relentlessly unforgiving desert, with almost no natural water. To beautify Kuwait City and its sprawling suburbs, the government planted more than a million trees and shrubs, watering them with desalinated water from the Persian Gulf. The vegetation was also intended to help screen the luxurious private villas, three-star hotels, space-age skyscrapers of marble and glass, and six-lane freeways from the mists of dust and sand that infiltrate even the most hermetically sealed spaces during summer sandstorms. It is a land of few hills and no mountains, of monotonous flatness.

Though Kuwaitis were fond of noting that their temperature was milder than the rest of the Gulf, summers there can have weeks of almost unbearable humidity. And the country endures *shamals*, the strong northeasterly winds from Iraq, which blow sand and dust in all directions. A summer temperature of 115 degrees is not unusual, and British diplomats who served in Kuwait before the advent of air-conditioning recall sleeping on the roof of their embassy's villa to catch even a hint of breeze.

It was not an easy place to inhabit. So Kuwaitis became great travelers, especially during Ramadan, the Muslim month of fasting from dawn to dusk, and in summer, when they fled by the thousands to the French Riviera, the mountains of Switzerland, and to their beloved London. Only Emir Jaber al-Ahmad al-Sabah remained steadfastly in Kuwait—he hated to travel.

The transformation of Kuwait from Bedouin tents to boomtown was brought about, as in Iraq, by oil. Though commercial production of crude oil began only in 1949, Kuwait had become the world's sixth largest producer two decades later. In contrast to Saudi Arabia, which invested massively in oil-related industries, modern infrastructure, weapons and largely unprofitable domestic businesses, Kuwait created two giant investment funds, of roughly $40 billion each, to channel oil profits into investments abroad. One of them, the Fund for Future Generations, the interest and principal of which were not to be touched until 2001, received roughly 10 percent of Kuwait's oil revenues every year. Because the Kuwaitis chose their investments and investment advisers wisely, these revenues from abroad gradually exceeded those from oil. Thus, Kuwait had little incentive to permit oil prices to rise precipitously, as Iraq desired, since such price increases would have depressed the stock, bond and currency markets upon which its major source of income depended.

Kuwait's almost unimaginable wealth prompted envy not only among its relatively poorer neighbors, but more problematically, among the emirate's non-Kuwaiti residents as well—particularly the more than 350,000 Palestinians, 300,000 Egyptians, and 200,000 Indians, Pakistanis and Filipinos, who tended to perform menial tasks in the oil fields and in related industries. The word they used time and again to describe their Kuwaiti employers was "arrogant." Kuwaitis, said the foreigners who actually drew the precious oil from the earth, did not work. In fact, Kuwaitis comprised only 18 percent of the work force. Citizenship, moreover, was a question of blood, not of longevity or loyalty. Even the Kuwaiti-born sons and daughters of non-Kuwaitis could not normally become citizens. Guest workers complained bitterly, often justifiably, about having to pay their Kuwaiti employers to extend their visas. Politically "undesirable" foreigners were often tossed out after their contracts expired. Non-Kuwaitis could not own land or homes.

The eruption of hostilities between Iran and Iraq in 1980 had a terrible effect on Kuwait. Although Kuwait was formally neutral, the emir armed and supported Baghdad wholeheartedly, as did Saudi Arabia and all the Gulf states. Together, Kuwait and Saudi Arabia shipped about 310,000 barrels of crude oil a day for Iraq. So the war was not long in coming home to Kuwait City.

In 1983, there were suicide-bomb attacks against the U.S. and French embassies, the airport and the oil installations, in which six people were killed and more than eighty wounded. The bombings stunned Kuwait, which immediately blamed Iran and its supporters. A year later, a Kuwaiti Airways plane was hijacked to Tehran. This was followed by more bombings and mysterious explosions, all traceable directly or indirectly to Iran. Later there were two more hijackings. Finally, terrorists staged a suicide car attack on the emir himself. He was only slightly wounded, but the attack rocked the ruling family and the country to its foundation. Less than a year later, the Sabahs decided that at a time of rising terrorism and falling oil prices, having a parliament was a luxury the nation could ill afford.

"Democracy is shaking," the emir said, dissolving the parliament and imposing press censorship on his country's feisty papers and magazines. Some forty-nine leading editors and journalists—all expatriates, many of them Palestinians who had given the press its flair and distinctly independent voice—were expelled. The depth of the trauma was reflected in the press's support of the censorship and of the suspension of parliament. "Go ahead, and we stand by you," declared *al-Seyassa*, a leading and previously nervy Kuwaiti paper. "We do not wish to see a society fragmented and scattered under untapped slogans of freedom of speech." As one acerbic foreign resident in Kuwait told *The New York Times*, "Kuwaitis prefer cash to democracy." But the bombings continued and so did the crackdowns. Police officials reported that some 26,898 people were deported in 1986 for security reasons.

Kuwaiti Shiites, who comprised about a quarter of the population in this Sunni-led emirate, were increasingly regarded by the majority as a potential fifth column in the country. One wealthy Shiite businessman, Saleh Selman al-Attar, took out a front-page announcement in the Kuwaiti newspapers in 1987 to offer an apology for his people and to pledge loyalty to the emirate. A few days earlier, a member of his family, along with another Kuwaiti Shiite, had been killed while trying to detonate a car bomb outside the Air France office in Kuwait City. "If this accident was aimed at Kuwait and its people," Attar wrote, "then they have been judged by God. And if they were misled by some elements or factions that want to harm Kuwait, then we declare our support for all our people and for our emir and his crown prince and the Kuwaiti people." The government began excluding Shiites from sensitive jobs in the military and security service, fearing that their loyalty lay secretly with the Shiite rulers of Iran rather than with the Sabahs.

Despite the growing insecurity at home, however, Kuwait demonstrated throughout the war years a surprising toughness. Some seventeen supporters of the Iranian-based Shiite group Al-Daawa were arrested, tried and convicted for the 1983 bombings of the French and American embassies. The Daawa demanded that the seventeen be released, warning they would do whatever was necessary to liberate their comrades. Kuwaiti officials knew that many of the subsequent explosions and terrorist attacks had been staged to underscore this determination, but the Sabahs would not budge. Unlike other countries that released suspected and even convicted terrorists to prevent attacks in their countries, Kuwait refused to make deals.

Two of the seventeen were finally released in December 1988, but only after they had served their full five-year prison terms. The rest, three of whom had been sentenced to death, remained in Salibeyeh prison until Iraq's troops stormed Kuwait City. The fate of the terrorists was in dispute in late September. Some Kuwaiti refugees said that the prisoners had fled the Kuwaiti prison after the Iraqis occupied the capital and had disappeared. But a Bush administration official who follows Iran closely said that the Iraqis had deliberately taken the fifteen from prison within forty-eight hours of the invasion. In late August, he said, the terrorists were moved to Baghdad, where the Iraqis cynically gave them back to the Iranians to help win Tehran's support in circumventing the United Nations sanctions against Iraq.

In foreign policy, Kuwait also steered its own quirky course. While it was among the Gulf's largest importers of American consumer goods, its political rhetoric—perhaps due to the hundreds of thousands of Palestinians in its midst—was often among the most stridently anti-Israeli and anti-American in the Arab world.

After the Arab-Israeli Six-Day War in 1967, for example, Kuwait cut off oil shipments to the United States and joined with gusto in the pan-Arab effort to boycott Israeli goods and companies that do business with Israel. Kuwait's Boycott of Israel Office was still issuing proclamations as late as 1988. In September of that year, for example, the office finally lifted a twenty-one-year ban on Coca-Cola, one of the Arab world's favorite drinks.

In August 1983, Kuwait rejected the nomination of Brandon H. Grove, Jr., as U.S. ambassador because he had served as the American consul general in East Jerusalem, a rebuff that infuriated Washington. In 1984, David Ottaway of *The Washington Post* observed that Kuwait was "accustomed to blaming the United States for all the ills afflicting the Arab world, and the gulf in particular." Only Iran's growing attacks on Kuwaiti ships prompted Kuwait to tone down its diatribes against American imperial power.

Kuwait got away with its rhetorical militancy because it had also managed to continue its time-honored tradition of playing off the superpowers against each other. The United States, it seemed, was destined to assume Britain's traditional role as Kuwait's defender and, like Britain, could be goaded into action by the prospect of Russian aggrandizement. In 1984, for example, Kuwait sought to purchase highly accurate Stinger anti-aircraft missiles and F-16 jet fighters from the United States, but Washington rejected these requests, offering instead an $82 million air defense package that included less sophisticated technology. As Theodore Draper reported three years later, "Then Kuwait went to the Soviet Union and arranged for the purchase of arms reported to be worth $327 million. With the arms came Soviet technicians and advisers." After learning of the deal, Washington speedily reversed itself, selling some $1.5 billion in military equipment to Kuwait by 1985. This maneuvering, Draper argued, was basically a "dress rehearsal" for the much riskier decision by the Reagan administration in 1987 to protect oil shipments in the Persian Gulf by putting some Kuwaiti tankers under an American flag and sending American aircraft carriers into the Gulf to ward off Iranian attacks.

Once again, Kuwait had decided to protect itself by pitting the superpowers against each other and entangling them in the Iraq-Iran war. When Kuwait's initial requests for reflagging its ships elicited a slow response from Washington, Kuwaiti officials turned to Moscow. After Washington learned that a deal had been struck with the Soviets to charter at least three Soviet tankers, the Reagan administration decided to outbid the Soviets. Five days after the Soviet offer became known, the United States announced it would put the U.S. flag on eleven Kuwaiti vessels to protect them—the very figure that Kuwait had initially proposed. After the U.S.S. *Stark* was hit (apparently accidentally) by an Iraqi missile, the Reagan administration stepped up its military presence in the region to protect those ships under American flags.

In what can only be seen in retrospect as a supreme

touch of chutzpah, Sheik Saad al-Abdullah al-Sabah, Kuwait's prime minister, disassociated his country in July 1987 from any hostilities in which the United States might become involved while protecting Kuwaiti shipping in the Gulf. "These are now American vessels," Sheik Saad said, referring to the eleven reflagged tankers. "We are not ready for either air bases or naval bases."

After the 1988 cease-fire between Iran and Iraq, Kuwait shifted course yet again. The threat posed by Iran had passed. Iraq, Kuwaiti officials reasoned, would be preoccupied demobilizing its military and rebuilding the country. American ships were therefore asked to leave the area and gradually did so. The Gulf Cooperation Council, a Saudi-led political and military alliance of Kuwait and five other Gulf states, went into low gear. Relief now swept through Kuwait and through much of the Gulf. Kuwaitis returned to their favored pastimes, among them driving out into the desert in four-wheel-drive air-conditioned jeeps, pitching tents and picnicking. The Al-Sultan all-night department store did a booming business. The press became more daring again.

The conversation changed among Kuwaiti men and women at their evening Diwaniyas, a century-old tradition of nightly gatherings which were the true heart of this very special society. During the war, a solemn mood had prevailed. Kuwaiti men who visited friends and dignitaries spent much of the time discussing the Iranian threat to their lives and economy. Leaving their sandals at the door, they would sprawl across silk-covered divans, cigarettes in one hand and worry beads in the other, drinking tea, snacking on dates, nuts and raisins, and pondering the latest Iranian offensive, the Iraqi response, the tanker war and the "war of the cities," the campaign in which Iraq and Iran had hurled missiles at each other's capitals.

After the war, the conversation became more varied. Diwaniya-hopping came back into fashion. Even more gossip was traded, business ventures were hatched, grievances were aired, and political opinions were exchanged and formed. And most important, something new was in the air: talk of "democracy."

By March 1990, the Diwaniyas had become one of the main vehicles for spreading the word about democracy in Kuwait. They were also a major source of pressure on the Sabah family to restore the parliament and lift the censorship imposed in the name of war. The Gulf, indeed, the entire Arab world was buzzing with daring talk—was it possible that the democratization movement that had swept through Eastern Europe and much of Latin America in 1989 might finally touch Arab shores?

At a Diwaniya last February, hundreds of Kuwaitis flocked to the home of Ahmad al-Khatib, a former member of parliament, to listen to his fierce denunciations of one-family rule in Kuwait and life without real freedom. "We are like the *intifada,*" Khatib said, using the Arabic word for the Palestinian uprising in the West Bank and Gaza. "First we have broken the barrier of fear, then we will go on. The people of Kuwait deserve something better than rule by decree. We have a democratic tradition, thousands of educated men and women, and a right to rule ourselves."

Those who could not squeeze into the room that night to hear his fiery oration listened to him on special FM radio banks in the Mercedes sport cars and BMW sedans parked outside. Women, segregated in separate rooms, a Kuwaiti Diwaniya tradition, watched him on an internal video system.

Night after night, the Diwaniyas of democracy spread across Kuwait City. Thousands of university students and their Palestinian and Egyptian teachers attended rallies and signed petitions calling for the restoration of democratic institutions. Merchants joined their ranks: democracy had to be good for business, they argued.

By March, Crown Prince Saad al-Abdullah al-Sabah sent signals that the ruling family was willing to discuss the restoration of parliament, provided such a move would not challenge its right to retain power. In April, the newly constituted National Assembly convened its first session, with fifty elected members and twenty-five Sabah appointees.

Pressures were building for far more sweeping reforms, since the new Assembly was neither as democratic nor as powerful as the old parliament had been. Jassem al-Qotami, a former member of Kuwait's parliament, stated that he and others wanted to go further: the ruling family should become a constitutional monarchy. "Are we better than Britain?" he was quoted as saying at the time. "They have a free parliament that can control, criticize, and represent the will of the people and they have a respected monarchy. This way we can make sure no ruler abuses his authority and join the civilized world. Why not us?"

Months later, Youssef Ibrahim would observe in *The New York Times* that "what was really being questioned in Kuwait was not the right of the Sabahs to rule, but the degree of power they should have." The Sabahs were largely accepted by the Kuwaitis because unlike the Saudis, who had triumphed militarily over the other tribes in the Arabian Peninsula, the Sabahs had achieved their power through negotiations with the other powerful merchant families. They ruled, therefore, by tradition, not by force, and through the acquiescence of the Kuwaiti people, a rarity in the Arab world.

The Saudis and the other Arab rulers were unnerved by such bold talk in Kuwait, for it was contagious. Arab intellectuals throughout the Middle East were beginning to challenge the legitimacy of their rulers. They were asking, in effect, whether monarchies or dictators were the only choices available, and whether they owed loyalty to these often corrupt regimes simply because they had won the nation its independence. These were truly revolutionary, and hence frightening, thoughts to the ruling elites.

"There is no doubt in my mind that the pressures for democratization in Kuwait would have continued building," said Ibrahim. "Kuwait, which was already the Gulf's most urbane, sophisticated place, was ready to go much further." But the democracy movement was among the saddest casualties of Iraq's invasion. Along with the palaces and villas and skyscrapers, the banners and leaflets and ideas that were taking hold in Kuwait were crushed under the weight of more than 2,000 Iraqi tanks. Iraq not only murdered a state, it extinguished a dream.

By all accounts, Iraq's invasion was, in the words of one senior U.S. military officer, "a cakewalk." Within five hours, 100,000 Iraqi troops—some in buses—crossed the border and encircled the capital. "They definitely made an effort to capture the royal family—to literally and metaphorically decapitate the enemy," said a military expert on the House Armed Services Committee. Only three or four members of the 1,000-strong Sabah family, however, were apprehended. The emir's younger brother Fahd was killed defending Dasman Palace, but the emir and several other members of the ruling family escaped in a limousine cavalcade across the Saudi border—reportedly a scant six minutes before the Iraqis reached the palace.

The scattered and disorganized Kuwaiti army, outmanned 26 to 1, was almost immediately overrun. The only island of resistance was the air force, which put up a short-lived, valiant defense. "The air force cratered the runway in the northern air field in the opening minutes of the war," the House military expert said. "Then they ran one bombing run against the Iraqis, came back, reloaded their planes by hand, and ran a second run. In two hours, they ran two missions before their airport was overrun. Considering that the attack occurred between 1 and 3 A.M. and that this was a very inexperienced air force, it was pretty damn impressive." In the southern air field, missions were also run before the pilots were forced to flee to Saudi Arabia with their planes. Within two to three hours after arriving, resistance groups were already being formed. "That was a lot faster than the French in World War II. And there were no mountains or jungles where you could hide. This was a city resistance," he said.

The Iraqis apparently employed three waves of troops: first across the border were the Republican Guards, the elite attack forces, battle-hardened veterans of the Iraq-Iran war; then came the People's Army, made up of ragtag, ill-disciplined peasants and thugs under the leadership of Ali Hassan al-Majid; and finally there was the regular army and the dreaded Mukhabarat, the secret police, who supervised detentions and torture.

Stories of looting, rape, execution and torture dribbled out slowly over the next few weeks, along with the grim cavalcade of fleeing refugees. There were weeping mothers and fathers whose sons had been taken from them at the border, and fresh and searing memories of friends and loved ones left behind. "They took my best friend, Bedar, and the next day they dropped his body in the street," a Kuwaiti doctor told *The New York Times.* "They had wrapped his head in a Kuwaiti flag and fired three bullets into his skull."

Another exile, twenty-five-year-old Jamal al-Ibrahim, pulled up his shirt to show the *Times* reporter, James LeMoyne, what the Iraqis had done to him and the other young men they had rounded up and interrogated. "The man's back and arms were covered with black-and-blue lacerations from what appeared to be a terrible beating," LeMoyne reported. "It looked as if a small tank had repeatedly rolled over his flesh, leaving tread marks." Ibrahim said that Iraqi soldiers had beaten him repeatedly and tortured him with electric shocks after they found a photograph of the emir of Kuwait in his car.

By mid-September, American officials openly speculated that Iraq was trying to depopulate Kuwait so it could move its own people in, as it had previously done with the Kurds in northern Iraq—a brutal Iraqi version of creating facts on the ground. American officials said that the Central Intelligence Agency had estimated that about 100,000 Kuwaiti citizens had been out of the country on summer vacations when Iraq invaded, and that by mid-September, about 200,000 had been forced out of their country. "They wanted them out," one administration official said. "They went right after the birth and nationality records. And part of the massive looting and burning was designed to ensure that these people would have absolutely nothing to come home to."

Ironically, though, by late September some American officials were actually hoping that most Kuwaitis would leave if they had the chance. Those who refused to abandon their country, these officials said, would be treaty harshly, even by Iraqi standards. "They have assigned Majid, the Butcher of Kurdistan, to oversee the quashing of any resistance there. Those poor people have no idea what they're in for," one said softly.

*

Kuwait, more than any other state, should have suspected Iraq's intentions. But the Kuwaitis, too, were totally stunned by the invasion. On three occasions before August 2, State Department officials had met with Kuwait's ambassador to Washington, Sheik Saud Nasir al-Sabah, to inform him of the ominous Iraqi troop movements. Each time, American sources said, the ambassador consulted with his government and assured the United States that the Iraqis were simply trying to bully his country into yielding to their demands, a conclusion with which the Bush administration agreed.

The United States did stage maneuvers in the Gulf in July to warn Iraq against military action toward the United Arab Emirates and Kuwait. And Kuwait did briefly put its forces on alert in response to the Iraqi buildup. But then the maneuvers ended, the American destroyers left, and Kuwait's army went off alert. Kuwait finally asked for U.S. military help—one half hour after Iraq invaded.

"The Bush administration should not be as tough on itself as it has been about 'missing' the warning signs," said one State Department official who has served in the Gulf. "If anyone should have anticipated what happened, it was the Arabs, and all of them misread the situation. And among the Arabs, Kuwait had the best reason to find out what Saddam Hussein intended. The fact is: we all missed it. But for Kuwait, the miscalculation has been catastrophic."

Non-Kuwaiti analysts argued that Kuwait had made a series of fatal mistakes. The first, said Joseph Kostiner, an Israeli historian of the Gulf, was in failing to grasp Iraq's determination after the war to get the money it needed for redevelopment and to gain a permanent, secure outlet to the Gulf. "They failed to see that for Saddam, access to the Gulf was his form of *Lebensraum*," Kostiner said, referring to Hitler's argument in the 1930s that the German people needed "living space." "Saddam knew that the Shatt al-Arab was not navigable, that he was deeply in debt, that Kuwait was the solution to both these problems."

Second, Kostiner maintained, Kuwait had grown "overconfident" during the Iraq-Iran war. If Saddam thought that Kuwait was not sufficiently grateful for Iraq's costly victory over the Iranian menace, Kuwait's rulers believed that Saddam would never act against the country that had contributed more than $10 billion in aid to his country. "Kuwait developed what was, in retrospect, an unjustified sense of security because of its role as donor and mediator," Kostiner added. "It provoked Iraq by starting to build a city on the island of Bubiyan, disputed territory in Iraq's eyes."

Finally and most fatally, Kuwait had ignored the lesson of its own history. As Theodore Draper argued in 1987, Kuwait, which enjoyed professing that its foreign policy was nonalignment, was "too rich to be left alone and too weak to defend itself." In other words, a small, weak and oil-rich country in the most turbulent part of the world would always need an obvious protector. In 1899, it had the British. In 1987, it had the Americans. In 1990, it had no one.

Conclusion

President Bush offered several explanations of his decision to send ground forces to the Persian Gulf, a decision he made without consulting either the American people or their designated representatives. After trying out several variations on different themes, he settled on the deployment as a means of preserving our "very way of life."

He could have put it more directly: Americans went to the Gulf for oil, on which our "very way of life" so greatly depends.

But this president could not afford to confront the American public so bluntly—indeed, no American president could. The nation's dependence on petroleum in readily available amounts and at relatively low and steady prices has been a mainstay of American foreign policy since the end of World War II. Yet reminding Americans of their well-known addiction is not good politics. Nor is asking them to die for it.

So, as Theodore Draper wrote about a related foreign-policy crisis three years ago, the administration felt compelled to drag out and play at full blast "the whole doctrinal organ music—'national security,' 'economic disaster,' 'freedom of navigation,' 'commitment' to the 'peace and welfare' of our friends and allies, preservation of 'peace.' " Caspar W. Weinberger, then secretary of defense, added one that his successor Richard

Cheney might well have used: "leadership." What was at stake, Weinberger told a congressional panel, was "the leadership of the free world to resist the forces of anarchy and tyranny."

A sure sign that a doctrine was being applied mechanically, Draper observed, was the language being used. If words like "vital interests," "national security," "free world" and "peace is at stake" were not hauled out, he said, "it might be necessary to do some thinking and explain the policy in less simplistic and apocalyptic terms."

Some of the president's men have spoken more plainly. "Of course it's about petroleum," said Secretary of Commerce Robert Mossbacher, who, like President Bush, was an oilman before coming to Washington. "Crass or not, it's oil that keeps everybody going."

Thinking through the motives demands, first and foremost, eliminating the alleged but spurious reasons for our presence in the Persian Gulf. To begin with, the United States has not sent more than 150,000 men and women to the desert because Saddam Hussein is a thug who heads a vicious regime. Yes, Saddam Hussein is a thug. And he does run a brutal dictatorship in which thousands of his citizens have suffered and died. But Saddam was a thug when Washington decided to "tilt" toward Iraq in its war against Iran. He was a thug when the Defense Department was giving him information gleaned from spy satellites that helped him in the war he was losing. He was a thug when he used poison gas against Iranian soldiers, then against civilians, and finally on his own Kurdish citizens, months after the cease-fire was signed. He had personally killed and tortured opponents. And he had used terrorism as a legitimate arm of foreign policy. Yes, he had turned his country into a bastion of intimidation and fear in which the cult of his personality supplanted the Baath party's and Iraq's culture and institutions.

But none of that prevented Washington from, in the words of a White House official, "recognizing that he is there, that he is the head of a powerful country in the region, and that we had to deal with him."

The world is full of thugs in high places, perhaps not quite as brutal as Saddam. But the fact that Hafez al-Assad of Syria is also a thug, and probably twice as shrewd as his mustachioed Baathist counterpart in Iraq, did not stop Secretary of State James Baker from hustling to Damascus in September to curry his support in the international campaign against Iraq. The wily Assad, of course, would probably have been delighted to undermine his long-standing rival, even without Baker's personal encouragement. Was it necessary for the American secretary of state to meet with the man who has played and continues to play gracious host to the terrorist group that blew Pan Am flight 103 and hundreds of Americans out of the skies?

At this point, White House officials said, Assad was the lesser of two evils. But that is exactly what a previous administration had said of Saddam Hussein, when it seemed that Iran's Ayatollah Ruhollah Khomeini would overrun Iraq and triumph in the war. In enlisting Assad as a political foot soldier in an American-led effort to force Saddam out of Kuwait, America has shown that its choice of thugs is, to be charitable, opportunistic. So it cannot be argued persuasively that the United States went to the Gulf because Saddam Hussein is evil. That he is truly terrible may make Americans feel better about the decision to deploy forces, but it should not be confused with the reason for our presence there.

Nor can it be said that American forces are in the Gulf, as the president has said, to restore the legitimate government of Kuwait. Defenseless Kuwait was among the most civilized places in the Gulf—indeed, throughout the Arab world. It had accepted vast numbers of Palestinians, whom many other Arab states had refused to take in, states that had paid cheap lip service to their cause. The Sabahs, Kuwait's ruling family, had ruled by tradition and consensus since 1752, longer than American leaders and obviously longer than Saddam's brutal Baathists. Kuwait was a genial, generally tolerant place run by merchants, not military men.

But the United States did not send forces to the Gulf because Kuwait was a nice country that had been made to disappear from the map. Although no country since 1945 had been "murdered," as French analyst François Heisbourg put it, other nice places have disappeared. Consider Tibet. Few tears are shed in Washington over its demise as a sovereign entity.

Moreover, the dust of the last Iraqi tank had barely settled before Arab intellectuals began attacking Kuwait as an anachronism, a feudal monarchy that had quashed democracy under the pressure of the Iraq-Iran war. What was so "legitimate," they asked, about the Sabah family's rule? "Almost everyone agreed that even if Saddam withdrew his forces tomorrow, it would be hard to return to the status quo ante in Kuwait," said Fouad Ajami, a perceptive analyst of both Arab and American politics. "The pressures building there for more modern government would almost surely have to be addressed." Honest analysts acknowledge that had Kuwait been, for example, a country in sub-Saharan Africa and without oil, not a single American soldier would have been deployed to protect it. So the United States did not become entangled in the Gulf to defend the principle of sovereignty or to restore Kuwait's rulers to their genial department stores and palaces.

Nor were American forces there to defend the "legitimate" government of Saudi Arabia, a truly feudal monarchy without even the semblance of Kuwait's fragile democracy. Did Washington really care about defending the House of Saud's right to ban all forms of religion but Islam, its systematic repression of women, or its stoning of adulterers or amputations of the hands of thieves? Did Washington care about the lack of a dissenting voice in the desert kingdom? No American official has dared argue that the president sent forces to preserve freedom and human dignity in Riyadh.

Rather, President Bush was responding to a combination of factors that came into play in Iraq's invasion of Kuwait. He acted because Saddam Hussein, this particular thug, chose to swallow up Kuwait, that particular defenseless country, in the part of the world that happens to contain 40 percent of the planet's petroleum reserves.

In short, American forces had been sent to Saudi Arabia to protect the nation's access to oil.

Had the United States heeded the lesson of the oil crisis of the early 1970s, when its reliable access to oil at low and steady prices was challenged, peaceably, for the first time—by ostensible American supporters in the region—the Bush administration might not have felt compelled to do what it did in early August. For the confrontation in the Gulf was prompted partly by greed—Saddam Hussein's and America's. Under the Reagan administration, the nation embarked on a heady oil binge. The notion of "saving" lost any remnant of grace. Oil prices fell; conservation dropped off the national agenda; and dependence on imported oil, and on Persian Gulf oil in particular, increased markedly. If after the previous energy crisis, Washington had kept the price of oil high through an oil import fee and gasoline taxes, if Congress had imposed conservation measures and created incentives for wise energy use, if the government had tried to diversify energy sources—into solar, natural gas, coal, and even nuclear—we would not be in our current mess. But President Bush, who found the courage to stand up to Saddam Hussein, could not summon the political courage to talk straight to the American people, to say that the hour is late and the party is over.

An astute, pragmatic foreign policy would have grasped that regional rivalries and the gap between rich and poor within societies and among nations—not to mention the presence of Israel so infuriating to the Arabs—ensured that the Middle East would continue to be racked with conflict. Embracing that elementary truth might have led the United States over the past decade to follow a different strategy from Ronald Reagan's "yuppie" consumerism. It would have argued for a deliberate, sustained and economically painful effort to reduce dependence on Persian Gulf oil.

Perhaps then Americans might have asked themselves some tough questions. Why, for example, should cheap oil be one of the nation's "vital interests"? Or on what basis and for which goals should America and the other industrial powers expect to form a consensus for intervention in the Gulf? Should it be for the sake of uninterrupted access to Persian Gulf oil? Or should it begin with the certainty that such access will be compromised by the vagaries of Middle East politics?

Instead, the United States and most of its major allies remain mesmerized by the idea that it is possible to retain in perpetuity their control over the supply of low-cost oil from the Gulf. In considering the litany of alleged "policy failures" of the Bush administration's handling of the current crisis, all pale in comparison with the Reagan and Bush administrations' unwillingness to face geographic, economic and political reality. Middle East oil may simply no longer be within the control of its consumers.

Even after the crisis erupted, President Bush sent a bizarre signal to the nation about energy policy. If our national interests were at risk by Saddam Hussein's stranglehold on our precious oil, why was his sole domestic energy policy response to call upon the oil companies for "restraint" in pricing policy? And why, when Americans were watching the price of gas soar, despite Bush's limp calls for restraint, did he persist in skimming along the coast of Kennebunkport in his gas-guzzling Cigarette boat?

Since the crisis began, Washington has been engaged in a favored pastime—political scapegoating. "You can already feel a little bit of 'Who lost Kuwait?' in the air," said Representative Les Aspin of Wisconsin, referring to the famous "Who lost China?" campaign by which the right wing attacked Presidents Truman and Eisenhower after the fall of Chiang Kai-shek.

Many have been accused: the U.S. ambassador to Iraq for faithfully following her conciliatory instructions from Washington and failing to hear or to heed Saddam's threats; the assistant secretary of state for Near Eastern and South Asian affairs, for doggedly carrying out the administration's policy of accommodating Saddam's regime long after there was a plausible reason to do so; Secretary of State Baker, for virtually ignoring a part of the world where, as we have now been repeatedly told, the nation's "vital interests" are at stake; and President Bush, who sent "our boys" to the Saudi desert, perhaps to fight, maybe to win and possibly to die, without any persuasive plan for bringing them home again. There may well be more than enough policy blame to share, or with luck, perhaps, some glory to share.

The administration's response to the rather gentle criticism expressed so far is interesting. Some officials have defended as simply "realistic" the policy of attempting to "moderate" Saddam by seeking warm or at least working relations with him. After all, Iraq finally agreed that never again, except in extremis, would it use chemical warfare after Washington demanded such a pledge. Saddam's government might have defaulted left and right on loans to other countries's banks and governments, but it scrupulously paid the United States. Everyone, not just the Bush administration, was unprepared for and stunned by his invasion, they argue. All true enough.

Some officials go further and argue that even if Washington had pressed Saddam in the months before the invasion not to attack Kuwait, and specifically, had the administration issued the strongest warning possible against military action in the Gulf, the brutal Iraqi would have taken Kuwait anyway. On the other hand, there is no way of knowing what Saddam would have done *had* he been warned, because he was not warned. The world will never know what he would or would not have done. It knows only what he did, absent a credible warning.

Further, if Saddam was going to invade no matter what the United States said or threatened to do, then Bush's policy of appeasing him in the hope of "moderating" his regime was, ipso facto, deficient—indeed, pointless. If Saddam was going to pay no heed anyway, Washington might just as well have pressed far harder than it did to stop his egregious human-rights abuses, his relentless campaign to buy or steal what he needed to build his chemical, biological and nuclear arsenals, and his incessant bullying of his neighbors. To say that Saddam would have invaded Kuwait no matter what we told him is to admit that our policy of appeasement had been futile all along.

In retrospect, a strong U.S. position consistent with stated American principles on human rights and regional stability might have been heard in Baghdad, which, as policymakers have argued, was eager to maintain its lucrative economic ties, credits and political contacts in America. Admitting our failed policy does not justify or excuse Saddam's invasion of his neighbor. But it raises the question of why the administration clung for so long to a policy which Saddam could so disastrously misread.

Only if Saddam Hussein had been compelled to invade Kuwait for the very survival of his country—rather than as a relatively cost-free solution to his indebtedness and virtual landlocked geography—might he have been deterred by strong and credible warning from a nation as powerful as the United States? If Saddam considered America a "paper tiger," as a senior Iraqi official suggested, then critics of the administration's Middle East policy are correct to say that Bush's coddling of a dictator was misguided, ineffective and inconsistent with America's stated values.

Now that several hundred thousand soldiers from many nations are in Saudi Arabia, the United States must now deal with the consequences of its failed policy and with Saddam's aggression. Kuwait, as well as other Gulf states that sought implicit American protection but rejected an overt American presence, must understand that they helped bring about their own plight. A small and weak nation in a tough, tumultuous part of the world cannot afford to have all things all ways. Moreover, the absence of a parliament and a spirited political debate at home not only meant that the Sabah family's misguided foreign policy went unquestioned but also that Kuwait's critics had grounds on which to challenge the government's legitimacy. Parliaments and democratic institutions may be little more than window dressing in most parts of the Arab world, but Western resistance to Saddam's overthrow of the

Sabahs might have been more heartfelt had they existed.

The Saudis should be asked to acknowledge that, for the moment, they need America as much as America needs their oil, and that some accommodations must be made to American soldiers defending their frontiers. Chaplains should not be asked to remove crosses and stars of David from their uniforms, or to call themselves "morale officers" simply because the practice of religions other than Islam is forbidden by the Saudi interpretation of Muslim law. The 900 Jewish soldiers defending Arabian oil should not have to be spirited away on Rosh Hashanah and Yom Kippur to observe Judaism's most holy days in secret, as though Judaism were some sort of conspiracy against Riyadh. American women soldiers maintaining the planes that Saudis fly should not have to swelter in 120-degree heat because a Saudi soldier might faint at the sight of bare shoulders.

The United States should by now have recognized that selling vast quantities of sophisticated weapons to people lacking the knowledge or will to use them may help America's balance of payments crisis, but does little to shore up an ally's defenses. Kuwait, after all, purchased millions of dollars worth of Hawk missiles in the past decade, most of which fell into Iraqi hands after Kuwaiti forces fled into Saudi Arabia. Yet only congressional pressure in September, to some extent reflecting Israeli wishes, forced the administration to defer until 1991 half of some $20 billion of new weapons sales to Riyadh.

Washington must also decide whose interests are being protected in the Persian Gulf. If America's European allies are more heavily dependent than the United States on Middle East oil, then a collective security arrangement that reflects those economic and political realities should be devised. What was only half jokingly known as Secretary Baker's "tin-cup exercise," pleading with Japan and the Western European democracies to offset the cost of American forces in the desert, belied the administration's implication that "the West" shared his estimate of its collective peril. The reality is all too familiar, as the analyst Thomas Omestad recently noted: "Washington continues waging a geopolitical struggle while key allies focus on economics." In other words, the United States, as usual, bears the enormous cost of maintaining the security of the industrial world, while its allies pursue their own economic advantage. If the so-called civilized nations feel threatened by Saddam's invasion of Kuwait, then they should pay proportionately in men and money to stop him. If they choose not to, then perhaps the threat is not quite so great as President Bush claims.

There are at least two powerful and legitimate justifications for having sent American troops to the Gulf, though they have been the most poorly articulated by policymakers. The first is that President Bush's attempt to impose economic sanctions against Saddam would probably not have worked had it not been reinforced by military power. Absent Bush's snap decision to send American soldiers to the region, America's Arab partners would probably not have had the courage to stand up to Saddam and devise an "Arab position" to oppose him. Saudi Arabia would never have agreed to sever Saddam's pipeline that runs through its country. In short, sanctions, the nonmilitary and theoretically preferable way of forcing Iraq to withdraw, would not have been an effective option for stopping him.

The second justification was alluded to last February by Saddam himself when he noted that the Soviet Union's decline would change politics in the Middle East. With the waning of Soviet power and the end of the Cold War, the rules that had for years governed the conduct of nations are no longer obviously in force. After the sudden collapse of repressive East Bloc regimes in 1989, analysts in Washington hoped that the end of the bipolar world would mark the beginning of a less fractious one, of a more stable order. But now, it seems, the opposite might be true: the fear of nuclear annihilation through which the superpowers had once deterred each other had lessened, and without the restraining hand of the superpowers upon their shoulders, former client states felt more free to meddle in their neighbors' affairs.

Whatever the case, the end of the Cold War and the collapse of the Soviet Union as a superpower mean that nations will learn new ways of relating to one another—in effect, new rules of world politics. Still, as Raymond Aron once observed, "The stakes of war are the existence, the creation or the elimination of states." If Saddam's annexation of Kuwait were permitted to stand, Washington reasoned, wholesale disavowals of old colonial borders and land grabs throughout the Middle East and the rest of the Third World might become commonplace. It was up to the United States, the Bush administration believed, to ensure that international crime did not pay—that Saddam be forced to withdraw unconditionally from Kuwait without a hint of a trophy from his aggression. (It is true, of course, that Washington did not hesitate overmuch when it decided to remove the unpleasant leader of Panama by invading his country and replacing him with men more to its liking.) The rule was straightforward: big countries should not be permitted to gobble up small ones, especially not in oil-rich parts of the world. But there was a larger issue, one that other nations quickly grasped. National boundaries, increasingly fragile in a world of shifting allegiances, had to be respected.

President Bush understood instinctively that depriving Saddam of victory had to be, and to be perceived as, a multilateral action; for the United States to act alone would arouse resentment of American "imperialism" on the Arab "street," the fashionable expression for the older leftist term, the Arab "masses," though as it has turned out, such resentment has arisen anyway. But Bush also believed that only the United States, one of the victors of World War II and the sole surviving superpower, could galvanize world opinion, take the lead in defining the new rules or restating old ones, and enforce compliance with them.

So, the administration chose to stand against evil and on international principle in justifying its decision to become, once more, the world's policeman. It may well have been necessary for the United States to play this role given the importance of oil and Saddam's clear aggression. But there was in President Bush's pronouncements something of an understated swagger, a bit of Clint Eastwood's deadly squint as interpreted by a president eager to distract the country from the inevitability of higher taxes and other forms of economic hardship, brought on in part by a vast financial scandal in which his own son has played an increasingly prominent part. Bush seemed to relish playing Dirty Harry. And how much more satisfying it was to turn his scowl against a truly evil man in the name of principle, not petroleum.

For all his swagger, though, Bush has privately expressed the deepest concern about an escalation of the conflict into actual combat with its thousands of American casualties. Some in Washington and elsewhere have argued that the United States, having sent forces to the region, should now eliminate what they see as a long-term threat to the region's peace and stability. That view is held by many Europeans as well as by most of Saddam's neighbors, and not by Israel and its American supporters alone, as some American conservatives have suggested. There is much support in Washington for getting rid of Saddam, permanently. War fever was palpable by the summer's end. Inevitably, there was the usual talk of "surgical strikes." R. W. Apple, Jr., of *The New York Times* quoted an American pilot who had flown many missions against Hanoi, who said such strikes "only exist in think tanks and mental institutions."

President Bush, having decided to set rules of behavior for the post–Cold War world, having mobilized the nation's and the world's resources to stop Saddam from controlling the world's oil and extending his power over the Gulf, now seems no less trapped by his own policies than Saddam Hussein. An "Arab solution" to the crisis, which would almost inevitably reward Iraqi aggression by enabling him to withdraw with considerable booty, would be an obvious victory for Saddam. It would mean that he, not Bush, made the new rules. And it would mean that his neighbors, and ultimately the world, would likely have to contend with him another time, possibly when he is stronger, richer, and a nuclear power.

A few analysts—such as Kevin Phillips, the Republican strategist—have warned that even if Bush accomplishes his goals, the nation must understand that it no longer has the resources to play its habitual role as international cop. During the Korean and Vietnam wars, Washington did not plead with other countries for financial help. But in this crisis we were a superpower for rent. "We came perilously close to having it look as if the Arabs had hired us to do their fighting for them," said Senator Daniel Patrick Moynihan.

Though the United States may be the sole remaining superpower, said Phillips, it is also the world's largest debtor nation, a faltering economic power whose profligate consumerism has at last undermined what for forty years had been the world's dominant economy. Phillips, for one, described the crisis in the Gulf as the "first war this country ever fought (overtly at least) over economics—over oil, in particular," almost a throwback to the nineteenth-century confrontations in which empires fought over control of scarce natural resources and trade routes. "If America's chancy Mideast involvement ends with military success, Saddam Hussein will pay the price," Phillips argued. "But from an economic standpoint, U.S. Persian Gulf military involvement looks like the classic overreach of a declining superpower going into debt to maintain yesteryear's prestige." His words echoed Paul Kennedy's observation in *The Rise and Fall of the Great Powers,* when he noted that the "test of American abilities will be the greater because it, like Imperial Spain around 1600 or the British Empire around 1900, is the inheritor of a vast array of strategical commitments. . . . The United States now runs the risk, so familiar to historians of the rise and fall of previous Great Powers, of what might roughly be called 'imperial overstretch.' " This vision requires that the United States reaffirm for itself an imperial role in a post-imperial age.

But in September these words had little resonance. Most Americans, like their president, yearned for displays of principle and grand actions. The thought that the foray in the Gulf might be one of America's last such adventures undertaken in the twilight of its short-lived empire remains unspeakable to most Americans. Yet perhaps this crisis in the Gulf will begin to force our country to face facts, to begin to abandon the myths about ourselves and our motives that have misled us so long so disastrously. No matter what happens in the Gulf, we postpone that reckoning at our peril.

Appendix

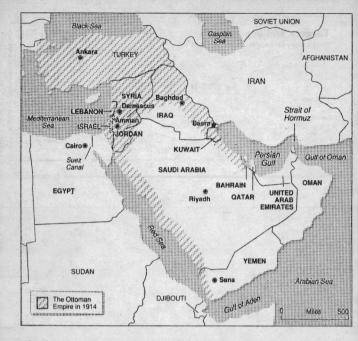

The borders of the Arab countries of the Middle East
were drawn largely by Britain and France after
World War I, when the League of Nations allowed
them to carve up the Ottoman domains there. In
Syria and Lebanon, France tried to establish
republics; in Jordan and Iraq, Britain set up
monarchies and installed members of the Hashemite
family that had led the Arab revolt against Turkey; in
Egypt, central Arabia and Kuwait, London backed
other traditional rulers with whom it had long
friendships. All these countries are now fully
independent, but force or conservative inertia, rather
than the practice of democracy, have proved to be
the decisive factors in how they are ruled; to one
degree or another most remain authoritarian. Map
and caption text copyright © 1990 The New York Times.
Reprinted with permission.

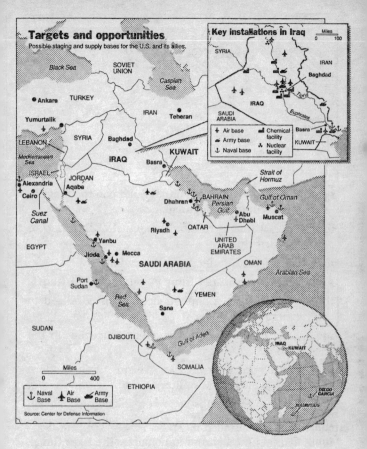

Map copyright © 1990 The New York Times. Reprinted
with permission.

Chronology

1534   The Ottoman Turks, under Suleiman the Magnificent, conquer Baghdad.

1917   The Ottomans relinquish control of Baghdad to the British.

1920   Iraq placed under British mandate.

1921   The British install Emir Faisal as king of Iraq.

1932   Iraq declares independence and is admitted to League of Nations.

1933   King Faisal dies; his son, Ghazi, succeeds to the throne.

1936   Bakr Sidqi overthrows government in modern Arab world's first military coup.

1937   Saddam Hussein is born in a village near Takrit.

1941   Several hundred Iraqi Jews are killed in riots.

1956   Gamal Abdel Nasser nationalizes the Suez Canal, and Egypt is invaded.

1957   Saddam Hussein joins the Baath party.

1958   The Iraqi monarchy is toppled in a coup led by General Abdul Karim Qassim.

1959   Qassim survives an assassination attempt by a Baathist hit team, one of whose members is Saddam Hussein.

1960 Organization of Petroleum Exporting Countries (OPEC) is founded.

1961 Iraqi army launches first major offensive against the Kurds.

1963 A Baathist coup overthrows Qassim, and is itself toppled nine months later.

1964 Michel Aflaq recommends elevation of Saddam Hussein to inner circle of Baath party leadership.

1966 Saddam founds the party's secret police.

1967 Six-Day War with Israel results in military rout for the Arabs.

1968 Baath party again seizes power; Ahmad Hassan al-Bakr becomes president; Saddam Hussein is made number two.

1969 War with Kurds intensifies; show trial of "spies" is held, public hangings follow, including more than a dozen Iraqi Jews.

1970 Baath party reaches autonomy agreement with the Kurds.

1972 Iraq Petroleum Company is nationalized.

1973 Nadhim Kzar, chief of Iraqi internal security, is executed along with others in the wake of an attempted coup. October War breaks out between Arabs and Israelis; an oil embargo is declared.

1974 Kurdish autonomy accords collapse; full-scale fighting breaks out; hundreds of thousands of Kurds flee Iraq; atrocities are rampant.

1975 Iraq and Iran agree at Algiers that Iran will end its support of the Kurds, and Iraq will give up half of the Shatt al-Arab waterway.

1978 Baghdad summit condemns Egypt for signing the Camp David accords; the Ayatollah Ruhollah Khomeini is expelled from Iraq.

1979 The shah of Iran flees Iran; Khomeini returns. Saddam Hussein succeeds Bakr as president of Iraq and promptly purges party elite.

1980 Iraq invades Iran, launching the bloodiest war in the history of the modern Middle East, lasting eight years.

1981 Israel destroys Iraqi nuclear reactor in lightning air raid.

1982 Israel invades Lebanon.

1988 Kurds are gassed by Iraqi army in first-ever use of chemical weapons by a state against its own citizens. Iraq-Iran war ends in August when both sides agree on a cease-fire.

1990 Saddam Hussein invades Kuwait, and declares its formal annexation as Iraq's nineteenth province.

Human Rights in Iraq

The following is reprinted with permission from Human Rights in Iraq *by Middle East Watch, published by Human Rights Watch/Yale University Press in November 1990.*

When he was released on October 18, 1983, after being held for 110 days in a Baghdad security prison without ever having been charged, Robert Spurling told U.S. diplomats that his treatment at the hands of his Iraqi jailers was "nothing" compared to that meted out to Iraqis and other Arabs he saw there. Spurling, a U.S. citizen, was then fifty and the technical director of the luxury Baghdad Novotel Hotel. He was on the point of boarding a flight to Paris on the night of June 29–30, 1983, together with his Belgian wife and children, when he simply disappeared. Unbeknown to his family, he had been deftly diverted down a ramp where security agents and a car awaited him. Mrs. Spurling frantically sought the assistance of U.S. diplomatic representatives in Baghdad. More than a week passed before Iraqi authorities answered their inquiries and acknowledged that Spurling was being held. They never explained why he was detained.

Spurling later told U.S. officials that he was abducted, blindfolded, and driven to what he assumed to be the headquarters of the Baghdad security forces. There, he was interrogated and tortured repeatedly, pressed first to confess to spying and later simply give information on others. "On July 6 and 23," he later testified, "I was given blows with a rubber truncheon on the soles of my feet, electric shocks were applied to my hands, feet, kidney region, genitals and above all to my ears, blows with the forearm to my head, four blows with a rubber truncheon on the upper part of my feet, two blows to the ears with boot heels, blows to the ears with cushions resembling boxing gloves and violent slaps." Spurling was threatened with mutilation and was told that his wife and children had been arrested and would be mistreated unless he cooperated. (This was untrue; Mrs. Spurling remained in Baghdad throughout her husband's detention, and while Iraqi authorities encouraged her to leave they did not harass her.) Spurling was fed half portions for a time and then fed irregularly. On several occasions he was given spoiled and heavily salted food to induce nausea and thirst. More fortunate than most, he was given a cell to himself, which he shared only briefly with an Iraqi political prisoner, but the cell had a external temperature control which enabled his jailers alternately to make it very hot or very cold. And "time after time I had to listen to the cries and noises of other prisoners while they were being interrogated under torture."

Because Spurling was a U.S. citizen at a time when the Iraqi government was looking to improve its relations with the United States, he was—as he himself stated—dealt with far more gently than others in his place of detention. The United States pressed the Iraqi government hard for access to Spurling. Before producing Spurling for his first meeting with U.S. diplomats, his Iraqi jailers gave him medical treatment for the wounds on his feet. At that meeting he obeyed their order to say that he was being well treated. But at his second meeting with U.S. representatives, Spurling defied these warnings and revealed that he had been tortured. According to a U.S. official present at the meeting, Spurling's revelation caused Iraqi officials acute embarrassment. The United States immediately lodged vigorous diplomatic protests and demanded Spurling's release. After that he was well treated. When released several weeks later he was in relatively good shape, although scars on his feet were quite visible and were seen by U.S. diplomatic personnel in Baghdad.

Spurling was examined by an Amnesty International physician in Paris on October 25, 1983, one week after his release. His only problems then were digestive troubles, pains at the base of his spine and in his feet, lack of feeling in his right thumb, and difficulty in bending one finger.

Peter Worth, a British civil engineer employed in Iraq, reported having been arrested, beaten, and tortured by electric shock in 1981. His reported offense was to have leaned against a wall at a construction project, accidentally causing a picture of Saddam Hussein to fall to the ground. Speaking of his ordeal, Worth later said: "I felt the . . . electric shock go through my arm, then other parts of my body, including my private parts." Worth said he signed a bogus confession to spying and was deported.

Not so lucky as Peter Worth or Robert Spurling was Neji Bennour, reception manager at the Novotel Hotel, who was arrested a few weeks before Spurling. A Tunisian citizen, Bennour was dealt with in the manner accorded Iraqis and other Arabs. According to his later testimony, he was arrested while at work after having been tricked into going to the hotel's parking lot, where he was forced into the trunk of a car and driven to what he assumed was the security police headquarters in Baghdad. There he was beaten before being put into a

cell jammed with more than two hundred other prisoners. He was held there for ten months. He later testified
to Amnesty International that he was tortured repeatedly, some one hundred times by his count. He stated
that he was given electric shocks on his ears, thumbs,
little fingers, nipples, and between his big toes; beaten
on the head and legs with a bare cable; repeatedly hit
with fists and rubber truncheons, including on the soles
of his feet and on the cervical, dorsal, and lumbar verte-
brae for long periods, and kicked on the face, head,
back, hands, legs, and feet.

Bennour said that at first he was not even accused of
spying; all the security police wanted was that he collaborate with them and denounce colleagues at work. In
September 1983, over three months after his arrest, he
signed a paper confessing to espionage and rape. Then
torture ceased, and six months later, on April 2, 1984,
without ever having been formally charged or tried, he
was released.

When Bennour was examined by a doctor in Paris
seventeen days later, he was found to have a variety of
scars and to suffer from headaches, diminished hearing,
some loss of vision, spinal pain, pains in the heels and
feet, fatigue, and difficulty in breathing during exertion.
He complained of rapid heartbeat in the evenings,
nightmares and acute anxiety.

The Iraqi government consistently denies all charges
that its officials engage in torture. In the cases of Spurling and Bennour, an Iraqi official stated in a letter to
Amnesty International that the two men had been "arrested in accordance with regulations [and] were not
subject to any form of torture during their detention."
The official added: "We take this opportunity to confirm
what we have demonstrated before, that there is no
torture in Iraq."

Iraqi spokesmen invariably reply to reports of tor-

ture by citing a battery of legal provisions—Article 22 of
the Iraqi Constitution, which prohibits physical or psychological torture; Chapter 111 of the 1969 Penal Code,
which also prohibits torture; Article 323 of the Code of
Criminal Procedure, which prohibits the use of unlaw-
ful means to obtain a confession; Article 333 of the
Penal Code, which stipulates that any government em-
ployee who tortures is to be punished by imprisonment;
and Article 322 of the Penal Code, which prohibits government employees from taking advantage of their position to treat any person harshly or in a manner
detrimental to his honor or dignity or to cause him
physical pain. Iraqi spokesmen point out that their government has announced its voluntary compliance with
the provisions of the United Nations Declaration on the
Protection of all Persons from Being Subjected to Torture and other Cruel, Inhuman or Degrading Treatment or Punishment and is considering accession to the
Convention against Torture and Other Cruel, Inhuman
or Degrading Treatment or Punishment.

Anyone who has been tortured, Iraqi spokesmen
add, is entitled under the law to institute criminal proceedings against the torturer. Iraq told the U.N. Human
Rights Committee in 1986 that "[t]he party responsible
for ordering and carrying out the torture, even if it
were a governmental body, would be duly sentenced to
the prescribed penalty and would be held liable for any
incapacity or damages resulting from the offense." Iraqi
officials have said that persons have been found guilty
of assault on prisoners and have been punished, but the
government has refused to substantiate this claim, and
in no instance is anyone known to have filed suit in Iraqi
courts for damages from torture.

But while vociferously denying charges of torture,
Iraq has never allowed a private human rights group or
United Nations body to visit its prisons and to interview

prisoners or victims of torture. In the meantime, voluminous reports of torture committed over the years by Iraqi jailers continue to emerge—reports of victims of torture, from relatives of victims and from others, corroborated in many cases by medical evidence.

Nabil Jamil al-Janabi, an Iraqi poet living in exile in London, recently gave a public account of the torture he suffered at the security-force headquarters in Baghdad after his arrest in March 1976. Janabi, an Arab Iraqi, had read one of his poems to an assembly of Kurds at Sinjar, in western Mosul province. He was arrested and driven to Baghdad.

I was taken by two very big gunmen into a single, cold, dark cell with no bedding. . . . The door of the cell was opened at 3 A.M. They took me out, blindfolded, to an unknown place. . . . They started torturing me by attaching one end of an electric wire to my left big toe and the other end to my penis. They put the power on and I lost consciousness for about an hour, then they repeated this with the electric wire attached to my right foot. Again I passed out. While I lay half dead on the floor they tried to revive me by torturing me with cigarettes and steel rods. When I regained consciousness again, they tied my head and both legs together and put me into a tyre. They started to spin it; two men on either side kept spinning me round and round. In addition to all this, I was completely naked, they'd taken off my pants. Then they started to beat me. Two men were beating me with electric rods, hitting my testicles.

Nabil al-Janabi reported that he signed a piece of paper without knowing what was on it, was sent to a "revolutionary court" where he was tried without the assistance of a defense attorney, and was sentenced to five years in prison for publishing a poem "calculated to incite people to act against the government." After being released, he was arrested again in 1982, held for two weeks and again tortured. He fled Iraq for Britain in 1983. The physician who examined him there stated:

> Mr. Jamil suffers from hypertension, ischaemic heart disease and diabetes mellitus. He also appears to have a lumbo-sacral prolapsed intervertebral disc and problems with various joints, almost certainly related to the torture to which he has been subjected. . . . Mr. Jamil has been subjected to gross brutality and is now in a somewhat precarious state of health.

Many Iraqi torture victims do not live to tell their story. Ahmed Mattar, another Iraqi poet living in exile in London, wrote these lines in memory of a friend who died under torture in Iraq.

> They imprisoned him
> before they charged him
> They tortured him
> before they interrogated him
> They stubbed out cigarettes in his eyes
> and held up some pictures in front of him
> Say whose faces are these
> He said: I do not see
> They cut off his lips
> and demanded that he name
> those "they" had recruited
> He said nothing
> and when they failed to make him talk
> they hanged him.
> A month later they clear him

> They realized the young man
> was not the one they really wanted
> but his brother. . . .

Of course, of those who survive torture in Iraq's prisons, only a relatively few reach the West, and not all of those are willing to speak of their ordeal. One who did agree to give testimony to Middle East Watch, a former lecturer at Baghdad University, insisted on anonymity in order to protect relatives still in Iraq.

> They came to my house in Baghdad in December 1979 just after midnight. They broke down the door, searched the house, blindfolded and handcuffed me, hit me with a rubber truncheon and took me to Baghdad security headquarters. There I was taken to the third floor, my clothes were taken from me and I was given a traditional Iraqi robe. I was then told, "We have documents showing that you are one of the leaders of the Daawa party." When I denied it they said, "We give you a few minutes to think it over. If you don't confess we will torture you." I asked them to show me the documents, they replied they would do that once I confessed. After that for 35 days they tortured me every day or every other day. I was beaten on the feet and hung for long periods of time by my arms from ropes anchored in the ceiling; they debated whether to hang me from my arms tied behind my back, but I was much heavier then and they realized that if they did that the bones in my arms and shoulders would break. When they weren't torturing me they kept me in a cell with over 100 other people, with no sanitation facilities. At the end of 35 days they said they would let me go if I joined the Baath party. I refused but they

released me anyway, but every day a security officer came to my house to question me. Colleagues at the University warned me that I was going to be arrested again, so at the beginning of March 1980 I fled the country. [London, 1989]

In a report issued in 1981, Amnesty International summarized the testimony of fifteen Iraqi exiles—twelve men and three women—who had been tortured in Iraq in the preceding years. One of them, Burhan al-Shawi, a twenty-four-year-old journalist and writer who was arrested in Baghdad in November 1978 and fled Iraq in May 1979, agreed to have his name used in the account he gave. Amnesty reported:

During the first two days he was taken to different rooms and beaten with fists, rods and a whip. . . . In one room he was caressed and sexually fondled, before being taken out and beaten and kicked. The torture then became more systematic, taking place every one or two hours. His head was whipped and beaten so hard that he lost consciousness. . . . After regaining consciousness on one occasion he was aware that his trousers had been removed and realized that he had been raped. He was then made to sit on a cold bottle-like object which was forced up his rectum. He was also burned with a hard object about the size of a pencil.

Burhan al-Shawi and the fourteen other torture victims who gave personal testimony were examined by physicians in London who in all cases "found that the tortures described were consistent with the subsequent symptoms and the signs found during the physical examination."

For sheer horror, nothing is likely to surpass the nightmarish scene described by an Iraqi mother who went to the Baghdad morgue to collect her son's body in September 1982. The boy was arrested in December 1981 and held without charge or trial, and without his family knowing his whereabouts. Here is an excerpt of the woman's testimony:

> I looked around and saw 9 bodies stretched out on the floor with him . . . but my son was in a chair form . . . that is sitting form, not sleeping or stretched. He had blood all over him and his body was very eaten away and bleeding. I looked at the other stretched out on the floor alongside him . . . all burnt . . . I don't know with what . . . another's body carried the marks of a hot domestic iron all over his head to his feet. . . . At the mortuary the bodies were on the floor . . . one of them had his chest cut lengthwise into three sections . . . from the neck to the bottom of the chest was slit with what must have been a knife and the flesh looked white and roasted as if cooked. . . .Another had his legs axed with an axe . . . his arms were also axed. One of them had his eyes gouged out and his nose and ears cut off. . . . One of them looked hanged . . . his neck was long . . . his tongue was hanging out and the fresh blood was oozing out of his mouth.

The woman testified that "corpses were returned [to the families] in this horrifying manner" for about a month and a half, but later the practice stopped and the authorities began giving out only death certificates.

Large numbers of persons have unquestionably died under torture in Iraq over the past two decades. Each year there have been reports of dozens—sometimes hundreds—of deaths, with bodies of victims at times left in the street or returned to families bearing marks of torture: eyes gouged out, fingernails missing, genitals cut off, and terrible wounds and burns. The brazenness of Iraqi authorities in returning bodies bearing clear evidence of torture is remarkable. Governments that engage in torture often go to great lengths to hide what they have done by burying or destroying the bodies of those tortured to death. A government so savage as to flaunt its crimes obviously wants to strike terror in the hearts of its citizens and to inflict gratuitous pain on the families of the victims.

Torture has been reportedly used not only against men and women but also against children, either to obtain information from them, to punish them for acts of opposition, or to punish their parents. Kurdish children have been among victims of detention and torture. A former Baghdad University student, arrested as a sympathizer of the outlawed Kurdish Democratic Party and released in April 1985 after having been tortured, reported that his mother, aged seventy-three, three brothers, three sisters, and five of their children between the ages of five and thirteen were arrested, beaten, and subjected to electric shocks. This witness testified, "Infant children are kept in [the] detention center together with their parents. Usually they keep such children in a separate cell next to [the] mother in order to force [the] parent to confess. I saw a five-month-old baby screaming in this state."

In September and October 1985, some 300 Kurdish children and teenagers were reportedly arrested in Suleimanieh. The bodies of three children were reportedly found afterward on the outskirts of the city, blood-stained and bearing the marks of torture. Some of these children were transferred to a security prison in Baghdad, according to the testimony of a detainee released at the end of 1985, who described in these terms what he saw:

> Each hour, security men opened the door and chose 3 to 5 of the prisoners—children or men—and removed them for torture. Later, their tortured bodies were thrown back into the cell. They were often bleeding and carried obvious signs of whipping and electric shocks. . . . At midnight, the security men took another three of the children, but because they were so savagely treated they were taken from the cell to a military hospital. It was clear that the security authorities did not wish them to die like this. However when their wounds healed they were returned to the cell. Some children tried to sleep on the floor. A child who had been in the hospital lay down and finally, we thought, fell asleep. But . . . we knew he was dead. . . . When I was released, there were still some children in our cell. I don't know what happened to the others.

In January 1987, it was reported that twenty-nine of these children had been executed and their bodies returned to their families, some with eyes gouged out and other marks of torture. Although the Iraqi government vehemently denied these reports, the European Parliament deemed them sufficiently credible to speak out about them. In its resolution "on the detention and torture of children in Iraq," the European Parliament condemned "these crimes which disgrace the government which perpetrates them" and appealed for "the immediate release of all the children and young people detained on the basis of political activities undertaken by their parents or relations."

That torture is used routinely as a method of political

repression in Iraq, and that it frequently involves acts of great savagery, is credited by a wide range of nongovernmental human rights groups as well as the U.S. State Department. According to knowledgeable U.S. officials interviewed by Middle East Watch, torture is not limited to political and security prisoners; while anyone arrested for these offenses can expect to be tortured, criminal suspects are also frequently tortured and almost always subjected to brutal treatment, at least in the early stages of detention.

Torture, Ill-Treatment, and Death in Iraq

*The following extracts from Amnesty International's
April 1989 report entitled "Iraq: Children: Innocent Victims of Political Repression" are reprinted by permission. The full report (AI index: MDE 14/04/89) can be
ordered directly for $5.00 from Amnesty International,
322 Eighth Avenue, New York, NY 10001.*

For many years Amnesty International has received
reports of the widespread torture in Iraq of political
prisoners, among them minors. Some were reported to
have died in custody as a result.

Torture is prohibited under Article 7 of the International Covenant on Civil and Political Rights which
states:

"No one shall be subjected to torture or to cruel,
inhuman or degrading treatment or punishment.
In particular, no one shall be subjected without his
free consent to medical or scientific experimenta-
tion."

Torture is also prohibited in Iraq under the Constitution and in national legislation, and constitutes an of-
fence punishable in accordance with the provisions of
the Penal Code. Article 22(a) of the Constitution prohibits "any form of physical and mental torture." Article

127 of the Law of Criminal Procedures states that no illegal methods may be used to extract confessions from the accused, including ill-treatment, threats to cause harm, psychological methods may be used to cause harm, psychological methods or the use of drugs and spirits. According to the provisions of the Penal Code:

> "A penalty of imprisonment not exceeding one year and a fine not exceeding 100 dinars shall be imposed upon any official or person entrusted with a public duty who, taking advantage of his post, treats another person with cruelty, causing him moral or physical harm . . ." (Article 332).

> "A penalty of imprisonment shall be imposed upon any official or person entrusted with a public duty who inflicts or instigates torture on an accused person . . . to force him to confess to a crime . . . The use of force or the threat to use force are regarded as torture." (Article 333)

As regards juveniles, Article 383 of the Penal Code provides that a term of imprisonment not exceeding three years or a fine not exceeding 300 dinars be imposed on anyone exposing to danger the life of a person below the age of fifteen.

Amnesty International believes that the torture and ill-treatment of detainees in the custody of the security forces is routine and systematic in Iraq. Among the victims are political prisoners—including young people below the age of 18—tortured in order to force them to sign "confessions" or to renounce their political affiliation. Relatives, including children, arrested in lieu of suspects being sought by the authorities have also been tortured. Some are reported to have died in custody as a result. Interrogation methods used by the security forces are described as brutal, in some cases resulting in permanent physical or mental damage to the victims. Other detainees, among them minors, have also been tortured prior to their execution.

In a report published in April 1985, Amnesty International listed some 30 different methods of torture said to be used in Iraq. These range from beating to burning, administration of electric shocks and mutilation. Over the years, the Iraqi Government has denied allegations brought to its attention by the organization, including cases supported by detailed medical evidence. During a mission to Iraq in 1983, officials told Amnesty International delegates that complaints of torture and ill-treatment had been investigated and the perpetrators punished. They stated that no one could be arrested without a warrant, that detainees could contact their families immediately after an arrest, that they were allowed regular visits by relatives every 15 days and medical examinations within 24 hours after arrest, and that regular prison visits were made by independent officials. Nevertheless, the inconsistency between the government's statements and testimonies Amnesty International continues to receive from torture victims and their families remain marked. The government has declined to provide Amnesty International with documentation showing that torture allegations were ever investigated, and the organization is unaware of any instance where the perpetrators were brought to justice in accordance with national legislation.

Children and young people have also been subjected to torture while in custody. Allegations received have included the following: the extraction of fingernails, beatings, whipping, sexual abuse, electrical shock treatment, and deprivation of food and of the use of toilet facilities. According to the testimony of a former prisoner released in 1988, female prisoners, including young girls, have been hung upside down from the feet during menstruation. Objects have also been inserted into the vaginas of young women, causing the hymen to break.

Iraq legislation gives juvenile offenders the right to make complaints against ill-treatment while in custody. Article 41 of Act No. 104 of 1981 states that a juvenile (as well as adult) offender:

> ". . . may address to the competent Director General complaints regarding any ill-treatment inflicted on him or any offence committed against his person, and the Director General shall deal with all such complaints within seven days of receiving them."

Amnesty International is not aware of any instances where detained juveniles have been able to file such complaints or that any such complaints were ever investigated. In the organization's view, any detainee venturing to exercise this right would be placed at risk of further reprisals.

Children and young people, according to Amnesty International's information, are most commonly tortured in order to force their parents and relatives to confess to alleged political offenses. A former political prisoner, held at al-Karkh Security Directorate in Baghdad and released in April 1985, submitted his testimony to the organization. A former student at Baghdad University and a Kurdistan Democratic Party (KDP) sympathizer, he was detained for five months and tortured in order to reveal his political affiliation and the names of other activists. In addition to details of his own treatment in detention, he gave the following information about the torture and ill-treatment of his relatives:

"Members of my family, mother (73 years old), three sisters and three brothers with five children aged between five and thirteen, were arrested and brought in front of me. They were subjected to the *falaqa* and electric shocks . . . They also made me listen to a recorded cassette tape of the cries and moans of my family [undergoing] torture . . ."

His testimony also described conditions under which infants have been held at the detention centre where he was held:

"The detention centre is extremely filthy . . . infant children are kept in [the] detention centre together with their parents. Usually they keep such children in a separate cell next to [the] mother or father's cell and deprive [them of] milk in order to force [the] parent to confess. I saw a 5-month-old baby screaming in this state . . ."

In January 1986 Amnesty International called on the government to investigate reports that some of the 300 children and youths arrested in Sulaimaniya in September/October 1985 had been tortured, and that three of them died in custody as a result. The bodies of the three children were reported to have been found in the streets on the outskirts of Sulaimaniya, their clothes bloodstained and their bodies bearing the marks of torture. Others were allegedly beaten while in detention. The government denied these reports in its letter to the organization received in April 1986. There was no indication that the torture allegations had ever been investigated. Amnesty International subsequently received the testimony of a former detainee released from Fudailiyya Security Headquarters in Baghdad in late 1985.

Suspected of having contacts with members of the Patriotic Union of Kurdistan (PUK), he was detained for seven months and allegedly tortured in order to reveal the names of PUK members. He stated following his release that some of the 300 Sulaimaniya children had been detained at Fudailiyya with him and subjected to torture. The following are extracts from his testimony:

". . . we were forbidden to communicate with the children, who were treated with special brutality . . . the cell was so small that only a few children could sit down in turn on the floor which was cold and uncovered. The cell was windowless, except for a hole in the door for the security officers to keep watch on us. There was no air to breath.

"Each hour, security men opened the door and chose 3 to 5 of the prisoners—children or men— and removed them for torture. Later, their tortured bodies were thrown back into the cell. They were often bleeding and carried obvious signs of whipping and electric shocks. We always tried our best to help them.

"At midnight, the security men took another three of the children, but because they were so savagely treated they were taken from the cell to a military hospital. It was clear that the security authorities did not wish them to die like this. However, when their wounds healed, they were returned to the cell.

"Some children tried to sleep on the floor. A child who had been in the hospital lay down and finally, we thought, fell asleep. But . . . we knew he was dead. No one knows what happened to his corpse.

"During the next few weeks our situation did not change. Three times a day we had meals thrown at us: breakfast was a piece of bread to be shared between every four prisoners; lunch was a pear or five grapes for each one. Whenever there was a complaint about the food, the complainant received a blow instead of food.

"We were only allowed to go to the toilets when the security men allowed us to do so, rather [than] in accordance with our needs. And they seldom allowed us to do so. For the children this was especially difficult and some children occasionally dirtied themselves. The prison chief ordered us to punish them for this by whipping them with a rubber whip. Those who refused to join in the punishment were themselves tortured.

"When I was released, there were still some children in our cell. I don't know what happened to the others . . ."

In January 1987, 29 of these children and youths were reported to have been executed and their bodies returned to their families. According to accounts received by Amnesty International, some of the victims had their eyes gouged out and their bodies bore marks of torture. The government did not respond to Amnesty International's renewed call for an investigation into the torture allegations The detention and torture of these young detainees were condemned by the European Parliament in a resolution passed in April 1987. . . .

The Death Penalty

. . . In March 1988, Amnesty International received reports of the execution of 17 minors aged between 14 and 17 in the period of November and December 1987. A number of these executions constituted extrajudicial killings. The victims were among some 360 people reported to have been executed at the time in seven separate incidents. The majority of the victims were Kurdish political prisoners from the province of Sulaimaniya, Arbil, Kirkuk, Duhok and Zakho. However, scores of political prisoners including Arabs, Kurds and Turcomans, were reported to have been executed in Abu Ghraib Prison on 30 and 31 December 1987 alone. According to reports, some of the victims were executed without charge or trial, or after having been sentenced to death by military court following summary proceedings. Others were said to have been executed after having been sentenced to terms of imprisonment. Some of the victims' bodies bore the marks of torture.

Nariman Othman 'Abdallah and Fallah Wali, two Kurdish youths from the town of Shaqlawa (Arbil Province), were reported to have been executed between 14 and 18 November 1987. They were aged 16 at the time. They were among a group of 32 Kurds arrested in the second half of October 1987 and executed by firing squad in the city of Arbil. The executions were said to have been carried out in reprisal for an earlier attack on Iraqi personnel in the area by the Kurdistan Democratic Party's Pesh Merga forces. The bodies of the victims were returned on 18 November to their families, who were asked to pay 50 Iraqi dinars each upon receipt. They were prevented from holding public mourning or burial ceremonies.

Five Kurdish youths aged between 15 and 17 were reported to have been executed between 10 November and 28 December 1987. Isma'il As'ad and Latif 'Adel, both 15 years of age, were executed on 18 November in Fa'ideh Garrison, located between the cities of Duhok and Mosul. Segvan Khaled 'Ali, aged 15, and Hewul Misho Miho, aged 17, were also executed in Fa'ideh Garrison on 10 December. Rizgar 'Abdallah, aged 16, was executed in Mosul Training Camp on 28 December. The five youths were among 31 Kurds, suspected of being KDP sympathizers, who were said to have been sentenced to death by military court following summary proceedings. They were executed by firing squad.

Eight children aged between 14 and 17 were among some 150 political prisoners reported to have been executed in Abu Ghraib Prison on 30 and 31 December 1987. The eight were Kurds from the province of Sulaimaniya whose bodies were handed back to their families in early January 1988. The family was asked to pay 300 Iraqi dinars per body upon receipt. The eight victims, all secondary school students, were: Karawan Nawzad Hama Agha, aged 17; Dara Muhammad Sadeq, aged 17; Ribwar Muhammad Karim 'Aziz, aged 16; Shirko Rida Ahmad Rida, aged 17; Rizgar Anwar Haji Rida, aged 16; Jamal Hama Saleh, aged 15; Dana Haji Sidiq Ma'ruf, aged 14; and Luqman Haji 'Ali, aged 16. . . .

Over a number of years, Amnesty International has also received reports indicating that the Iraqi Government has repeatedly resorted to the poisoning of its opponents as a method of eliminating them. The most widely used poison, thallium, is a heavy metal commonly employed as rat poison. Amnesty International first appealed to the Iraqi Government to investigate reports of thallium poisoning of political opponents in September 1980, after receiving detailed evidence that former political prisoners had been victims. There was no response to these appeals from the government. Similar reports continued to be received since then, the most recent reported incident having taken place in November 1987. In this instance, Amnesty International was able to document in detail and obtain medical evidence of the poisoning. It was an incident in which Trifa Sa'id Muhammad, a 14-year-old Kurdish girl, was an innocent victim.

According to Amnesty International's information, she was one of ten Iraqi Kurds who were poisoned with thallium on 24 November 1987 in the town of Marga (Sulaimaniya province). The poison was said to have been put in a yoghurt drink by a female agent of the security forces working at the home of a member of the Patriotic Union of Kurdistan (PUK). The victims included members of the PUK and the Kurdistan Socialist Party—Iraq. Three of the victims died within ten hours of drinking the poisoned yoghurt, one of them being Trifa's grandmother who was aged 60 at the time. The seven survivors suffered a range of symptoms associated with thallium poisoning, including vomiting, fever, neurological disorders and loss of hair. They were eventually taken to hospitals in Tehran, but subsequently the three most serious cases were flown to London for urgent treatment, among them Trifa's uncle. The consultant physician who treated them in London confirmed that the three patients were "seriously affected" as a result of "acute thallium poisoning."

Trifa Sa'id Muhammad was transferred to hospital in Tehran in late February 1988, some three months after being poisoned. Winter conditions had made travelling earlier impossible through the mountainous terrain of the Kurdish region. The report on Trifa's medical condition, based on an examination conducted on 5 March 1988 in Tehran, stated that she had "arrived too late to benefit from therapy" (the antidote to thallium, known as Prussian Blue, is only effective when administered within 2–3 weeks after poisoning). Diagnosis of her condition was as follows:

". . . both legs involved with serious loss of sensory and motor functions. In addition [to] hair loss there is muscular atrophy [in] upper arms and some evidence of ascending paralysis . . . further treatment and rehabilitation strongly recommended . . . [Trifa] presently in wheelchair . . . [It is] expected that hair loss will recover spontaneously but neurological damage can only be treated palliatively with physiotherapy. Dryness of the eyes and mouth can be addressed with some oral hygiene and eye drops . . ."

In early May 1988 Trifa Sa'id Muhammad was flown to the Netherlands where she continues to make gradual recovery through physiotherapy. The following are extracts from her testimony:

"After the meal I travelled to another place in Kurdistan. I didn't know I was poisoned as well. After three days my hair began to fall and at the same time I felt weakness in my legs and I walked as if I was drunk. After seven days all my hair was lost and when I walked the problems in my knees were so bad that I fell after a few steps.

"The pain in my legs was terrible and because of the pain I could not stand any more. Every movement was giving me a lot of pain and I cried and shouted when my legs touched one another or touched the blanket.

"I was at this time in a little village near Marga, this place was under the control of the Pesh Merga. After this first week I was sure I was poisoned as well. I didn't have any appetite at all and was getting weaker and weaker. The movements in my legs were getting less and less. After three weeks I was completely paralyzed in both my legs.

"This was all when I was with the Pesh Merga and all the help I had was infusion and some tablets for the pain. They wanted to transport me to Tehran but this was impossible because of the bad weather conditions. Roads were hard to travel, snow was falling and of course the war in the area was dangerous. I couldn't ride a donkey in my condition, and had to be transported lying down.

"After four weeks my condition was getting very bad and they decided that they should try to transport me. But after a couple of hours they had to stop because I was frozen and the pain in my legs was unbearable. They couldn't give me anything else in Kurdistan, only some tablets and infusion. On 20th February I arrived in Tehran. The journey [to Iran] took four days and I travelled on a donkey. This time I managed because the weather was milder and there were more people to help me.

"First I came to Sardasht and after one day to Tabriz. After one night in Tabriz I was brought to Tehran by aeroplane. I went to Luqman Hakim Hospital and stayed there for two months until 4th May . . ."

On 13 January 1988, Amnesty International called on the Iraqi Government to investigate reports of the security forces' use of thallium poisoning against political opponents. There was no response from the government. However, Iraq's ambassador to the United Kingdom stated, in press interviews, that the allegations were "false" and "bizarre."

Further Reading

Abdulghani, Jasmin M. *Iraq and Iran: The Years of Crisis*. Baltimore: Johns Hopkins University Press, 1984.

Abu Jaber, Kamel S. *The Arab Ba'th Socialist Party: History, Ideology and Organization*. Syracuse, N.Y.: Syracuse University Press, 1966.

Aflaq, Michel. *Fi Sabil al-Ba'th*. Beirut: Dal al-Tali'ah, 1959.

Ajami, Fouad. *The Arab Predicament: Arab Political Thought and Practice Since 1967*. Cambridge: Cambridge University Press, 1981.

Amnesty International. *Iraq: Evidence of Torture*. London: Amnesty International Publications, 1981.

Batatu, Hanna. *The Old Social Classes and the Revolutionary Movements of Iraq: A Study of Iraq's Old Landed and Commercial Classes and of Its Communists, Ba'thists, and Free Officers*. Princeton: Princeton University Press, 1978.

Berque, Jacques. *Arab Rebirth: Pain and Ecstasy*. London: Al Saqi Books, 1983.

Blair, John M. *The Control of Oil*. New York: Pantheon, 1976.

Crystal, Jill. *Oil and Politics in the Gulf: Rulers and Merchants in Kuwait and Qatar*. Cambridge: Cambridge University Press, 1990.

Dann, Uriel. *Iraq Under Qassem: A Political History, 1958–1963.* New York: Praeger, 1969.

Devlin, John. *The Ba'th Party: A History from Its Origins to 1966.* Stanford: Hoover Institution Press, 1976.

Dickson, H. R. P. *Kuwait and Her Neighbours.* London: Allen & Unwin, 1956.

Dickson, Violet. *Forty Years in Kuwait.* London: Allen & Unwin, 1963.

Draper, Theodore. *A Present of Things Past: Selected Essays.* New York: Hill and Wang, 1990.

Friedman, Thomas L. *From Beirut to Jerusalem.* New York: Farrar, Straus and Giroux, 1989.

Fromkin, David. *A Peace to End All Peace: Creating the Modern Middle East, 1914–1922.* New York: Henry Holt and Company, 1989.

Glubb, Sir John. *A Short History of the Arab Peoples.* Briarcliff Manor, N.Y.: Stein and Day, 1970.

Halliday, Fred. *Arabia Without Sultans: A Survey of Political Instability in the Arab World.* New York: Vintage, 1974.

Hameed, Mazher A. *Arabia Imperilled: The Security Imperatives of the Arab Gulf States.* Washington, D.C.: Middle East Assessments Group, 1986.

Helms, Christine Moss. *Iraq: Eastern Flank of the Arab World.* Washington, D.C.: The Brookings Institution, 1984.

Hewins, Ralph. *A Golden Dream: The Miracle of Kuwait.* London: W. H. Allen, 1963.

Iskander, Amir. *Saddam Husain: Munadhilan, wa Mufakiran wa Isanan.* Paris: Hachette, 1981.

Ismael, Tareq Y. *The Arab Left.* Syracuse, N.Y.: Syracuse University Press, 1976.

———. *Iraq and Iran: Roots of Conflict.* Syracuse, N.Y.: Syracuse University Press, 1982.

Kelidar, Abas, ed. *The Integration of Modern Iraq.* London: Croom Helm, 1979.

Kelly, J. B. *Arabia, the Gulf and the West.* New York: Basic Books, 1980.

Khadduri, Majid. *Arab Contemporaries: The Role of Personalities in Politics.* Baltimore: Johns Hopkins University Press, 1973.

———. *The Gulf War: The Origins and Implications of the Iraq-Iran Conflict.* New York: Oxford University Press, 1988.

———. *Independent Iraq: A Study in Iraqi Politics from 1932 to 1958.* 2d ed. London: Oxford University Press, 1960.

———. *Republican Iraq: A Study in Iraqi Politics Since the Revolution of 1958.* London: Oxford University Press, 1969.

———. *Socialist Iraq: A Study in Iraqi Politics Since 1968.* Washington, D.C.: The Middle East Institute, 1978.

Khalil, Samir al-. *Republic of Fear: The Politics of Modern Iraq.* Los Angeles and Berkeley: University of California Press, 1989.

Kimball, Lorenzo Kent. *The Changing Pattern of Political Power in Iraq, 1958 to 1971.* New York: Robert Speller and Sons, 1972.

Kimche, Jon. *The Second Arab Awakening: The Middle East, 1914–1970.* New York: Holt, Rinehart and Winston, 1970.

Kirk, George E. *A Short History of the Middle East: From the Rise of Islam to Modern Times,* 6th rev. ed. New York: Praeger, 1963.

Lacey, Robert. *The Kingdom: Arabia and the House of Sa'ud.* New York: Harcourt Brace Jovanovich, 1981.

Lamb, David. *The Arabs: Journeys Beyond the Mirage.* New York: Random House, 1987.

Laqueur, Walter Z. *Communism and Nationalism in the Middle East.* London: Routledge and Kegan Paul, 1956.

Lenczowski, George, ed. *Political Elites in the Middle East.* Washington, D.C.: American Enterprise Institute, 1975.

Lewis, Bernard. *The Arabs in History.* 2nd ed. New York: Harper and Row, 1967.

———. *The Middle East and the West.* New York: Harper and Row, 1964.

Longrigg, S. H. *Iraq, 1900 to 1950: A Political, Social and Economic History.* London: Oxford University Press, 1953.

McLachlan, Keith, and George Joffe. *The Gulf War: A Survey of Political Issues and Economic Consequences.* The Economist Intelligence Unit Special Report no. 176. London: The Economist, 1984.

Marr, Phebe. *The Modern History of Iraq.* Boulder, Colo.: Westview Press, 1985.

Matar, Fuad. *Saddam Hussein: The Man, the Cause and the Future.* London: Third World Center for Research and Publishing, 1981.

Mortimer, Edward. *Faith and Power: The Politics of Islam.* New York: Random House, 1982.

Mosley, Leonard. *Power Play: Oil in the Middle East.* New York: Random House, 1973.

Niblock, Tim, ed. *Iraq: The Contemporary State.* London: Croom Helm, 1982.

Nyrop, Richard, ed. *Iraq: A Country Study.* Washington, D.C.: Foreign Area Studies, American University, 1979.

Penrose, Edith and E. F. *Iraq: International Relations and National Development.* London: Ernest Benn, 1978.

Quandt, William B. *Saudi Arabia in the 1980s.* Washington, D.C.: Brookings Institution, 1981.

Roux, Georges. *Ancient Iraq.* Harmondsworth, England: Penguin Books, 1980.

Sader, Makram. *Le développement industriel de l'Irak.* Beirut: Centre d'Études et de Recherches sur le Moyen-Orient Contemporain, 1983.

Safran, Nadav. *Saudia Arabia: The Ceaseless Quest for Security.* Cambridge: Harvard University Press, 1985.

Said, Edward W. *Orientalism.* New York: Pantheon, 1978.

Sampson, Anthony. *The Seven Sisters.* New York: Viking, 1975.

Sawdayee, Max. *All Waiting to be Hanged: Iraq Post Six Day War Diary.* Tel Aviv: Levanda Press, 1974.

Seale, Patrick. *Asad: The Struggle for the Middle East.* Los Angeles and Berkeley: University of California Press, 1989.

Sluglett, Peter. *Britain in Iraq, 1914–1932.* London: Ithaca Press, 1976.

———, and Marion Farouk-Sluglett. *Iraq Since 1958.* London: Kegan Paul, 1988.

Tahir-Kheli, Shirin, and Shaheen Ayubi, eds. *The Iran-Iraq War: New Weapons, Old Conflicts.* New York: Praeger, 1983.

Tarbush, Mohammad A. *The Role of the Military in Politics: A Case Study of Iraq to 1941.* London: Kegan Paul, 1982.

Utovich, A. L., ed. *The Middle East: Oil, Conflict, and Hope.* Lexington, Mass.: Lexington Books, 1976.

Weissman, Steve, and Herbert Krosney. *The Islamic Bomb.* New York: Times Books, 1981.

Winstone, H. V. F., and Zahra Freeth. *Kuwait: Prospect and Reality.* London: Allen & Unwin, 1972.

Acknowledgments

No book comes into the world easily. The pains of writing this book were probably more intense than most, but they were compensated by a sense of urgency and the brevity of the time available. Our greatest appreciation is due those we cannot name and those we did. To begin with, we are grateful for the research assistance of James Rosberg. Others shared their keen insights about Iraq and the Gulf with us, especially: Fouad Ajami, Amazia Baram, Lowell Bergman, Jill Crystal, Charles Francies of Hill & Knowlton, Joseph Kostiner, Hisham Milhem, Ali al-Sabah, Uri Savir, and Avi Yaari. *The New York Times* provided aid and support, in particular Martin Arnold, Leslie Gelb, Courtney Kane, Carolyn Lee, Howell Raines, A. M. Rosenthal, Ann Rubin, William Safire, and the talented staff of the Washington Bureau. A word of special thanks to Abe and Tony Chayes, Robert Denison, Karin Lassakers, Martin Meyer, and Carolyn Seely, for the fax and friendship. And to Richard Leone of the Twentieth Century Fund we are indebted for much-needed research support.

Jerome I. Levinson, who was largely responsible for the drafting of chapter 10, "Black Gold," is the author of an unpublished work on U.S. foreign policy. In the 1970s, he served on the staff of Senator Frank Church, whose hearings on the role of multinational corporations included a major inquiry into the origins of post–World War II U.S. foreign policy in the Persian Gulf. He is currently of counsel to the Washington law firm of Arnold and Porter. We would like to thank him for his generous help in the crucial stages of putting this book together.

In order to write this book so quickly, Judith Miller was primarily responsible for drafting the Introduction, chapters 1, 8, 9, 11, and the Conclusion. Laurie Mylroie drafted chapters 2, 3, 4, 5, 6, and 7.

Finally, we would like to thank all the people at Times Books and Random House who worked so remarkably and so selflessly to bring this book to the attention of as wide a public as possible. We are particularly grateful to Peter Osnos, associate publisher of Random House and Times Books, for his enthusiasm and good cheer; to Paul Golob, associate editor of Times Books, who always found the right word and unmuddled the thoughts; to Jason Epstein, whose superb cooking, skepticism and constant encouragement kept us going; and, most of all, to Steve Wasserman, editorial director of Times Books, the architect of this book, without whom it would never, ever have been created.

ABOUT THE AUTHORS

JUDITH MILLER joined *The New York Times* in 1977. Since then she has reported extensively from Paris; the Middle East, where she served as Cairo bureau chief; and Washington, where she served as deputy bureau chief. Currently the *Times* special correspondent covering the Persian Gulf crisis, Judith Miller is the author of *One, by One, by One: Facing the Holocaust.*

LAURIE MYLROIE, a former assistant professor of government at Harvard University and currently a Bradley Foundation Fellow at Harvard's Center for Middle Eastern Studies, is the author of a forthcoming book on Saudi Arabia and Persian Gulf security.